BACKYARD RACEHORSE

THE TRAINING MANUAL

Written by Janet Del Castillo
with Lois Schwartz

Illustrated by Janet del Castillo

Copyright: 1992 by Janet Del Castillo
               First Edition
Copyright: 1993 by Janet Del Castillo and Lois Schwartz
               Second Edition

Published by:
               Prediction Publications & Productions
               3708 Crystal Beach Road
               Winter Haven, FL 33880

Library of Congress Catalog Card No. 93-086831
ISBN No. 1-884475-00-0

ATTENTION

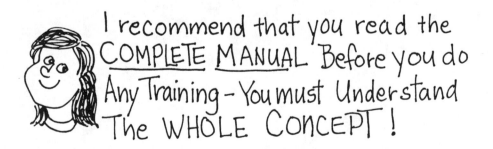

I recommend that you read the COMPLETE MANUAL Before you do Any Training - You must Understand The WHOLE CONCEPT !

INTRODUCTION

The intent of this manual is to have a friendly dialogue with people who share my love of horses. It was written for the hands on horseperson. My desire is to encourage the COMPETENT HORSEPERSON to consider racehorses. If you have competed in Rodeo, Hunter-Jumper Events, Horse Shows or other equine competitions, and have done the preparation yourself, you are able to consider some racehorse training. It will depend on how experienced you are.

The manual will teach you to adapt your own circumstances to train a useful racehorse. You may have your own property or have to keep your horse at a boarding stable. Either situation can work.

Whether you are training Appaloosas, Arabians, Paints, Quarter Horses or Thoroughbreds, a horse is a horse is a horse. Basic horse sense and training development are the same. The personalities of the various breeds differ. Thoroughbreds and Arabians are the most hot blooded.

We all have been intimidated into believing the only place to train a horse is at the racetrack. Expensive for us. . . and unnatural for the horse. The joy of doing it yourself, in your own environment is a major part of training. Your sense of accomplishment, when the horse you trained wins, will never be matched or forgotten. With this in mind, come with me. . .let the games begin!

FORWARD

Many factors went into my decision to write this manual. First the need for more communication with those outside the racehorse industry who were considering becoming a part of it. I recalled those days of innocence when we naively said, "Let's own race horses!" The learning process that took place was slow, painful and filled with disappointment. Since I started with mares and foals, it took a long time to get to the reality of the race track. Along the way, my family and I learned about fencing, animal feed, mare and foal care, breaking and training.

The responsibility of raising and caring for animals was a good discipline for us all. The animals always had to be taken care of first. Our plans had to fit around their schedule. The children were able to earn a little towards their college, while being a part of our side business. Tax wise, this helped offset income from other sources.

We read trade magazines and discovered how successful stakes horses were. We also always found some famous horse who was related to our own backyard stock. They all are related, if you go back far enough.

The real trial and tribulation came when the horses had to go to a trainer. So much happened to slow down the process of winning races. There were so many little accomplishments that had to be overcome before the big day. There was another complete language to learn at the track. Terms like, "break his maiden", or "fire the legs" or "blister the knees." What did it all mean? When I questioned, I was patted on the head and assured I didn't need to worry my pretty little head about such things. I was told, "Just send the check."

Since I was the interpreter between the person who paid the bills, my husband, and the person who wanted the bills paid, the trainer, I found myself always having

to enable him to run. This was not a pleasant position. Especially when you are married to a doctor who is high strung, volatile and doesn't want excuses - just action. Still in my mind, fifteen years later, is my husband, as he closed the encyclopedia after reading that Thoroughbred horseracing is the sport of the kings. "Well," he said, "we have breeding that goes back to Kentucky Derby winners on both sides. I want my horse trained for the Kentucky Derby. With good breeding and good blood there is no reason he can't win."

With that thought in mind, he had numerous conversations with the trainer, telling him to train the horse for nothing less than the Triple Crown. After a few months of this dialogue, the trainer finally said, in exasperation, "Doctor, this horse can't even beat my pony horse. He's not fast enough to work yet." At that point, my husband decided this man hadn't enough belief in our horse to do a good job. We found someone else who was willing to tell my husband what he wanted to hear.

Another thing that I remember about our first trainer is the creativity he used in billing. In the 1970's he was charging $35 per day in base costs. He then itemized and charged for extra bandages, safety pins, electrolytes, and legitimate items such as shoes and vet costs. In his own way, he got even for having to put up with such a silly man.

So we went to the races. The hardest part for us was to have to face reality. After investing $18,000 in the horse, he was going to have to run for a $3,500 claiming price. The horse we put $18,000 in was going to have to run for $3,500. How could that be? The concept that someone could claim away our horse, after all our sweat and money, was beyond comprehension. If you have been raised around the track you understand . . . outsiders don't . . . and newcomers don't. We had to learn, "Put the horse where it can win." We didn't want to, but after a few humiliating races, we allowed the horse to be dropped where he became a useful claimer. Not the Triple Crown - but once in a while he helped to pay his board bill.

The illusion of racing and the reality of racing were so different that soon my husband refused to accept the collect calls from the trainer. He no longer wanted to hear the word "horse" spoken in his presence. Surreptitiously I had the horses shipped back and did what I could on the farm. About that time, my husband and I parted ways, for reasons that had nothing to do with the horses, and I decided to give myself two years to see if I could train and support the small farm myself.

At that point, I started looking for books on how to train racehorses. There were books that interviewed famous trainers, and books about famous horses, and one that had the routine of a known trainer. But nothing worked in my situation. So, by luck, observation, and hard work, my own style of training evolved. I've done my homework and in the following pages will share my knowledge and observations with you. **I will continually stress that my way is not the only way.** In fact this is one of the most important lessons for you to learn. There are many ways to "skin a cat." Open your mind. See how my suggestions relate to your circumstances. Don't be afraid to try your own ideas. Keep the welfare of the horse in mind. If the horse is happy and healthy you have a chance to win!

On The Right Track

In response to the letter to the editor on Tom Ivers (EQUUS 70), I would like to state that the probable reason that he has not yet made his mark in the racing world is that he is experimenting with "cheap" horses—the kind of breeding that would not impress anyone at a county fair track, let alone the "Grand Circuit" stock. But he is in fact making waves.

My experience at the racetrack is that a horse costing $300,000 is lucky to win in a race of maidens five years old or under. I am working in a stable of 40 horses where the *average* yearling price is $100,000. Nearing the end of the season we are racing seven of them because the rest of them literally have "pulled themselves apart." And every other stable on the grounds is thinning out rapidly. But no one admits to this problem, as it reflects a trainer's ability. If you took the lame horse out of training you could not fill the races at meets and would have only the horses left who could not "go fast enough to hurt themselves."

Today's horses are trained the way they were trained 100 years ago. It's about time someone revolutionized the racing world, and I think progressive trainers such as Ivers are on the right track. Please give them time to prove their theories. When people finally get enough confidence in them to get them to train the kind of horses that can be competitive, my opinion is that they will come into their own as leading trainers.

name withheld on request

This was a letter sent to Equus Magazine in November of 1983

Please understand the significance of this paragraph!
37 pulled themselves apart!
7 were still racing — not winning — and they cost an average of $100,000.00!

We can do Better than that!

I wrote this letter in response to the letter above. Even in 1983 I was training from the farm!
My training has changed somewhat since then!

'Disposable' Attitude

I was thrilled to read the trainer's letter entitled "On The Right Track" (EQUUS 72), since I always take one year to gallop, swim and condition a horse, before asking for speed, and always seem to have to justify myself as to why I gallop five to 10 miles for each horse. All of my racehorses have been cheap—but they have been honest and sound and are still running. What disturbs me is the "disposable" attitude of so many trainers who feel there are always other two-year-olds to break down when their present ones fall apart.

Another point: I am a Florida trainer and yet I could not run my fit, sound, "cheap" filly at Calder because they put in an eligibility rule that eliminated many local ship-ins from running—yet the barns are filled with two-year-olds breaking down daily because of the big money in two-year-old races. I feel like a stepchild when I arrive at the track on the day of the race, unload my horse, run and come home to turn her out in a pasture that night. I get a lot of strange looks from trainers when I try to explain why I prefer to gallop them at home for mileage—they are closer to being in their natural environment. Horses who are raised this way do fine and can continue life after the racetrack as nice rideable animals.

Janet Del Castillo
Winter Haven, Florida

THANK YOU!   THANK YOU!   THANK YOU!

Though I sometimes think I'm all alone and shouting against the wind, that is not so. I have a wonderful support system of family and friends who have encouraged me in my endeavors. To them I say thank you. . . it is important that someone somewhere thinks what you are doing has value. These people have all, at various time of highs and lows, been there to give me the energy to carry on.

Mom and Jim - who have always been ready to pitch in when the going gets rough.

My children - Alex, Nando and Victoria. . . they have certainly shared in the overall adventure. . . the earning of the knowledge and experience I have put in this manual. We are all better people, in spite of the struggle and hardship we have endured, to have gotten to this point. Adversity builds character. . . isn't that so?

Walda, Barbara, Marlene, Lois, Ubie and Jackie . . . all have helped in their very special and unique ways.

Many, many others . . . owners and trainers who put up with my unusual methods, racetrack track personnel, entry clerks, stewards, stall men, grooms. . I've learned from all of them. The exchange of experience and sharing of ideas is what helps us become more educated about horses and training. I hope my manual is the beginning of an open forum. . . to share hands on knowledge that will help all of us improve the plight of the horse and the future of HORSERACING!

THE IMPOSSIBLE DREAM
by Alex Del Castillo

I shouldered my sea bag and waved one last time at my ride as it disappeared over the hill. Home at last! I drank it all with a thirst that was born from a long absence and made more acute by the rigors of Navy life. My steps carried me through the white pillars marking the entrance to our drive. Home was Rancho Del Castillo, all white board fence and lush green pasture and, of course, the horses. They were in large open paddocks along either side of the drive, trotting about with their ears perked up, placidly munching grass or fussing with a friend over the fence. Just doing horse things and being horses. What looked to be an older two year old took notice of my presence, stuck his head through the top two boards and gazed at me expectantly. That earned him a pat on the neck and a rub behind the ears as I murmured in the low, soft tones that I had always used with our animals. As he nuzzled me in return, I found myself savoring the not unpleasant smell of a healthy horse. That may sound silly to someone who has never spent much time around the animals, or is so familiar with them that one stops noticing it. However, being on leave from the Navy, where cold metal, gray paint, hydraulic fluid and PineSol are the order of the day, a soft nuzzle and the scent of a horse's breath had the same effect as a home cooked meal. You have to understand, I feel pangs of sentiment when I catch a whiff of horse manure at a parade.

When I got to the house there seemed to be nobody around. This was not unexpected as both my sister and brother had long since moved out and on to lives of their own. I had hoped to catch my mother between trips to the track, but instead only got a glimpse of her in the sharp white and red diesel pickup with a matching

trailer as she pulled away from the barn and started on the oft traveled trek to Tampa or Calder, Hialeah, or Gulfstream in Miami. It was still relatively early and both sides of the two horse-trailer were occupied. I considered what this meant with regards to when my mother might return. It was March, so first of all her most likely destination was Tampa Bay Downs, then in season and an easy hour or so away. The early hour meant Mom probably intended to work at least one of her charges through the gates or get a timed work before the racing started at 1:00 p.m. If neither horse were in a race that day, then she could arrive at the track, work the horses, take care of any business on the "backside" and probably be home early in the afternoon. If she had a race her return would be delayed on the outcome of the race. Things had not always been so predictable. As a teenager I had spent my school weekends and summers, as had my siblings, helping Mom campaign our then meager, retinue of "cheap claimers". In those days that "crazy lady from Winter Haven" would show up at the receiving barn in a tired old Wagoneer and equally battle scarred red trailer. Old track hands would snicker as the harried red headed mother of three would direct her kids in the unloading of the horses from the trailer and then see to the transfer to stalls in the receiving barn. "You see", they would say, "she's got it all wrong, race horses belong at the track, where they race; you can't ship in the day of the race and win". They would continue on about her other "silly notions", but were tolerant, albeit condescending to this outsider. I noticed that many of these sage old experts had holes in their shoes.

In spite of the common wisdom, we did begin to win; nothing spectacular mind you, but just enough to keep the bill collectors at bay. My mother's convictions, which fundamentally were based in the tenant that horses should be allowed to be horses, pure and simple, had begun to pay off. Early in the game she noticed that many horses kept at the track developed vices and personality problems. She always said a good racehorse need not be psychotic.

Training at home consisted of runs through the adjacent orange groves, swimming in the lake and, perhaps, most importantly, spending most of the day in open paddocks as opposed to being cooped up in a stall all day and asked to go all out for one of the twenty-four hours. It was no wonder to me that horses kept at the track tended to be more high strung. A trip-wire psycho horse is not necessarily any faster than a sane one. I suspect many such horses expend themselves in antics before the race. As time went on, my mother carved a respectable niche for herself and her methods. She was not alone in her philosophy of training and people were starting to pay her to train horses for them. Her reputation was that of an honest trainer with somewhat of an unorthodox method. She shunned gimmicks and drugs, preferring to get many honest runs out of a healthy horse rather than racing an unfit, injured horse maintained by painkillers or questionable surgeries. The key to her method was that of a sound foundation - her horses didn't start racing until they were fully developed and fit, somewhere around three years of age. While it is true that three year olds race in the Kentucky Derby, many people don't realize how many youngsters are broken down and rendered unfit to race before their first win. It is only

the exceptional and precocious that can be so successful at such an early age. Poor folks can't afford to pick the stars out of hundreds of horses. We have to do the best with what we've got. I shudder to think how many viable (not Derby winners, but horses that might have had respectable and profitable careers), horses that have been squandered by having been pushed too hard, too soon. The fact that Mom is still in business without ever having to pay big bucks for "Blacktype" horses or stables of yearlings, proves the validity of her philosophy. It should also be noted that not one of the horses she instills with the aforementioned "sound foundation" has ever broken down at the track. This is no small feat.

As I write this, I gaze out to the back pasture. Down near the lake a small unassuming gray mare munches on grass, now and then swishing her tail at the occasional fly. It occurs to me her story will help illustrate my remarks thus far, as well as bringing me to the point of these ramblings. Paul Marriott (right, the hotel guy) donated what seemed to be an unpromising member of his extensive stable to the Florida Boys Ranch, where Mom was a volunteer, for use as they saw fit. The director of the facility realized that he could not afford to keep this animal and another filly, and offered them to us for $5000 "on the cuff". Although, at the time, against the ropes financially, my mother took them on credit. Both fillies were entered into Mom's regimen and it soon became apparent that one of them, although fit, didn't have what it takes to win races. The other, a little gray named First Prediction, after months of jaunts through the grove and swims through the lake, seemed ready to prove her worthiness at the racetrack. After a second and a third place showing at Tampa Bay, a trainer offered us $25,000.00 for the filly. Although the ten fold return was tempting, the resounding consensus of my sister, brother, and me was "Oh, Mom, don't sell the filly"! Though based on sentiment, that decision proved to be wise financially. First Prediction, with her unremarkable size and tremendous stretch run, came to be a leading Stakes filly in Florida. She was dubbed "The Iron Maiden" for her ability to run and consistently win as often as every eight to ten days or so. Of course, with every win the Boy's Ranch received a consummate donation. Now retired after some one hundred plus races and over $300,000 later, First Prediction is the embodiment of Mom's racing philosophy. Were it not for the unlikely chain of events and gut feeling, this horse would have been doomed to obscurity, profiting no one. How many other First Predictions are out there, needing only the individual training and sound foundation that big money owners and trainers can't give them?

You say, "gee, well, that's a nice story, but I'm not a trainer and don't know much about racing, etc.". If you have bothered to read this far, I expect it is safe to assume you have some interest in horses. No doubt many of you compete in shows or the like. I did, but eventually lost interest in merely winning ribbons and trophies. I don't mean to disparage showing in any way; it builds horsemanship and allows one to be rewarded and recognized for his or her labors and efforts. My point (I know, finally!) is that training Thoroughbred racehorses and campaigning them offers all of that and more. Nothing can compare to the thrill of the home stretch run. The horses giving it their all in the finish - necks outstretched, ears pinned back and hooves thundering.

viii

Jockeys clad in brightly colored silks, perched high and forward on their mounts cajole them for that last bit of speed as they vie for position. The noise of the crowd crescendos to a roar as people cheer their picks. Then on the outside of the pack you see it, it's your colors (there is no mistaking as no two designs are the same) on your jock, on your horse. The leaders are beginning to tire and your horse is inching past the pack, fourth, third, second, and now neck and neck with the leader. "GO, GO, GO!" you scream, flailing your arms, pounding on the person next to you who doesn't notice, caught up in the moment himself. Fifty feet to go, jockey and horse are one, and yes, did you see, they nose ahead and then finish . . .!

I can't do justice to that feeling, your heart is in your mouth, there is just nothing like it. You have to experience it. I don't mean to give anyone the idea that racing is all sweetness and light. There are tough breaks and lots of hard work to get through before you step in the winner's circle for the picture. Thing is, the effort that goes into training a racehorse at home is comparable to that of preparing a serious show horse. The rewards from racing, however, far exceed those of showing. I mean besides the emotional high, there is, of course, the money. Few horses conventionally trained ever win, much less show a profit. Most of our horses are of lack-luster backgrounds and have won at least once. If you show or just keep a horse, why not give it a shot; the horse eats everyday whether you race it or show it or just ride it. Don't think you can race to pay the rent, but if you are lucky and work hard, anything you get is pure gravy. Just because you train your thoroughbred to race doesn't preclude it from other endeavors if it just doesn't win. Many of my mother's horses have gone on to become very competent and fit hunter jumpers after their racing days are over.

You may never win much, but that just sweetens it when you finally do step into that winner's circle. Besides, you never know, you might find your own First Prediction, we're still looking for another one.

TO BEGIN THE GREAT ADVENTURE. . .

One goal of this manual is to help you avoid suffering the many humiliations I have endured over the years. My mother came along on one of my first trips to the track. She was not a horse person but I was short of help and was stuck depending on her extra set of hands.

Two horses had to work that morning. I was cooling one when the other came back from the track. "Here Mom, walk this horse for a few minutes while I take care of the other one." I was busy on the backside of the shedrow. The horse my mother took was on a very long lunge line, I was also short of proper equipment. As I returned to see how my mother was doing, to my horror, I saw she had tied the horse to the bumper of my truck. One end of the lunge line was connected to my bumper, and twenty feet away the other end was connected to the horse...who was, at that moment, starting to graze. "Mom, quick, go to the horse's head." too late. As we watched, the horse took a few turns in a circle, and effectively wrapped the nylon lead around his legs. More and more, with each turn. Finding his legs restrained by the line, he did what any thoroughbred would do . . . he had a fit. He fought and carried on until the rope around his legs and his own violent struggling caused him to thump to the ground.

This whole, embarrassing, scenario did not go unnoticed by anyone within a thousand feet of the receiving barn, (surely half the population of the backside of the track). I stuck the horse I had into the nearest open stall and ran over to the struggling animal . . . who was flailing his legs to release them from the line . . . which was by now wrapped in a tight tangle around all four legs. With the whole world watching, I cautiously freed the animal. . . trying to keep an impassive look on my face, (Ho hum . . . horses try to hang themselves on my bumper all the time).

The horse escaped with nylon rope burns on his legs, (which swelled to twice the normal size by the next day). "Mom", I said, "What possessed you to tie the horse that way? You never, ever tie a thoroughbred . . . especially not with a long rope!" "Goodness", Mom said, "I see cowboys tie their horses like that all the time on T.V. I didn't know I shouldn't. Besides. . . my back was bothering me!" It took years to live down that terrible display of poor horse management. To this day, I blush when recalling the "Show" mother and I put on for the backside!

There is a lesson or two to be learned here. One is never tie up a horse with enough rope to hang himself. The other might be to never take your mother to the backside. "Well", Mom says, "She doesn't ask me to help her anymore!" Seriously, it is never have people working around your animals who don't have horse sense.

This manual should help you avoid making my mistakes and hopefully, will help you avoid making some of your own.

A Trainers' <u>Role</u> is to Develop the <u>Personal Best</u> of each horse <u>WITHOUT</u> Breaking him down in the Process!

TABLE OF CONTENTS

A Message

To: Owners
Trainers
Veterinarians
Farm Owners
and Farm Managers

Frolicing is Fun!

A MESSAGE TO FARM OWNERS AND MANAGERS

Today, horse farms are struggling to keep going. There are major problems with labor and Workman's Compensation. If you understand the concept of the training presented in this manual, then you will realize there are many ways to continue training at the farm and cut down the costs of riders by two thirds. If a twice a week riding program is initiated, the labor and stress of getting out, galloping, bathing, and leg wrapping young animals every day is eliminated. At the same time you will find that your horse develops progressively, at the rate that his structure can tolerate. You are training horses while listening to their individual responses to the stress put to them. Many tune up more quickly than anticipated . . . they show no filling with each progressive gallop and therefore can continue right on to the races.

Since you are turning them out on the off days, there is no need to wrap and paint legs. They will adjust to the work load. Be sure you or your employee monitors and charts any filling and waits until it is down before galloping again.

It costs you less to handle horses this way and they are in real training. They are growing, developing and thinking. You will be pleasantly surprised at how little expense there will be to treat and medicate these animals. You're not over stressing them so they have strength to resist major infections. Again, the free movement and being outside a good portion of the day, in itself, will improve the animals' life style.

Whether or not you race off the farm will be a decision that you and your owner make. Obviously, I prefer it. Keep in mind, once your horses learn the track rules and routine, they really don't have to be cooped up at the track between races. Some may need a gallop or speed work between races (every horse is different). Depending on your location, you should be able to handle the logistics. Horses, living at the track, only get about fifteen minutes actually on the track on any given morning. You could arrange for riders at the farm to do more and develop them better with the twice a week schedule and the free time in between. Most rack personnel cooperate with ship-ins. You may schedule your trips to the track so that you, too, only go once a week to work horses or combine a work in the morning with a race in the afternoon. Sensible work and good rest keep people and horses fresh.

A MESSAGE TO TRACK TRAINERS

Many times, as you train, you find you are having to treat problems that are created by track circumstances. A problem, my horses have only had at the track, for example, is cracked heels. At some tracks, the dirt has stones or bits of shell in it. When the horse gallops on this surface every day, the cuts and bruising become chronic.

If, as in my situation, I haul them over and gallop or work them on the track but then take them home, they can be turned out and heal from the trauma between visits to the track. The routine I suggest allows them to recover from the experience and be healed by the next race.

One track was famous for making horses sore in the shoulders and stifles. Trainers had no choice but to use the track and contend with muscle soreness. On the other hand, my horses would run or work and go home. They were usually sore the day after the work and fine by the second or third day afterwards. They walked and grazed while healing. They went into races feeling good and could take it easy until the next race or work. It was not necessary to give any kind of medications, because the horses were always bucking and kicking and feeling good by the third or fourth day. By noting their movement on the chart, patterns would emerge indicating how much time each horse needed before he was ready to run again.

Some tracks put chemicals on the surface to be able to race in the winter. These chemicals again cause burns and chronic problems when horses must train on the surface every day. Washing hooves with castile soap and rubbing them with bag balm or other lotions to help the injured tissue is very time consuming and work intensive. These problems slow down training.

Please be open to working with owners who want to bring horses to you and be somewhat involved. This can be a source of more horses to actively race in your stable, then everyone gains from the compromise.

Turn out is a very important part of TRACK TRAINING - It allows rebuilding from the Track pounding between Works and Races !

VETS, OWNERS AND TRAINERS . . . THE RELATIONSHIP

As you read this manual, do not misinterpret my feelings about Veterinarians, Owners, and Trainers. In my desire to educate you, **the "worst possible scenario" is used when presenting cases**. My goal is for you to make your own informed decision as to how you want your horse treated. Your expectations about how your horse will perform must be tempered by the reality of his talent and soundness.

The trainer's role is to develop the horse to his personal best. Most trainers have the horse's welfare at heart. Their position is very challenging. Many trainers must move from track to track, depending on the season. They must pack their belongings and find a new place to live every three to six months unless they are lucky enough to have their own farm near tracks that are open year round. The logistical and financial problems are great. Compound that with the challenges of training young horses every year. . . horses that will have their own normal setbacks, as they grow into useful animals. Every time there is a problem or slow down with the horse, (which is to be expected), the trainer must call the owner with the "Bad News". So many trainers, myself included, find this one of the most difficult parts of training. **We don't like to deliver bad news.** We don't like the fact that the horse is showing problems or weaknesses and we don't want to stop him. Yet we must do what we perceive is best for the owner and the animal. How I dreaded the silence on the other end of the line when I said, "His shins are sore. He has a cough." or "He needs time." I am aware that the owner is thinking of the per diem costs while the horse rests. These are normal and expected occurrences in the process of developing and maintaining a horse.

IT IS VERY IMPORTANT THAT THE OWNER AND TRAINER HAVE A MUTUAL RESPECT AND TRUST. Each must understand the philosophy of the other. The owner must believe that the trainer is doing an adequate job and the trainer must understand the owner's intent in owning a race horse. For example, many owners tie the hands of the trainer when they won't allow him to run the horse in a particular race. The owner generally thinks his horse is worth much more than the claiming price. It simply doesn't matter how much the horse cost or how much you have invested in him. He must run where he can win, where he can justify the training bills. Statistically, it is going to be a lot less than his cost. So trainers have the unpleasant task of having to tell the owner that his twenty thousand dollar investment should start running at five thousand if any money is to be made. It is possible that the horse will work his way up the ladder but the start must be realistic. This is one of the many problems that appear between owners and trainers. **We all want to get the "Big Horse' and when that doesn't happen there is a disappointment on all sides.** The reality is that few will justify the cost, but the good one can pay for many if we can only find him!

The other really unpleasant task trainers have is reporting to the owner that the horse didn't win. An excuse is expected. Many times the horse has run a good race, but just wasn't good enough to win. What can a trainer say? The horse was outrun. If the owner is at the track, he can see for himself. That can make it easier . . or more difficult. . . depending on the sportsmanship of the owner.

We trainers want to win . Each time we bring a horse over to run we are hoping he will jump up and win, even when the form clearly shows there are more talented horses in the race. It does happen. Then the bettors mumble about how the trainer must have set that one up . They don't realize we're just as surprised as they are. The better is convinced that the trainer had a large bet on the horse and "made a score". It does happen, but not as often as you think.

My racing career began as an owner. I knew nothing about racing or the track. I loved my horses and wanted to win with them, just like in the movies. An owner expects the trainers to know everything about the horse. That may eventually be true, but at first, the trainer is learning.   Each horse is different. His idiosyncrasies must be observed through trial and error. The trainer must decide on the distance of the race, the equipment and the style of riding that suit the horse. He learns this as the horse progresses. As frustrating as it is, owners must be patient with trainers and understand the horse tells us things with each race. We all learn by doing. Some of our perceptions about a horse are incorrect and we have to go back to the drawing board. **Eventually, the horse, trainer and owner should evolve an understanding that will be beneficial to all.**

A major problem is when the owner pushes the trainer and demands action when the trainer feels the horse isn't ready. This can be disastrous. Mutual respect and communication will alleviate this problem. An educated owner is much easier to deal with. Since they are paying the bills, they should be kept as informed as they want to be. Some owners don't want or need frequent updates. Others want to be very involved. Matching the trainer's style to the owner's expectations is an important part of good rapport.

Owners are paying the bills. It is their right to know how their horse is handled. They may be in racing because they love to go to the backside and walk their own horse or bring him carrots. They may only want to be in the winner's circle. **Seek out your own kind of trainer. Look for mutual benefit.**

Owners, please remember a trainers can do everything right and your horse can still have problems or not be a runner. If this happens, don't blame the trainer. The possibility of winning is slim. Be fair and understanding with your trainer. Something may happen to the animal after much hard work on the part of the trainer . So the owner bad mouths the trainer. Be fair, **there is a great deal of luck involved in training**. High strung, honed animals can be difficult to handle. The horse can be his own worst enemy.   Just rolling in his stall he can injure himself for life. Things happen with the best of care!

Trainers have expenses like everyone else.   Don't get a horse unless you understand what the projected costs will be. Don't expect your winnings to pay for training. **Figure out how far you can go with no economic compensation and discuss that with the trainer. He can tell you how realistic your goals are.** Always be prepared for the worst case scenario . . . then you'll be pleasantly surprised when things turn out better. Hopefully with my methods, your horse will not have as much breakdown as is typical, and that it will not take nearly as long to establish his

ability and usefulness at the track.

The veterinarian who practices at the race track has special challenges. He knows and generally keeps up to date on the best therapy for the horses. He is aware that sometimes rest and turning the horse out are easy rational solutions to many problems. Mr. Green (the pasture) is one of the greatest "cures" of all. But he can only recommend such solutions. If the trainer and or owner does not concur, he tries the next best treatment. **The fact is that racing is a business in which horses are expected to produce. Financial pressures cannot be ignored.** Veterinarians can advise various treatments to help a horse run better and without pain. Much of the therapy is very good. A great deal of the medication is therapeutic and helpful. Tell your trainer and vet what you are willing to pay for, what kind of treatment you want for your horse and whether or not you are open to allowing time and rest to be a part of the game plan. Veterinary medicine has made great contributions to the racing industry. Many horses have had successful surgeries allowing them to be useful and capable of earning on the racetrack. **Trust and a clarification of the owner's philosophy is necessary so that there are not misunderstandings later.** Whether to operate or not, weighing the economic impact in relation to the horse's earning power, can only decided when all the facts are presented. Removal of spurs and chips may return a horse to a very competitive level with little trauma and expense in relation to overall cost and time lost. My suggestion is to get opinions and information on problems and make informed decisions. Veterinarians work with the trainers but are generally happy to discuss and explain cases and options with owners. As an owner, be clear about your decisions and what kind of vet bills you are willing to pay. If you don't want your horse run with painkillers and steroids, make it clear! It may save the soundness of your animal if you chose competent training over masking medications!

If you are reading this manual, it is because you want to be an informed owner and or trainer. Communication and knowledge are the key to successful relationships between the owners, trainers, and veterinarians. Each person has a very important role to play for the horse and the racing industry. If we work together we can strengthen our positive impact on the sport of horse racing.

Trainer, Owner, and Veterinarian —
The Relationship!

GOOD COMMUNICATION! A MUST!

The Horse...
WHere to Get Him...
What to Look For!

Sales
and
Bloodlines

Catalogue
Sales page

SALES AND BLOODLINES

When buying a horse for someone else, I am still a bargain hunter. This doesn't mean I want the cheapest horse around, which can turn out to be very costly. It does mean I want the most horse for the money, whether it is five or fifty thousand dollars.

Before going to a sale, study the catalog. It is not mystical. The catalog tells you a great deal about the animal's history and family connections in the horse business. Generally there are anywhere from 100 to 1,000 horses listed in the catalog, depending on the size of the sale.

Much more weight is given to the dam's (mother's) side of the family than to the sire's (father's). It is generally believed that the dam influences the talent of the offspring more than the sire, except when the sire is very dominant and all the offspring look like him, act like him, and have his build.

Many people put a lot of weight in black type. This means that the animal whose name is written in black type is a winner of a stakes race (a race in which entry money was paid). This is considered the most difficult and prestigious type race.

Any horse with "black type" on his page in the sale is considered more valuable. You must observe where the black type occurs; the closer the blood relation to the animal, the better.

When we look in the catalog and see that the horse in question has black type in the first paragraph, it generally means that the dam, a brother, or a sister, has some running ability. If the black type appears in the second dam, you are into grandmothers, great aunts, and cousins. It is important to establish how close the relationship is to the animal in question.

The catalog sales page tells all about the sire and how successful his offspring have been. It will also give his racing history.

Look for a dam who has run, and has had offspring who are runners. They can be very useful even if there is no black type.

So, first look for horses who have dams and sires who have run successfully, and then dams who have useful offspring who "last" and have run. Look for soundness and talent in a bloodline. If various offspring have made $20,000 or $30,000 within a few years, they are useful horses. If they make that much in a year and have run for four or five years, better yet!

Go through the catalog and fold over the pages of horses that you like. Sometimes I'll like a particular sire because of characteristics I have seen in his offspring. For instance, "On to Glorys" have heart are extremely strong boned and resilient. Certain animals run well on a particular track. We all want success, so performance counts.

Once you have marked off the horses you like in the catalog, go to the barns and look at each horse. Ask the handler to take each horse out and watch him walk, check his legs, and note your observations on his page in the catalog.

If you see a horse with a flaw you can't live with, put "no" by his name and don't consider him.. . even though he may go for nothing later. Examine every horse

Typical Sales Page

Hip No.   Barn
40   **Chestnut Colt**   4

Relatives —

Half-brother to 8 winners, including Key Policy ($82,875). Out of sister to OUT THE WINDOW ($408,353, Laurance Armour H., etc.), Let Me In (dam of GUARDS UP, $150,825; CUT THE MUSIC, $131,377; HOW TO KNOW, $126,615), half-sister to Excluding (dam of TAIPO, $60,498).

The horse —

		Raise a Native
Exclusive Native		Exclusive
Qui Native	Qui Blink	Francis S.
		Winking Star

Chestnut Colt
April 26, 1989

		*Shannon II
Clem's Ex (1967)	Clem	Impulsive
	Exclusion	Shut Out
		Bee Ann Mac

Father →

By **QUI NATIVE** (1974). Stakes winner. Sire of 9 crops of racing age, 135 foals, 102 starters, 72 winners of 313 races and earning $3,324,011 in N.A., including Native Mommy ($491,430, Mutual Savings Life Ladies H. [L] (FG, $60,000), etc.), Sheena Native ($393,782, Majorette H. [L] (LAD, $53,100), etc.), Exclusive Greer ($241,138, Pioneer H. [O], etc.), Native Drummer ($110,257, Forego S. (LAT, $12,058), etc.), stakes-placed Link [L] (3 wins to 3, 1991, $148,693), Qui Square [O] (8 wins, $107,205), etc.

Mother →

1st dam
CLEM'S EX, by Clem. Sister to **OUT THE WINDOW**. This is her 13th foal. Dam of 11 foals to race, 8 winners--

Half brothers and sisters {

Key Policy (c. by Diplomat Way). 6 wins, 4 to 7, $82,875.
His Ex (f. by True Colors). 8 wins, 2 to 8, placed at 9, 1990, $76,005.
Mischievous Saint (f. by Explodent). 5 wins, 2 to 5, $73,933. Producer.
Colorex (c. by True Colors). 5 wins, 2 to 6, 1991, $73,638.
Batchelorette (f. by On to Glory). 7 wins, 4 to 7, $56,230.
R. T. Saxon (c. by Royal Saxon). 6 wins, 4 to 6, $49,425.
Babblejack (c. by Sezyou). 9 wins, 3 to 5, 1991, $46,571.
Johnny Two Dance (c. by Pollux). 16 wins, 2 to 8, $45,637.

good!

Grandmother on Mother's side

2nd dam
EXCLUSION, by Shut Out. Placed at 3. Dam of 10 foals, 7 winners, incl.--
 OUT THE WINDOW (c. by Clem). 22 wins, 2 to 7, $408,353, Laurance Armour H., Stars and Stripes H., Better Bee H. twice-once in ntr, etc. Sire.
 Excluding. 2 wins at 3, $9,925. Dam **TAIPO** (c. by *Ballydonnell, $60,498).
 Oui Madame. 18 wins, $53,448. Dam of **Oui Henry** (c. by Flag Raiser, $94,-330, 3rd Hawthorne Juvenile S.-G3, etc.). Granddam of **WHITE MOMENT** (f. by Balance of Power, $51,440), **OUTOFAJOB** (c. by Marshua's Dancer, $30,880), **Whodatorsay** (f. by *Star Ice, $223,936), etc.
 Let Me In. Dam of 10 winners, including--
  GUARDS UP (c. by Cornish Prince). 7 wins, 2 to 5, $150,825, Jerome H.-**G2**, Keystone H., 2nd San Pasqual H.-**G2**, Leland Stanford H. Sire.
  CUT THE MUSIC (c. by Stop the Music). 5 wins, $131,377, [Q], 3rd [Q].
  HOW TO KNOW (c. by Green Ticket). 25 wins, 2 to 8, $126,615, Lakefront H., 3rd Thomas Edison H., Midwest Championship H.
  Back Out. Dam of **Closed Corp** (c. by Affiliate, 5 wins, $88,002, 3rd [Q]).
RACE RECORD: Has not started.
Engagements: OBS Championship S., Florida Stallion S.
Registered Florida-bred. ← *Fees have been paid for these Engagements!*

ahead of time so you don't buy a horse foolishly in the heat of bidding. At that point it is too late to examine him properly. It could be that he is really worth the money, but unless you have examined him thoroughly ahead of time, resist the urge to buy. They all look good under the lights in the auction ring. It is very deceiving.

Now, with the catalog pages folded and notes on the horses, you sit down for the auction. Wait until the bidding settles on a horse you like and if it's in your budget, go for it. Know ahead of time your limit for each animal, taking into account bloodline, conformation and your gut response to the animal.

If you buy a horse, go immediately to the barn and have a vet check him out. For about $200 he can take X-rays of joints, scope the horse and look for any problems that would keep him from being a useful race horse. If he has a paralyzed flap or other listed problems, you may be able to return him to the seller. This examination must take place within a very short period of time, so do it at once. Depending on sales rules you will still have time to buy another horse, if this one turns out to have a problem.

Read the front pages of the catalog for the rules and regulations regarding buying horses.

When you buy privately, you still should have the horse vet examined and scoped before closing the deal. It is money well spent, if you avoid spending all of your time on a horse with built in problems. A legitimate seller will allow such examinations. If you know nothing about conformation and how it relates to racing, try and find an astute person to help you.

Do not buy a horse if you don't know what to look for!

Conformation

Conformation —
What to Beware of
Physically
Mentally

CONFORMATION

Many books discuss the conformation of horses. Some go into great detail about angles and relationships of degrees of slope of shoulder to length of leg, etcetera.

Generally, form and function do go hand in hand. But, I have seen some poorly conformed horses beat handsome ones time and time again.

My uncle, a breeder of Quarter Horses, once said that good conformation doesn't get in the way of being a good runner. Indeed, good conformation has little to do with the innate gift of speed a horse may have. Poor conformation will perhaps hinder a horse from lasting long term, but he could have a world of speed.

Many trainers are frustrated by horses with high speed and crooked legs. Why? If you have a car with one bald tire and three good ones you can probably go many miles with the bald tire as long as you don't go fast. Zoom to ninety miles an hour and you may have a blow out. Racehorses are somewhat the same. As long as you don't redline the system, the horse will last. When you start racing and asking for high speed at a sustained distance, your weak "tires" may become critical factors. When I started training, I used to gallop my horses six miles at an open gallop and they flourished. Then, when pushed to high speed, the stresses on imperfect joints began to take a toll.

As a trainer, you must consider conformation carefully. Some flaws are easier to live with than others. There are horses so talented that they run faster than the average horse without redlining their systems. As your horse becomes progressively more competitive he will, by the nature of the sport, find himself in tougher races. As you win on one level you progress to another, you find where your horse should be running, in claiming races or allowance races.

Wise trainers with less than perfect horses try to keep them where they don't have to run too hard to win. Some horses are so honest and game that they will try no matter what. The trainer who is attentive and monitors the horse's legs can tell when a race has caused damage.

Now, let's talk more specifically about structure. We must judge those conformational faults we can live with and those we can't. **My judgments are based purely on personal experience and are by no means the only accepted opinions.**

My first choice among horses would be a **well balanced horse with very correct legs.** If both the sire and dam were Stakes winners, their well built offspring should have an edge. Yet, we need to remember that if both parents were great, they could be a hard act to follow.

If our first choice is not affordable, what do we settle for?

A horse must fit together well. This sounds very unscientific but as long as his parts seem to blend together, he can be useful. For example, I've seen many Quarter Horses bred and fed to have huge muscle mass. They look great at first glance. They have a burly chest and big hind quarters, but from the knees down the horse will have light cannon bones and small feet. This kind of horse will not stand up to racing and I doubt that he will be able to do much performance work since his body mass and bone structure are so out of balance.

At the other extreme, a light boned horse is useful only if legs and frame are in proportion.

I had a mare so light framed she probably didn't weigh over 900 pounds. Her bones were like titanium. She was very correct and very tough. She never had any kind of leg problems. As a unit she worked great. She was a useful claimer who ran every ten days comfortably.

Northern Dancer was actually a small horse. Photos show he is a well balanced package on sturdy legs. (Though he did toe out.) That type is a joy to ride. They are even and solid in movement.

Some horses have unusually long backs and short legs. This type horse is prone to sore backs since the span between the front and rear legs is long and less efficiently supported.

When you come across a huge two year old, be careful. **A big boned horse generally needs more time to develop.** The pressure on his joints is greater. This type horse may gallop "heavier" and is harder on himself than a lighter horse. Just as with a gangly teenager, this one must work harder to get his act together and to coordinate himself. He may take longer to find his stride. **Size does not guarantee speed.**

If you see a Thoroughbred with large muscle mass like a Quarter Horse, he may genetically have more of a tendency to "fast twitch" muscles. He may be more efficient in sprints than in long races. There are many theories about fast twitch and slow twitch muscles, and whether training tends to encourage one type muscle over the other. It is said that long gallops develop slow twitch, long distance muscle bunches, and speed work develops fast twitch, quick responding muscle bunches. Since more than just muscle goes into developing a racehorse, I would train the horse the way I suggest and then go into speed spurts and let the horse tell you whether he wants to run long or short. (See Section on Second Phase Training.)

The other type of Thoroughbred commonly seen is lanky, with smooth slab-type muscles and a svelte look. His muscle, even developed, will not be bulky. A trainer might suspect that he will develop into a distance horse. Of course, the bulky look can sometimes be created with steroids. (See Section on Medications.) All sorts of varieties come in between these types. I have a filly with a tremendous chest and no rear end. She has the lungs but no rear power. She will not be much. Another horse may have a huge rear and a weak front. **All parts of the horse must fit together smoothly for the exceptional horse.** But, imperfect animals may find their own competitive level...and, in the right hands, do very nicely for a long time.

We should all look for a horse with an intelligent eye, large nostrils and plenty of room and width in the jaw, (more than 8cm is desirable).

If you find a horse that seems to be acceptable to your overall goals, go for it! As you get to know him, see if you recognize "The Look of the Eagles" in his eyes. I know that sounds romantic, but anyone in horseracing is going for "The Impossible Dream"!.

SPECIFIC CONFORMATION TO BEWARE OF

Front legs with tied in tendons

The horse may be light boned or heavy boned. However, if the tendon is tied in behind the knee, it could be a point of weakness, when red lined. Of course, a good training foundation always helps. Look for solid short cannons with parallel lines when the horse is viewed from the side.

Over at the knee

This flaw may improve with exercise. The horse can always improve with a good foundation.

Back at the knee

This is a problem to avoid. It will cause pressure on knees and ankles. Even though exercise and fitness help, it is easy for this type horse to tire and chip joints when red lined. He is a very poor racing prospect. If you see this in a stallion who has not raced, don't breed to him. He probably couldn't hold up to racing himself so why look for trouble.

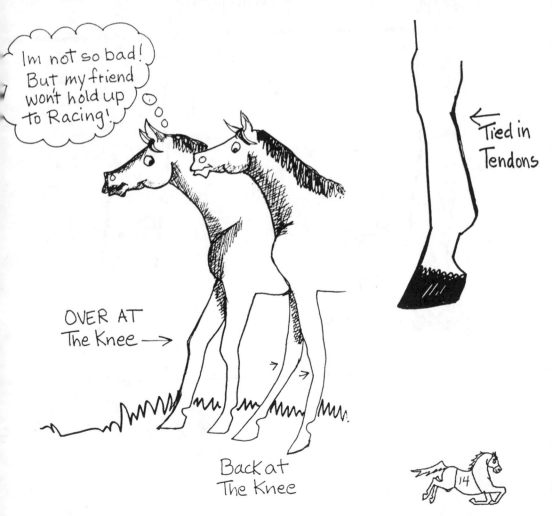

Long pasterns

The horse will be comfortable to ride. However, in racing you must make sure he is very fit. When he starts to tire, his fetlock will drop and he will have a tendency to run down on it when he is redlined. This means the fetlock hits the track surface and the horse can get burns or open wounds from his effort in a race. I have seen this type of horse being cooled out after a race, with tremendous tissue damage in the fetlock area. You can help this problem by putting on bandages with pads to protect his fetlocks. After a workout or two at the track, you'll be able to see if your horse has this tendency. If he does, always protect him. (See Section on Bandaging.)

Short upright pasterns

Horses with these come with their own set of problems. If the horse is upright, he will tend to pound and be choppy on his front end. As well as providing a more uncomfortable ride, this conformation puts a great deal of **stress on the joints.** The shoulder could become sore easily, especially if the horse is running on a hard track. He just **doesn't have good shock absorbers** and may run better on a heavy track or on a turf course. These surfaces are kinder to his joints.

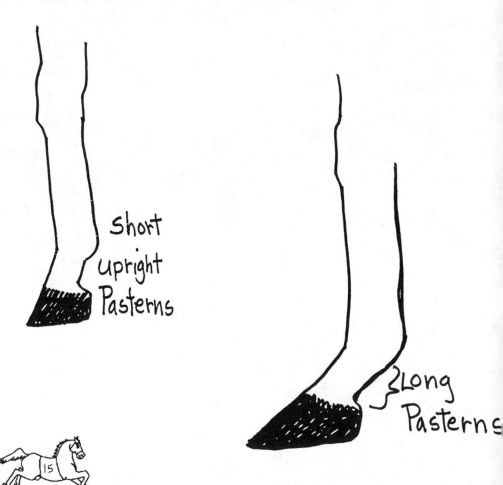

Short upright Pasterns

Long Pasterns

15

Straight or shallow at the hind end

These horses seem weak in the rear. They tend to have stifle or hock problems.

Cow hocked

Horses with this problem seem to be very agile and athletic and to run just fine even though they wouldn't win any Conformation Classes.

Cow Hocked

Inefficient flight pattern

If you look at some horses from the rear, it appears that their flight pattern is very inefficient when they walk and trot. It looks as if they make a circle with their hoof, before they put it down for the next stride. A **toed-in** horse circles the foot to the outside, which is called **paddling**. A **toed-out** horse circles the foot to the inside, which is called **winging.** I tended to eliminate these kinds of horses, because I thought the trait showed inefficiency of movement. Having been forced to train horses like this, I learned that **many horses look inefficient at a walk and trot, but when at a gallop or run, the pattern was completely different.** The legs were two solid pistons, straight in their flight pattern at high speed and very efficient at covering ground. So, don't lose hope even if your horse looks like he will trip over his own feet. When he grows and develops, he may be great.

Remember that horses have been bred for speed over the years. **Many crooked legged horses have tremendous speed. We must not eliminate horses just because of less than perfect angles. When we know they have weaknesses in their structure we must give them time for the bone to mature and more preparation with long, slow gallops during their early training.**

Toe in   Toe Out

Some horses seem to withstand and tolerate their conformational flaws. Others **show warning signs right from the beginning.** If you have a horse with a crooked knee that carries heat in the knee after each work, you are being warned. **The horse is telling you he can't tolerate that level of stress.** If you continue to redline a horse in this situation, **he will break down before he runs.** Unfortunately, some trainers will drill to the point of breakdown, rather than tell the owner the horse won't stand up to training. Others will recommend surgery, injections, etc.

My own feeling is that if a late two or three year old **shows these problems in training,** especially my kind of training, **he is not a good candidate.** I advise owners to **get out now**, rather than spend another year of training and medical problems. They may **ruin the horse** anyway. Many horses can't stand up to the rigors of training and racing. If this is the case, find them a home where they can be useful as pets or riding horses.

Telling owners not to put money into a certain horse has been one of my biggest problems. They don't want to hear this and for sure they will find another trainer willing to try.

TRAITS TO BEWARE OF

Horses are a lot like people. They have different personality traits, and just as **some people are hard headed, so are some animals.** If you perceive certain undesirable tendencies in your horse, don't continue training the animal. There are macho type people in this world, who believe they can "straighten' out a bad horse. There are some traits which cannot be straightened out. They are there in the animal and seem to appear when you least expect them. **Leave complex horses with difficult personalities to the professionals.** If you are new to training horses, it is not good to start out with high strung animals. I started with Quarter Horses. They are more tolerant of beginners. The mistakes you make during your learning process are not as crucial to a Quarter Horse or Appaloosa. Thoroughbreds can react so violently ,when mishandled, that they may injure you or themselves.

The nice guy

Indolent

Scared

Feminine

cranky

BROWN BAG

He was raised here, out of my first wonderful mare. The horse was never mistreated and seemed quite normal. He was uneventfully broken, started the trail rides properly, and was no more difficult than any of the other animals I trained that year. When we started to do long, steady gallops he would swerve left or right in a 90 degree turn. It didn't matter if there was a tree, a fence or any other obstacle, and there usually was.

Sometimes he would go days without doing this and then suddenly would do it again. We couldn't anticipate his behavior. It didn't seem to have any relationship with external stimuli, location on the route or whether it was early or late in the gallop.

When he misbehaved, I would yank, shank and spank doing everything to let the horse know this was bad behavior. He seemed oblivious to the punishment.

One day, when the horse was about 30 months old and nearing track time, I was riding him. (I am large and heavy and hoped this would make it hard for him to pull his tricks.) He bolted, and much to my disbelief, ran smack into a 12 foot high irrigation pipe. I had pulled to the right and to the left, but to no avail. The horse crashed into the pipe.

Hmmm- I Think I'll go That way!

Laying on the ground with my left foot on his belly, to keep him from stepping on me, I thought, "That's it! It is too dangerous to train a goofy horse." Two days later, he was sold to a trainer at the track.

The trainer was forewarned about the horse's problem, I explained in detail how the horse veered to the right or left with no warning. The trainer said, "No problem."

Later, I asked the trainer how the horse was doing. "Galloping fine," said he. "Has he tried his sharp turns yet?", I asked. "Nope," said he. " Do you warn the rider before you put him on," I asked. "Do you tell him about the horse?" He said. "Hell, no, he'd be afraid to ride the horse. I don't tell him anything."

This information made me very uncomfortable and is probably a reason I'll never be a trainer at the track. I am incapable of setting someone up like that. I couldn't put a rider on a horse that has a hang-up, and not warn him. I constantly hear trainers saying, "That's the rider's problem."

To make a long story short, the horse was put in his first race. Unfortunately, he got the number one hole. He broke out of the gates, hung a left into a rail and lost the race. The trainer sent him back to the gates, got blinker approved and

the horse won his second race.

He's back at the track again this year and is still as erratic as ever. He has won some races, but he still hangs a left or right when you least expect it. You never know if he will run or bolt.

Leave a horse like this to the professionals.

Interestingly enough, this horse's sire has thrown various runners with the same tendency. It seems to be a genetic trait. Good luck if you try to change something like that!

DOUBLE DEXTER

Who could forget Double Dexter? While in the receiving barn she dug eight foot holes. She was well known at the track. This filly was so erratic and nervous that no one believed she could possibly run, after expending so much energy waiting for her race.

Many felt Double Dexter would be better off living at the track. Little did they know that she already had. For the month she spent there, she would gallop, fret and dig in her stall until she was exhausted. Then the ding-bat would fall asleep, rest, awaken and start all over again.

Double Dexter was simply nervous and high strung. Interestingly enough, she was basically happy at the farm. She had her friends and I could keep good weight on her.

She was small, but an extremely plucky little filly, with bones of titanium. Never sore out of a race, she had tremendous resiliency, but she could lose a race at the gate, because she was so nervous.

Each year Double Dexter got progressively better. At five, she was almost manageable. If you drove in half an hour before the race and unloaded her to run, she didn't fret and went right to racing.

The stewards at Tampa Bay were good to me. They would let me arrive close

to race time, for which I was very appreciative. This helped Double Dexter tremendously. She won two or three races each year at Tampa and did pay her way.

One day someone offered two thousand dollars for her and the owner said to sell. As far as I know, she is running in Puerto Rico. She was sound enough to run for many years when she was sold.

This kind of horse is very tricky to handle and only good help should work around such a hyper animal. A horse like this is not mean, just over-reactionary, but still can be dangerous. If you are not extremely competent, don't put yourself in a threatening situation by trying to handle an "impaired" animal.

Double Dexter almost killed her owner in a trailer while being loaded. The horse lost control and overreacted hysterically to the tight quarters. She went into a frenzy and flung herself every way until she was cut loose. The owner was trapped inside the trailer with her and was almost crushed to death. Dexter "schooched" under the butt bar of the trailer to escape. Luckily, both owner and horse survived. That episode gave me half of my gray hair. Take heed . . . don't look for trouble . . . get a horse with a reasonable personality.

EPIDEMIC

There are probably people in Mountaineer Park who still remember Epidemic. He was a huge brute of a horse I bought as a maiden in October of his fourth year. In Florida, a horse must win a race before he is five or he can't run. So, I knew I would have to work fast.

Epidemic was a powerful broad boned hunk of a horse. He looked like he lifted weights in his stall, he was so muscular. Galloping him in the grove a ring bit meant nothing to him. Nor did the "silly" person on his back. He ignored me. It was like being on a runaway train, when he took off. Realizing the danger, I told my son Alex (the 6'4", 240 pound son) the horse needed some attitude adjustment.

Alex is basically gentle natured. He felt his sheer strength could handle anything this horse could try. Being 18, Alex knew bullets couldn't pierce his skin, so, he condescendingly agreed to give Epidemic a spin in the grove.

Ten minutes later, the horse came galloping back, riderless. Five minutes after that, with pieces of a tree sticking from his clothes, Alex came limping home. He mumbled about how the horse had no mouth, no feelings, and no response to anything.

So . . . I decided this horse would do better at the track.

Since he had run before, I took him to Miami and put him in a race. We threw the jock up on the horse's back, in the beautiful paddock area of Hialeah. The horse started to trudge off, and to our amazement, he literally knocked over the groom. The groom fell with arms and legs flailing. Epidemic stumbled over him, walked through the flowers and into the fence of the paddock.

I scurried through the flowers, following the horse. The jock was still sitting on Epidemic's back in amazement. As he jumped off, he said, "I'm not riding this ox!" I was left to try and haul the horse back to the parade area.

I managed to find another jock and the horse ran uneventfully, arriving 8th out of 10 horses. He did, at least, stay on the track when aimed in the right direction. Apparently, the only way to handle him was to run him.

When Tampa opened he had one month to break his maiden. Six days after the Miami race, he ran fifth. Five days later, he ran fourth. Four days later he was third. I reentered immediately and three days before the end of the year, on his last chance to win, he ran second.

A man from Mountaineer Park bought him for eight or nine hundred dollars and hauled him home. He won the first time out.

Later, the story was the horse had some kind of screw missing though he could run. The owners got rid of him, because he would walk over people and things. He simply wasn't controllable. None of this surprised me. He was another good horse to get rid of, even at a loss.

The older we get and the more experience we have, the wiser we become. There are many challenges I have undertaken out of sheer ignorance. Since I survived the ordeals, they were learning experiences - not to be repeated.

The message is this: observe and learn from everything you do. Remember what works and forget what doesn't. Don't berate yourself if you made a wrong decision. Ignore the "Monday Morning Quarterbacks". Just carry on. Learn from the past and dream of the future. Things will eventually work out.

FARM LAYOUT

Fence
 Wash rack Area
  Bathing Horses
 Barn and Stall Area
 The Gate
  The Chickens and Goats
  The Dogs
Visit from the Veterinarian

FENCE

Good visual board fences are my first choice. Their main drawback is maintenance and the fact that the older they are, the more brittle they become. When a horse, while frolicking or by accident, crashes into board fences there is a danger of being impaled. In major Thoroughbred farms, miles of double fencing is utilized. To keep horses from playing across the fences. It is an extra safety factor when fences are broken. Needless to say, it is expensive for most of us to put up board fences, let alone double fencing. There are new types of vinyl fencing. I have had no experience with them. They should be worth investigating.

Many types of wiring are being sold as fencing for horses. If horse wire fencing is used, it is desirable to run a wood sight board on top for visibility. Do not use goat, pig or chicken wire type fencing. It is very easy for a horse to stomp his foot through this kind of wire and, in the process, tear his skin and tendons. For obvious reasons, **I am adamantly opposed to any kind of barbed-wire fencing.** However, if you must use it, make sure you mark it clearly with bright rags or tape fluttering every few feet so that the horses see it. My vet friends say that barbed wire helps them pay their mortgages.

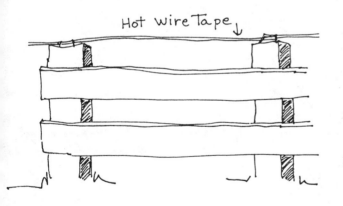

Hot wire Tape ↓

Double fencing is expensive. I use electric tape across the top of all my paddocks. It helps separate animals that want to horseplay across the fence. They may clunk their heads together but they respect the hot tape. I tried hot wire but found that it was a terrible danger when the electricity went off. The horses would fight and break the wire off the holders. The loose wire could easily tangle around a leg and sever a tendon. Ribbon or tape is more visual and will break rather than strangle or tighten. Hot tape can always be used temporarily until proper fencing is installed.

My horses are turned out all night in their individual small paddocks. The

paddocks are approximately 50x100 ft. When my farm is full, **every horse must have a stall during the heat of the day.** I also **put the horse in the stall to reinforce rest a day or two before a race.** They should take turns in a large grassy pasture, each spending at least an hour every day there. My farm has four grassy turnouts. The rest of the time they live in the paddocks behind their stalls.

Rolls of old conveyer belt is useful for lining the small paddocks. It discourages the biting of knees and lunging that young horses like to do. They can run freely, frolic and rear. Horseplay is necessary and helpful. However, we don't want them hurt. Horses love to roll in such close quarters - invariably next to the fence, because it's sandy and soft from their hooves tearing up the soil. They tend to roll into the fence and get their hind legs caught between the fence boards - no matter how close or far apart they are spaced. This can cause scraping of tissue and lacerations on their legs. The conveyer belt between boards proved to be good protection for horses who are allowed out. Those of us in racing are aware that **horses can inflict a great deal of damage on themselves just being horses.**

Every horse has access to water and a red mineral block in his turnout paddock. This is mandatory here in Florida due to the intense heat. The horse can regulate his own salt intake as necessary.

Each paddock has its own feed tub out of reach of neighboring horses. A rubber mat is placed on the ground under the tub. The hay ration is put on the mat. When the horses drop grain as they eat it falls on the hay. Hopefully, the mat will reduce the amount of dirt he ingests. It is important that each horse eat his food at his pace without harassment from his neighbors. Be sure that all nails or dangerous items are far from the inquisitive lips and bodies of your horses. Bored horses can get into trouble with anything in reach.

recycled conveyer Belt

Hot wire "ribbon"

Wood Board

Safe Paddocks

WASH RACK AREA

The wash rack area is one of the most important areas on your farm. Most of us must work alone, so it is essential that we utilize our layout efficiently. As you can see by the drawing, my wash rack consists of a large concrete slab, approximately 14 x 14 ft., covered with rubber matting. I have a sturdy round pole supported by two other sturdy posts. These can be wooden or steel pipe. Drawings are included of my wash rack to help you adapt your style according to your needs and availability of materials. Remember, **these are suggestions from which you may accommodate your own needs.** Certain points are essential. **The cross pole must be round** so that when you loop the lead shank around the cross pole you can easily pull it to control the horse and to make him stand closer to the cross pole. **You are also able to release him** quickly if it becomes necessary. My principal wash rack is completely enclosed by fencing. I use this rack with new and/or more fractious horses. **It is imperative that they learn how to behave** while being bathed or treated. At the track two people are usually needed for the young horses. They can't be tied and are very nervous. After a few lessons the horses learn that the rack is not to be feared and you will find yourself more comfortable bathing them. If they throw a fit at being confined, all they do is fight and pull themselves loose, if you allow them to. **They are still confined by the perimeter board fence** and the shank is still on them. It's easy to catch them again and loop the shank over the cross pole. Before my wash rack was confined, if the horse got loose, he could gallop all over place getting into trouble or harm. **Always close the gates and be sure the area is safe before you handle the fractious horse.** Even alone you will find yourself able to control the head while working on the back legs by looping a longer shank around the pole and holding it in one hand while you are at the rear of the horse. If your shank is 20 ft. long, you can teach the horse to move forward by looping it around the pole and using a buggy whip to tap him from behind. This way he learns that the tug on the head and the tap on the rear mean that he is to go forward.

If he has not been handled much, especially around his legs, you can loop the

Hose the face when you bathe your Horse!

shank around the poles to control him while you rub his legs and body with the buggy whip. If he kicks to the touch of the whip, yank, shank and sharply say, "No!" After a few lessons, he learns that the whip is an aid not to be feared and stops kicking at it. Another way to accustom him to having his legs and body touched, is to hose him all over until he accepts and enjoys it.

Have everything you need at the head of the wash rack; shampoo, hoof pick, and a grooming box. You never want to leave the horse unattended while you run to look for something.

Enclosed Wash Rack

You can handle a young horse by yourself if necessary with the proper Layout

BATHING HORSES

Always start with the horse at your wash rack area. In Florida, we bathe our horses very frequently. If they are not bathed every three or four days during the hot, rainy season, the horses may develop rain rot or some other kind of skin itch. Being outside a great deal, they get caught in the rain. When the rain is over they roll in the sand to dry off.

The soil nurtures many bacteria. **By scrubbing the skin of the horses every three days, we stir up and cleanse the surface.** My recipe is quarter cup of bleach to a gallon of water with a squirt of Palmolive liquid or some other common household soap. (Buy it on sale.) The bleach disinfects the skin, and hopefully, the cycle of itch is inhibited. This has shown definite results over the years. When I am lax during the rainy season, the itch moves in. If you prefer, Betadine or any of the liniments with disinfectant qualities should be fine to use instead of bleach in the rinse water!

To bathe the horse prepare the soap, water and bleach in a two gallon container.

Hose the horse very aggressively with a nozzle sprayer. **The skin should be drenched and stimulated by the hard hosing.** Dip a scrub brush in the solution and scrub the entire body with the mixture. Take the horse's tail and dip it completely in the bucket. The bleach is great for getting the grime off the tail. If you rinse in a reasonable amount of time, it doesn't bleach the tail. Then, having first picked out the feet, dip the whole foot in the sudsy bleach solution. Scrub all the feet with the brush. Using the nozzle at medium pressure, spray all over the body and rinse out the soap and bleach. The dirt pours off and the skin is stimulated by the water massage.

During the bath, try to hose water directly on the horse's face so that he will be accustomed to the sensation of water or dirt hitting him head on. This prepares the him for the sloppy water or mud that can be flying at him during the rigors of racing.

Bathing your horse, you can learn a great deal about the him. **If he is sensitive to being scrubbed or rubbed in a particular area, discern if it is because he hurts or he is just ticklish.** As you handle your horses, **you learn their personal idiosyncrasies. Learn to be tuned into how your horse reacts during baths and grooming. The clues he gives you help gauge his overall state of health.** The first thing most horses do when turned back out is to roll and get dirty again. . . probably to have a nice layer of dirt on to discourage flies. That's all right . . . at least you know they were clean!

Rubber Mats are placed
over concrete slab
My poles are welded
Steel !

Enclosed <u>Wash</u> <u>Rack</u>   Note how lead shank must
be wrapped

THE BARN OR STALL AREA

An ideal situation would be a paddock with a nice large stall. You could turn the horse out for a portion of the day or confine him. This should work for anyone with one or two horses.

A row of stalls with common walls can help utilize materials efficiently. Florida has such mild winters that our stalls can be very airy and open.

Mine is a two barn system. The lower barn is for the females - the girls dorm. Sometimes you will have help that doesn't quite understand who you said to turn out. Many crucial mistakes can be made. **A filly in heat turned out next to a racing colt can cause damage to both. Try and avoid accidents.** Always try to keep turnouts and stalls for colts and fillies completely separated. Young horses remind me of teenagers. **Constantly thinking of having a good time and procreating.** You learn when working around animals to **read body language. Be aware of what they are saying to each other with their tail switching and squeals. You could be hurt.**

The best barn is a large pole barn with a very high roof that is airy inside. Mine has four **stalls with small paddocks behind each one.** The stalls are 14 x 14 ft., nice and roomy. **The paddocks are 14 x 20, enough space for them to doze in the sun if they want, or sleep out under the stars, which they seem to prefer at certain times of the year.** Best of all, they choose to drop the manure in the far corner of the outside paddock rather than dirty the sawdust, helping it last longer. If your schedule gets hectic and you don't clean the stall paddock area for a few days, it is not crucial, they are not standing in manure.

My lower Barn!

4 stalls on either side of center aisle

sawdust dumped in center aisle

small paddocks behind stalls

All the horses that have been raised on my farm drop manure outside. If they are from the track, they tend to drop it in the stall. They had no choice for so many years.

The paddocks behind my stall area are completely lined with conveyer belting. These are active racing horses, they like to roll on their backs and could get their legs caught in the rails. Hot tape is secured to the top board so they don't lunge at each other too much. This arrangement is riskier than enclosing them in the box type stalls that most racehorses live in. **However, horses are herd animals. They like to nuzzle and talk to each other. Socializing keeps them mentally healthy and allows them more tranquility long term.** It helps them not to develop the vices so prevalent at the track. As they mature, they are more adaptable to the race track environment, at least their **formative years were more natural.**

There is an aisle in front of the four stalls. This was originally just hard packed dirt. It occurred to me to store the sawdust there until it was needed in the stalls. Now **whole loads of sawdust are dumped in the aisle.** This provides about two feet of sawdust that settles into a nice base. It lasts about two to four weeks. It is easy to clean stalls and **rake the sawdust from the aisles into the stalls.** This is very convenient and keeps the sawdust dry and protected from the elements. **This has cut my stall cleaning time down to almost nothing.** When dirt appears under the sawdust, its time to call for another load. **This simple adaptation has saved me energy, time and money.**

Salt)
Block

All my feed buckets clip into a screw eye. They can be removed and scrubbed when necessary. Hay is put under the feed buckets so that any spilled grain falls on it. **I am completely opposed to hay nets.** Horses are grazers, not browsers (though they can nibble leaves from trees). **They are built to eat off the ground.** Hay nets cause back problems. **The horses are not using their normal physical movements when they twist their heads and eat a shoulder level.** Ideally, both feed tub and hay should be on the ground. Certain adjustments can be made for convenience. When a horse has a back problem, he is fed on the ground or with the bucket in a hole. As he is eats, he is flexing and exercising his back. He does back exercises without even realizing it.

All paddocks and stalls have automatic watering devices. They can be easily installed with PCV and are real time savers.

Your own stable and paddock areas may differ considerably. Other parts of the country need different styles of stalls. Study your needs and make your areas as convenient and labor saving as possible! When you do everything yourself, you must be more efficient with your time and labor.

THE GATE

Everyone feels that it's necessary to have a gate at the farm. Frankly, **gate work is one of the last things you worry about in training**. It is always a good idea to **encourage your horse to walk into small areas** and to obey and learn that he doesn't have to fear such experiences. I have pretend gates.

The gates are constructed in wood. Use any materials you have around. My sides are padded with rug and **there is a guide board extending between the two stalls to encourage the horses not to veer when breaking**. At one time I had a barricade board across the front, supposedly we could yank it open and hustle the horses out. Experience has taught me this isn't necessary. **You need stalls, open as shown; to walk horses in, to stop them and back them out or to walk them through.** Eventually you can gallop them out. **Finishing touches of breaking out of the gate should be left for track training.** Experts are there and the gate crews need to have the horse work out with them. This is discussed more thoroughly in the Training Section.

My gates are positioned at the base of a hill. When the horses eventually learn to gallop out, they are going up hill, which will help strengthen their hind end. Some trainers believe that starting on a hill is very difficult on a young horse. Be judicious and make your own decisions based on how your animals handle the work!

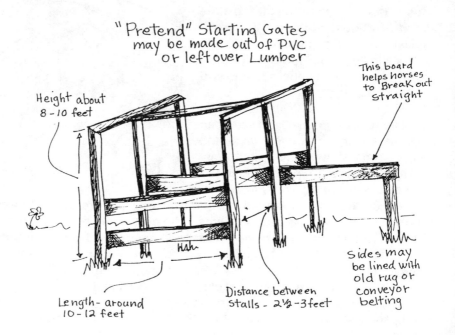

"Pretend" Starting Gates may be made out of PVC or left over Lumber

This board helps horses to Break out straight

Height about 8-10 feet

Length- around 10-12 feet

Distance between Stalls - 2½-3 feet

Sides may be lined with old rug or conveyor belting

31

THE CHICKENS

Anyone who has come to my farm knows I can't discuss its layout without telling about my chickens.

This all began when my children joined the Four H Club. One of their many projects was proper chicken raising. It was easier to turn the chickens loose when the Four H project was over, than worry about their feed and water. The chickens reverted to their clever, cagey ways in no time and soon took up residence in the hay barn at night. During the day they did "manure patrol duty". People even asked if I had trained them to seek out every pile of manure and very efficiently peck and scratch to break it down! Their work effectively broke up the piles in the pastures, thus helping control a fly problem.

The incessant raking on the part of stable help breaks up the fly cycle. **If an egg laid on manure is left undisturbed for 24 hours another fly is added to the population.** If the egg is disturbed by rain or by a little crew of chickens pecking to get undigested grain, the egg does not hatch.

Breaking up manure also helps the process of pasture fertilization.

There can be a danger of salmonella, from chicken manure. Investigate the situation in your area to decide if the effect is worth the risk. Never allow the chickens to contaminate feed and water areas. Use your horse sense.

Mother Nature controls the population problem. Sometimes we can become over cautious about the dangers in our environment. A healthy horse should be able to co-exist with a certain amount of bacteria. Horses adapt to chickens, their flapping and noisy conversation. They learn to relax and tolerate chickens. Actually, some become great friends.

THE GOAT

The goat is a good, if somewhat odorous, companion for insecure horses. They are easy to keep, are allowed on the backside and offer entertainment to both horse and barn help. If your horse is more tractable with such a companion, be sure to have him dehorned. Neutering is also highly recommended.

THE DOGS

Since we have discussed chickens, we should mention dogs. We have owned many dogs over the years. Certain types are very dangerous around horses and others rather non-threatening.

Shepherds have an uncanny herding instinct. One shepherd we hand raised from four weeks knew from the beginning that he shouldn't bother the horses. As he matured, he seemed to look and see if there were any humans around. If he thought he was alone, he would slink toward a horse grazing in the field. The horse would immediately sense the dog, react nervously, and trot away. The dog was then in his glory! Once the horse started to run, he would joyously chase him snapping at his rear legs.

There was no way to break him of this habit. It was almost as if he said, "The devil makes me do it!" This became such a problem and had to get rid of him.

Rottweilers instinctively want to bite the rear end of the horse. This is very dangerous, especially if you happen to be on a fractious two-year-old. It is upsetting to an old steady animal. I won't even consider having the breed around.

You can't fight instinct! The older I get, the more I try to eliminate trouble. Some dogs are jealous when you start handling your horses. They must be tied up before you begin your work. I no longer have that kind of patience. Too many horses have stomped on me, when they sensed a threatening animal sneaking up behind them. One of my horses ended up in the swimming pool because a dog chased him into a frenzy.

It's good to have dogs around horses. It's good for them to learn to get along. I have had more luck with large dogs that have no herding instincts. Through trial and error you will find what you can live with.

A VISIT FROM THE VET

The State Veterinarian for the winter meet at Tampa Bay Downs, Jerry Wessner, was kind enough to give me this information on vaccinations.

Jerry graduated from the University of Pennsylvania Veterinary School in 1965. He was a practicing racetrack vet for many years. His help with this section is appreciated.

COGGINS TEST

Every horse should have a Coggins Test. This test is named after Dr. Coggins who found the test for detection of "Swine Fever" or Equine Infectious Anemia (EIA). EIA is a viral disease transmitted from an infected horse through a blood transfusion. This transfer may occur by blood contaminated needles or syringes, mosquitoes, flies or any other vector or means that causes EIA contaminated blood to come in contact with circulating blood in the healthy horse. Horses that contract EIA have the virus in the white blood cells for life.

Usually an infected horse will show intermittent fever, depression, progressive weakness, weight loss, edema, and either progressive or transitory anemia. The disease may incapacitate or kill horses with the anemia or it may go quiescent and never cause anemia again. This quiescent stage is the most dangerous. Before the Coggins Test, many horses were infected through insect vectors or multiple use of needles and syringes. The Coggins Test detects both the carrier and the infectious state. Most racing jurisdictions will not allow horses to race if they have a positive Coggins Test. The majority of states allow the infected horses to live if suitable quarantine facilities are built and measures adhered to. However, most states prohibit the interstate shipment of positive Coggins horses. Although this disease will probably never be eliminated, economic losses of horses have decreased dramatically since the advent of testing was coupled with strict control measures. Some states require testing every six months, while others only require annual tests. Whatever your state requires, be thankful you will probably never see this disease.

VACCINATIONS

Vaccinations or immunizations are injections made up of either killed or modified live viruses or bacteria that do not cause disease in an animal, but offer the protection or immunity, as if the horse has succumbed and recovered from the disease. You should vaccinate your horse. The cost of the vaccination is much more economical than the cost or treatment of the disease.

TETANUS TOXOID

All horses should be vaccinated annually with Tetanus Toxoid. All the unvaccinated horse needs is a small non-draining wound or abscess in the foot or other part of the body and, if infected by the tetanus organism, the animal will have

a very painful and expensive illness. Symptoms of tetanus are a stiff saw horse appearance, rigid tail and flickering of eyelid over eyes when startled. Tetanus causes spasms and a great deal of pain. Inoculate during the first year and repeated in four weeks. Boosters are given annually.

BOTULISM

Botulism is caused by the same family of bacteria that causes Tetanus. It is characterized by muscular weakness that leads to paralysis. Death ensues from paralysis of respiratory muscles. A minute amount of toxin can kill a horse, so beware and vaccinate. Injections are given in the first year, repeated in four weeks, and boosters given annually.

POTOMAC HORSE FEVER (PHF)

This is a disease that originated in Virginia and is caused by pleura pneumonia-like organisms (PPLO) which are very similar to organisms that cause Rocky Mountain Spotted Fever. PHF is characterized by a severe diarrhea and sometimes laminitis (founder). Horses that have both diarrhea and laminitis are hard to save. An immunization is now available.

ENCEPHALITIS

Encephalitis means inflammation of the brain and coverings or meningitis. This virus causes horses to be very ill. Since the brain is involved, CNS signs will be evident: blindness, blind staggers, convulsions, circling, head pressing and abnormal behavior. There is a trivalent vaccine currently available...Eastern, Western, and Venezuelan. It is almost 100% effective when given early enough.

Injections are given in the first year, repeated in four weeks, and then given annually.

STRANGLES

Strangles is a respiratory disease caused by a bacteria called Streptococcus Equi. This disease is somewhat spotty now but if it does appear, your land and area will be contaminated for seven years. The disease is manifested by high fever and swelling and sometimes bursting of the sub-mandibular lymph nodes. Symptoms are fever and large swollen glands under the jaw. Three injections given seven to ten days apart the first year and then repeated annually are recommended.

FLU AND RHINO

There are thirty five viruses that can cause respiratory disease in the horse. These viruses offer no cross immunity. Theoretically, it is possible for a horse to be continually infected with 35 distinct respiratory viruses. Recovery from one would not offer any protection from the other diseases. The two main viruses are Flu and Rhino. Many two year olds at the racetrack seem to have chronic cough and respiratory disease. Discuss with your vet which way to prevent or control the Respiratory Disease Complex in young horses.

35

Anatomy

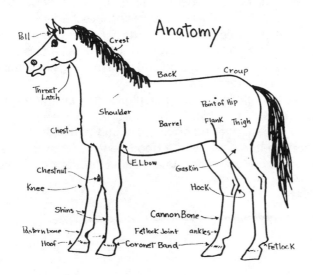

Poll · Crest · Back · Croup · Throat Latch · Point of Hip · Shoulder · Barrel · Flank · Thigh · Chest · Elbow · Gaskin · Chestnut · Knee · Hock · Shins · Cannon Bone · Pastern bone · Fetlock Joint · ankles · Hoof · Coronet Band · Fetlock

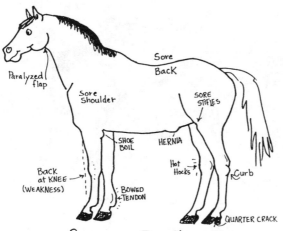

Sore Back · Paralyzed flap · Sore Shoulder · SORE STIFLES · SHOE BOIL · HERNIA · Back at KNEE (WEAKNESS) · BOWED TENDON · Hot Hocks · Curb · QUARTER CRACK

Common RaceHorse Problems

36

EQUINE DENTAL CARE

The horse's mouth can be the source of a great deal of trouble if the trainer is not on his toes. Many problems in controlling the horse may be related to his teeth and mouth. When a horse tries to bolt, swing his head or fight the bit, it may be simply because his teeth are bothering him. For a while, one of my horses would bolt and run all over the track uncontrollably. I was interpreting this behavior as fear and nervousness at the track. A pony and various other devices were tried to control him. The problem occurred when the jockey "took a hold" of him. It hurt his mouth. Had I been smarter, I could have avoided much time and effort solving his problem. Once his teeth were filed he was a different horse.

Signs of teeth problems include a change in chewing habits, dribbling of feed, washing feed in the water bucket, and holding the head to one side when eating. There could be excess saliva, halitosis, swelling of the face, and refusal to eat hard grain.

Your vet should be able to recommend a good dentist. Most racetracks have resident dentists. Ask in the office for information about the track equine dentist.

Open Wide!

Haynets
cause the wrong
kind of movement!

BASIC TRAINING

WEANLINGS TO Eighteen Months

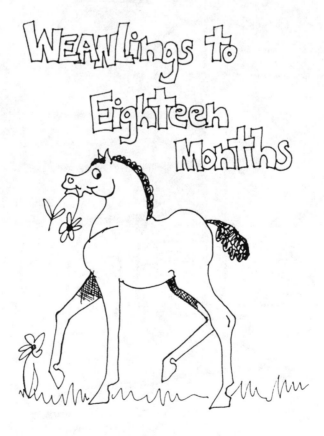

WEANLINGS TO 18 MONTHS- GROUND WORK

Frolicing is Fun!

If you have bred your own horses and have some youngsters out in the field, here are a few tips that might help those weanlings turn into better racehorses. If you have a big field, you can chase them or throw dirt at them and encourage them to run the perimeter of the field in a group. You can observe a lot about their personalities, learn which are dominate and which are not. By encouraging them to run you have also already started the process of disciplined galloping.

Make a special effort, when handling the weanlings, to teach them to lead like young ladies and gentlemen. Have them walk in and out of places like trailers, and to accept being tied. The drawing in the Wash Rack Section shows you how horses should be tied, in order to allow you to control them...or let them loose, if they are in a panic situation.

It's good to teach a horse to stand at attention and be confined while still very young. You can save a lot of tough training time by teaching a weanling that it's natural for you to lean on him, rub your hands up and down his legs, lift his feet, and generally hang all over him. All of this ground work accustoms the animals to being handled. It eventually becomes second nature to them. If you have a trailer, this is a good time to feed them in it, once in a while, and take them for a ride.

Even as weanlings they can learn voice commands, such as, "NO", for negative behavior. You can't expect too much more from them. Horses are animals God designed to be grazing or constantly moving. Try to keep them as close to their natural behavior and environment as possible.

Providing a natural environment is the foundation of my training Horses are natural herd animals. They like to be together, to jostle each other, to scratch each other on the back and to horseplay. Eventually, it will become necessary to isolate them, in their stalls. We want to put that off as long as possible and let them learn as many social interaction skills as they can.

A good book to read about handling horses from birth is Dr. Miller's *IMPRINT TRAINING OF THE NEWBORN FOAL.*

BASIC TRAINING

YEARLINGS

YEARLINGS - 18 - TO 24 MONTHS

Start yearlings with what I call free roundpenning. Free roundpenning is done in a rather large corral or small paddock without putting a lunge line on the horse. With a long whip, encourage the animals to gallop around in circles. Ask them to gallop steadily two to five minutes at a time. Doing this once a day, or once every couple of days, **encourages their bodies to learn the discipline of galloping at a sustained speed for an extended period of time**. Even as yearlings, we want them **to start developing their racing muscles**. In nature, horses like to frolic. They stop and start, run in spurts and whirl around. By imposing just a little bit of discipline on that natural activity, we are encouraging development of the galloping muscles. In addition to encouraging your horses to gallop around the field, you can begin to establish a few halter training points. After their gallop, they should be taught manners; how to walk, stop and back up on a lead. Always be sure to handle them all over.

For **free roundpenning**, use an area **at least 100 x 100 feet. Smaller circles are too tight**. You may use as large an area as you want. If it is too large, the horses will outsmart you and stand in a corner, unless you chase them - makes me wonder, "Who is roundpenning whom?"

Initially, your yearlings can be free roundpenned in a group. When they get older, they should be worked separately, because they frolic wildly and will kick each other. **There is a danger in galloping horses together at any age**. By the same token, **it teaches them to handle other bodies in close proximity**. Even if they get bumped or bruised, they have a good six to ten months to heal. It is important for them to learn to gallop and carry themselves together in a group. Many people will disagree on this point, but I believe in the school of hard knocks. **In my experience the more interaction the horse is exposed to when young, especially socially, the better adjusted he will be when he goes to the racetrack.**

When Thoroughbreds are what we term "hothoused", and prepped for sale, they are separated from their friends and not allowed to play with anyone or be turned out. I remember buying a yearling at a sale. I brought him home and put him in a medium size paddock that had a four board fence. Another horse was on the other side of the fence. When the new horse arrived, he was turned loose, he looked around, in amazement. As the neighboring horse came closer to say, "Hello", the yearling took one look at him, turned around, crashed through the four board fence and galloped down the road. He was terrified of seeing another animal coming at him. Fields are a safe place for your horses, if the fences are good and strong. The animals will get to know their environment.

The general consensus seems to be that, if a horse is nicked or scratched, it will detract from his overall value. In addition, yearlings are given all the food they want to fatten them up. This is where many future problems commence. A diet too rich in protein and calcium can start bone problems that appear later! Presented groomed and polished, they certainly look very beautiful.

About November or December in the yearling year, it's time to start putting the surcingle on their backs. This can be done in a small paddock. While being

being broken or when equipment is on, put the horses in separate paddocks. Let them wear the surcingle for a couple of days, in the paddock. You can use a pad, with the surcingle, until they are comfortable.

From the surcingle, we graduate to a saddle and weight on their backs. Put the saddle on for a few hours at a time and let them loose in a paddock. When they are fully accustomed to the tack, have them gallop, wearing first the surcingle and then the saddle. My preference is to start with a western saddle, without any stirrups but with the floppy fenders where the stirrups connect. This rig weighs a good 30 to 40 pounds. When the fenders flop, the horses react. Then they get used to it. Leave it on for at least a couple of hours every third day and handle them with it rigged.

Next put on a snaffle bridle with the reins through the hole in the pommel and over the saddle horn. It will take a couple of hours for them to get used to wearing a bit in their mouths and to having their heads restricted.

Some trainers like to "bit-up" a horse using the lunge line. They make the horse gallop in either direction with the surcingle and bridle, "setting the head" of the horse. My feelings are that a horse should not be forced to carry his head any tighter than is comfortable for him. Therefore, I do not lunge in this fashion. These are racehorses who should not have their natural movements restricted, especially their head movement and certainly not at first. Early in training they should learn to carry their heads naturally, in ways that allow them to run their best.

Another reason you should not lunge young horses in tight circles is because, at 18 months, bone is still developing. It could be damaged by the leg torque. You are better off using a large corral or small pasture to free roundpen young horses.

People spend thousands of dollars breeding the best horses for potential speed.

Then inhibit their natural ability, with counterproductive training. There are a hundred good books out there on how to train. This one contains my philosophy . . .developed through trial and error. It is not the only way, but, it has given me the best results. If you have a training method that has been effective for you, use it.

Shoes aren't necessary for young horses either. If the horse has a particular problem in his feet, or has splitting hooves, use protective front plates. Keep hooves well trimmed at a natural angle. Remember that the natural angle is the angle where the hoof continues on a straight line through the angle of the pastern. A competent farrier can help you. If you have a rocky soil or hard surfaces and must use shoes, by all means do so. I personally try to avoid it until the last possible minute.

Late in the yearling year, you're generally not doing enough work to over strain your horse. You are handling him only a half hour every third day. You don't want to do too much too soon. You have to give the animal time to develop. "No pain, no gain," is a saying that is true to a certain degree with young horses, but it is better to wait an extra day than to rush them. If you follow the every third or fourth day schedule, you are providing two or three days off for evaluating whether any damage is being done to the horse.

As you start free roundpenning, with a saddle and bridle, be aware of these things. You must learn to know your animal very well. Start feeling his tendons, around his sesamoid bones, his suspensory ligaments, his knees and his ankle joints. The day after you train him, it is very important that you observe whether your horse has a tendency to be congested in his lower leg near the ankle, or whether he is carrying a little bit of fluid in the tendon sheaths. If he does it is the reaction to the stress you have given him. Don't worry. After a day or two it should go away and his legs should be tight. If his legs show no filling and his skin is nice and firm around the tendons by the third day, go ahead and "insult" him again. You can confidently let him resume his galloping.

A late yearling with no weight on his back shouldn't show any kind of physiological change in the front legs. It should only commence later, as you start doing more aggressive training with weight on his back.

Many trainers tend to be too aggressive and demand too much, too soon. Remember, we have almost until the horse's third year to develop him. You want to develop him in a way that brings out his potential. Day by day you demand a little more and allow him to come back stronger. This is a very logical and easy process, if you have patience and do not overdo anything physically or mentally. Do not stress him too much. Do not ask him to gallop too long nor behave too long. Always praise him and leave your training on a positive note. He can not do much wrong at this point. He may be a little lazy, that's okay. You have plenty of time.

Until your horse is about 24 months old, he only needs to be free roundpenned every third or fourth day. Have him gallop a good steady, level gallop five to ten minutes in either direction. From training as a weanling, he should be used to having his feet cleaned, being bathed, groomed and loaded into a trailer. By now your horse has learned to respect the bridle. He has gotten bucks and kicks out of his system and accepts a certain amount of restriction with the bridle and saddle. Be sure you always

use good equipment. It would be a bad lesson for him to learn that he could buckoff a saddle and potentially the person on it.

While your horse is a yearling, leave him turned out with other horses of the same sex, or with geldings. There is a certain amount of risk, as I have mentioned earlier, but in the long run he will be healthier. There is no reason to stall him yet. The rough and tumble activity he gets will be good for him. So, turn him out as much as possible. If you are more comfortable turning him out at night than in the day, do so.

Now, a precautionary note with regard to your personal safety, when handling Thoroughbreds or Arabians. You must be more careful with them than when handling easy going, placid breeds. This holds for the most minute activities with the horse. You may be accustomed to having an Appaloosa, Quarter Horse, Paint or grade horse. Please remember that Thoroughbred and Arabian blood is "hotter" and they are more "thin skinned." This means they can be more reactionary or 'hyper' than other breeds. They tend to hysteria at the drop of a hat. **Never, ever tie a Thoroughbred or Arabian and leave him alone**. Cross-tie him with break away hay ropes, or tie him as shown in the section on wash racks. Never expect him to stand still very long, while he is tied . You must have a proper place to confine him. You cannot tie him to a tree with a long rope. It just doesn't work. Keep these things in mind with everything you do with hot blooded horses. You have to be more cautious and must always think ahead to avoid bad situations. This manual is written for any breed horse, but the Thoroughbred is the horse I have found most challenging to train.

Free Roundpen
with Saddle and Bridle

45

Goals 18-24 Months
(more or less)

You don't <u>have</u> to start this until
22 to 24 months
Have horse comfortable with being
<u>handled</u>, <u>bathed</u>, <u>Led</u>, and <u>saddled</u>

<u>Feed</u> in the <u>trailer</u> at times
Hopefully he will go into trailer
quietly!

Every <u>third</u> or <u>fourth</u> day
<u>free</u> round <u>pen</u> in a large area
Do about five minutes in each
direction at a gallop - or until
he gets into a "good" sweat

<u>Feel</u> and <u>Monitor</u> joints

Know what is "<u>Normal</u>" for your horse!

Keep young animals
<u>outside</u> and running
<u>free</u> as much
as possible

BASIC TRAINING

TRAINING

TWO YEAR OLDS

TWO YEAR OLDS - AT 24 MONTHS

As your horse is nearing 24 months, there is a certain escalation in his training. It is a natural progressive evolution that allows the horse to graduate to carrying weight on his back.

If you just got your horse, and he has had no training, in a month or two, try to cover the ground work discussed in the Yearling Section.

Remember there are many wonderful systems of training. If you have one that works for you, use it. My suggestions are for those who really don't know how to begin. You must have strong riding and training experience, if you plan to train your own horse. **Do not attempt to train, if you are not an extremely competent horseperson.**

A two-year old can carry a pretty large person. I was intimidated by an article that said no one over 90 pounds should ride racehorses in training. I weighed substantially more. I have found, through experience, that a young horse can carry a lot of weight. . . if it isn't for too prolonged a period of time..or too fast. If you weigh 150 to 160 pounds, you can start riding your horse when he is between 24 and 28 months.

Before you get on your horse it is **imperative that you put on your safety helmet.** This cannot be over emphasized. There are many different styles available. Any reputable tack shop will have them for sale.

When you mount your horse, remember to make all movements very clear. Be very patient with him. Try to think like the horse thinks. Never punish him for something he fears. If he is disobedient on purpose, say, "No!" and punish him firmly.

With young colts in particular, I look in their eyes, say, "No!" and shake my finger. I observe whether or not they tend to be respectful. If not, I brandish a whip. You must be very careful to not accept negative behavior in a two year old. They are like teenagers. They will try anything and everything until you draw the line. **It I s much easier to draw lines before they get bigger, stronger and smarter**. Their respect for you has to start now!

Since you are starting to ride, everything you do with the horse is crucial. Every movement you make must be very clear. He must not take advantage of you in any way, shape or form. Start to ride your horse for 15 minutes every other day, for the first month. Riding every day, or even every third day, is acceptable. The frequency is not crucial, at this point. Do not let him get into bad habits.

For the first month, ride him in a large pasture. Teach him to stop, turn around and back up. You might try some figure eights, at a trot. Basically, get him to understand all of your signals and to respect you. After a month or two, when you feel he is cooperating, you can walk, trot, canter and do figure eights. Then you can begin trail riding. (Phase I)

Positive imaging is very handy, when riding a two year old. Horses are somewhat psychic. If you are riding a two year old , and you see a piece of paper blowing in the wind or a cloth flopping in the wind, your natural instinct is to think, "Oh, my God, he is going to shy." What you do instead, is to think very positively and "image" your horse obeying you and going by that blowing cloth or paper. Put an image in your mind, and **mentally will the horse** to go right by whatever it is that frightens him. **You give him the courage to do it.** If you tense up and expect him to shy, he will fulfill your expectation. That is the message you have given him. It is a real

Teach Respect!

challenge, and exercise of mind over matter, for you to override your natural fear of the horse acting up, when logically he might. You must will him, with a tremendous mental power and body language, to go on and through whatever is frightening him. He must obey your signals and do what you command.

My daughter had a horse named Mullikin. She wanted to jump with him, but he had her over a barrel, because she was afraid he would baulk at the jump. She would get on the horse thinking," He's going to baulk, he's going to refuse to jump." Mullikin sensed her anxiety. He'd come up to the jump and refuse it, because it was the message he received. It took a lot of work to encourage my daughter to believe that this horse was going to jump over the fence. When she reached a fence, she learned to whack him on the behind while thinking, "YOU WILL GO OVER THE FENCE." Mullikin obeyed the command and they had no further problems. This is the attitude you must attain with horses.

The importance of being mentally positive and powerful, when you are teaching horses, cannot be overemphasized. It has nothing to do with body size. The smallest jockey can handle the largest horse. It has to do with a knack and finesse, in handling the animal.

There is a great deal of equipment out there to help you do this. I must admit to always using a chain over the nose on my horses. Before you jump to any conclusions, you are welcome to come and see that none of my horses have a ridge of scar tissue from chain abuse. It is seldom necessary to shank a horse hard, but when I need to, I can, if the chain is there. Most of the time, my horses are docile and completely willing to cooperate. Very early, in their training, they learned the ground rules are laid out. They must obey me. They must go where I tell them to go and they must follow where I lead.

One of the most important things for you to learn, at this point in training, is regular **daily monitoring of legs**. You will be asked to make this a nearly religious habit

49

throughout all phases of training. My pattern, for two year olds, when they begin to be riden, is as follows:

        The first day, before you ride him, run your hands around the knees, down the front of the cannon bone and around the ankle. Then go to the back of the knee and come down. Learn how your horse feels. His tendons and the skin over them should feel very tight You shouldn't feel any edema, pockets of fluid or sponginess. You should be able to cup your hand under the fetlock and feel very firm bone and tissue. This is a two year old, who shouldn't have infirmities . . . swelling or problems. When you ride him, which is only for about 15 or 20 minutes, your goal is to get him to obey you at a walk, trot, stop, etc.

        The next day, in the morning, particularly if he is stalled up during the night, you must monitor his legs. Again run your hands over the knees, the shins, run your hand down the back of the tendon and cup around the fetlock. On the day after you start riding your horse, or sometime within the first month, you may notice a little edema where you cup your hand under the fetlock or around the ankle joint. **It is normal to have some filling the day after you exercise your horse.** All you do is feel it and say, "Okay, he has some edema." Don't ride him, just turn him out. The next day bring him in and feel him again. The edema should be down, or almost down. It should certainly be less than the previous day. **You are learning how to monitor your horse's response to the training stress you are giving him.** Usually, by the third day the edema is gone and his legs are nice and tight. **This tells you his body is adapting to the "insult" you are giving to his system.** "No pain, no gain." This animal will become strong and adjust to carrying weight without damaging himself

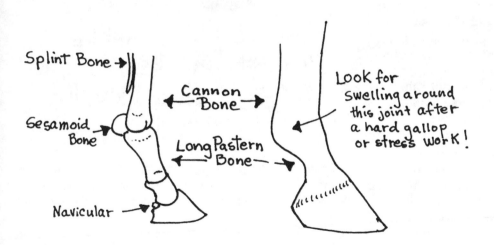

Splint Bone →

Cannon Bone →

Sesamoid Bone →

Long Pastern Bone →

Navicular →

Look for swelling around this joint after a hard gallop or stress work!

physiologically.

Often when people find edema the day after a horse has been ridden, they want to put on leg bandages. **Do not put bandages on two year olds when they have edema that is related to new work.** Monitor the situation. Within three days the edema should be gone and you can ride him again. Stress him again, by riding him 15 or 20 minutes. Possibly the next day he will have edema again. **You will find that the horse will slowly and surely adapt to the work he is doing.** As he becomes accustomed to the work, increase the time you are riding him -- just don't overdo it.

A certain amount of fluid retention around the sesamoid bones, where you cup the fetlock is perfectly normal, in front and rear legs. The filling should be equal in the two front leg joints, but not necessarily equal to the filling the two rear legs. It is only mild congestion in either set of legs. It is nothing to fear. **Frequently, you will find more congestion in the front legs.** The horse's legs should not be congested, in the first month. As you progressively do more work, you will insult the tissue more. **As long as you do not ride the horse until the edema is down, you will not harm your horse.** This pathological change that you see and feel in the legs, is a perfectly normal adaptation to the incremental stress of race training. If the horse only gets edema in one leg, or shows lameness or soreness, you have something different and should appraise it.

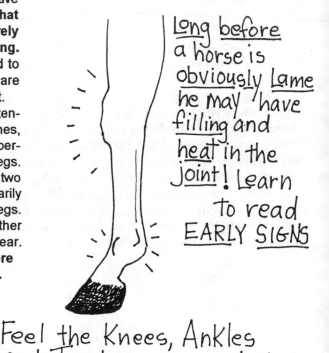

Long before a horse is obviously lame he may have filling and heat in the joint! Learn to read EARLY SIGNS

Feel the Knees, Ankles and Tendons every day Observe them before Training and after Training

For this preliminary Basic Training, work on having your horse obey commands while you ride him. He must be controlled. You must be able to stop him and to turn him. Don't leave your confined area until you and he understand the basics.

Then you graduate to the Trail Riding Phase.

51

MR. BLUEJEANS

This Section is for the "over the hill" trainers who can no longer ride their own two year olds. As I approach 50, it is necessary to find more ways to get the job done without injuring my body. I no longer ride two year olds. Since my children are grown, good help is sometimes hard to find. It has been necessary to evolve a way of preparing the 22 month old yearlings for riding. Saddling them with a 60 lb western saddle and free roundpenning them every third day is a good beginning. From the ground I can teach them to go forward, stop and turn. As they

Mister Blue Jeans

progress, it is possible to find riders willing to work on weekends. The midweek training session is done with Mr. Bluejeans on the western saddle. Mr. Bluejeans is easy to come by and to work with. You take an old pair of sturdy bluejeans, tie each leg at the bottom and fill with sand. When they are full, tie the waist and bingo - a midweek rider. Don't develop a hernia trying to lift this 80 lb. load of sand onto the saddle, becareful. You'll find a way.

Once Mr. Bluejeans is mounted, you tie his legs to the stirrup flaps and his waist to the horn. Then off he goes. The horse is now free roundpenned with at least 130 lbs. of weight on his back. Twenty minutes of galloping with Mr. Bluejean's weight flopping around, gives the hores's structure the weight bearing stimulation it needs. The horse also learns to accept weight without fighting a live rider. A friend of mine had saddle pads made to carry lead weights. He put weight on his horses that way.

Be innovative. Seek solutions. Always bear in mind the goals you want to achieve. Then find a way to achieve those goals, inspite of less than ideal circumstances.

You do what you have to do! Mr. Blue jeans can help!

The THREE Phases of Progressive Training

Trailriding phase
Aerobic phase
Speed phase

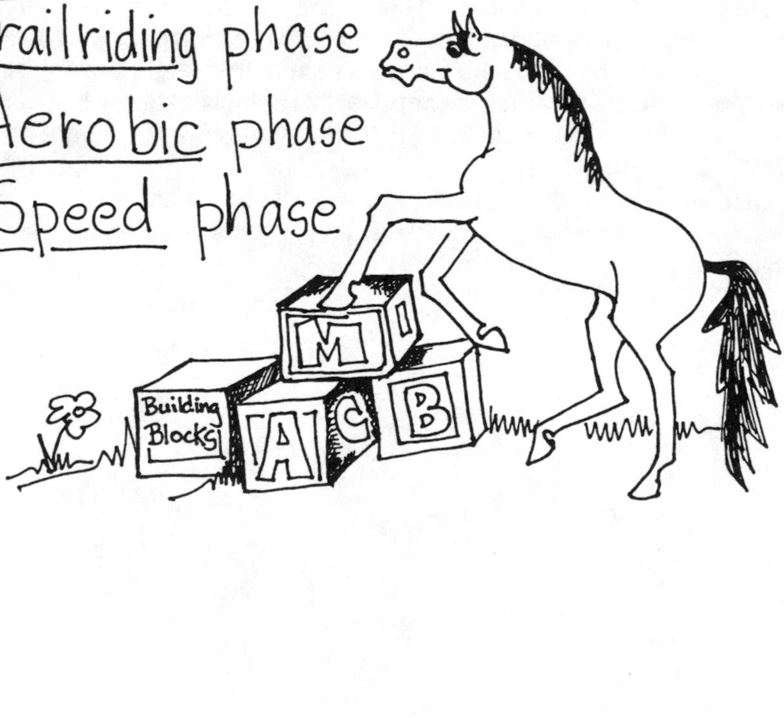

Building Blocks

M
A C B

THE THREE PHASES OF RACE HORSE TRAINING

INTRODUCTION

You have a green-broke two-year-old, at this point. He has been worked in a relatively enclosed area. For a month or two he's been taught manners. He's learned to stop, back up, do circles at walk, trot, canter and do figure-eights at a trot. You're ready to embark on an eight to ten month journey, to make a racehorse out of him.

The training is divided into three phases. Each phase has it's own logical goals, but is flexible, in terms of time, to allow for individualization.

In Phases I and II, from 24 to about 30 months, we are going to deal with going three miles at a walk and trot with a certain amount of galloping. **We will progressively increase the galloping every third or fourth day, until your horse can do a solid three miles in a relaxed gallop.** This will take about six months and is our goal in Phase II. You will have ridden over various terrains, up and down hills and included many left and right turns. Your horse will have learned natural lead-changing, and have developed superb balance and surefootedness. His mental attitude will be excellent and keen because he has been turned out and is "horse-happy." At no time during this period, have we asked your horse for speed. At no point during these six months does he need to see the racetrack. In Phase III, between approximately 30 to 34 months, (sooner if your horse has handled Phases I and II with no physical or mental problems) we develop speed in our athlete. Speed is where redlining and danger begins. It is the last thing we request.

My belief is that we should start with full weight in the middle of the back. As the horse becomes more fit, we begin to ask for more speed within the distance. Finally, at the track, we take off the weight. **Your horse has learned to carry heavy weight a long distance. Now, he hones into high speed, short distance and light weight.** My theory is to develop a very tough resilient animal. When we get to the track, the horse thinks, "Gee, this rider only weighs 100 lbs., I have been carrying about 175 lbs. over hill and dale and through sand. Here the track is flat and smooth. This is a piece of cake." If you have exposed your horse to a variety of trails and terrain, when he reaches the groomed track it should be easy. He should be able to continue soundly at whatever achievement level his conformation and genetic gifts allow. This is, after all, the most you can ask of any horse.

The Program

Day 1   Ride the horse –

2   Turn out
3   Turn out
4   Ride Horse
5   Turn out
6   Turn out
7   Turn out
Day 8   Ride the Horse
follow day 1–7

} Sample weekly exercise program

The horse is fresh and sound on each exercise day –
He recovers and rebuilds on rest days

He progressivly builds stamina with each ride

Work hard, Rest and Recover
Work hard again

As horse becomes fitter, in second and third phase –
He may need 4 or 5 days between Breezes

He must recover and rebuild from the stress His legs and attitude tell you when he can do it again!

Turn out is a kind of cross Training for a horse!

TRAIL RIDING PHASE

PHASE I -THE TRAIL RIDING FOUNDATION

You are ready for Phase I, when basic training has been completed. Basic usually takes a month or two. Your horse will go forward easily, walk, trot, canter, stop, backup and do figure eights. Now, at about 24 months, (his age may vary depending on the horse and circumstances) you start trail rides and establish your route. Find a route that will cover a minimum of three miles. I prefer five miles to allow for "warm up" and "warm down".

Only ride every third day, but whenever you put a saddle on your horse's back he should go at least three miles. Over the next two to four months, speed is gradually increased from walking, to trotting to a light gallop.

Your first goal is to get through three miles on your horse. At first, this may take an hour or two, depending on you, your horse and his attitude. As he goes out on the trail, he will shy, look around, react to every little distraction and generally be silly. Remember, he is young. This is all new and frightening, until he learns more about the big world out there. **If you have a friend with an older, steady horse, ask him or her to ride with you. The older horse will help calm the younger one.** If necessary, you can put a lead shank on your future race horse, and let your friend lead or "pony" him down the trail.

The first few times you traverse your route it will seem to take forever. Carry a riding crop and tap him on the rear to make him go forward (the same way you would if you were on the ground). Do not over react and get angry with the horse at this point. His wariness is normal. You don't want to start fighting with a horse who is not being mean. He's just cautious and insecure. **You must give him the courage and confidence to go forward. Always be positive and encouraging.**

Never pull back or stop a horse That is shying or Propping!

Always push young Horse FORWARD - Even when Frightened!

At the beginning, wear your stirrups long. **Your legs help control the horse and help you defend yourself, when he shies and acts like a two year old.**

Sit flat on the back of your horse. **Sit and put your weight in the center of his back.** You can use either an english or western saddle. Let him learn to carry your full weight.

At this early stage, do not make a big issue about elements that frighten him. For ex-

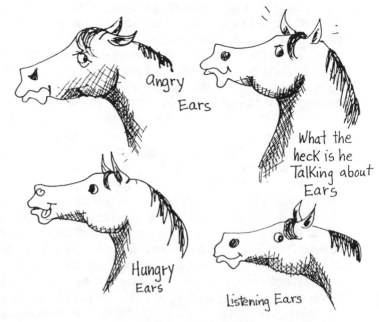

angry Ears

What the heck is he Talking about Ears

Hungry Ears

Listening Ears

ample, if he encounters a water puddle and refuses to cross it, let him go around it . Then approach it from the other direction and encourage him to step into it. However, if the situation threatens to become a "knock down, drag out fight', it's much wiser to gracefully avoid the conflict for the day. **Get him to like going three miles, without major problems or major fights.** After you feel he is more or less confident with the surroundings, start being more firm with him. **Start helping him overcome unreasonable fears.** Try to see how the horse perceives the environment. Have a comfortable, relaxed, trail ride (nearly an oxymoron on a two year old). Usually, after four or five rides, on the same route, the horse will begin to relax.

The horse's ears are his Barometer . When you first started riding him, his ears were so tense that they looked like they could "snap off". The ears warn you about his fear; they let you know what looks strange and could prepare you for the "propping" and "wheeling" that young horses are prone to do.

When the horse is relaxed, start asking him to gallop. Don't force things, just "cluck" or "kiss" and encourage him to go forward willingly. At first he will gallop in spurts, then he'll drop back to a walk as he tires. That's fine. When you think he has caught his breath, or has rested a little, encourage a trot or gallop again. Never stress him or ask too much. Just kiss to **urge forward motion**. Then drop back to a trot or walk. Then kiss to gallop again.

Your first goal was to get through three miles. Your second is to get through three miles, with as much trotting and gentle galloping, as your mount can tolerate comfortably. Never push for speed. A nice, light, relaxed gallop will do. At some point, usually after a month or so, you'll find you cover your three miles mostly trotting and galloping. Now you must try to bridge the trotting to all galloping. Again, always allow the horse to drop back to a trot when he wants. **He will willingly gallop further as he adjusts and gets fitter and stronger.**

You'll find that when you start galloping, some horses will dip their heads. . . be ready for a buck. When this happens, sit very far back in your saddle and pick up his head. He has to have his head down to buck. So, encourage him to gallop out.

Remember you only saddle and ride your horse every third day. Otherwise he's turned out. You may free roundpen him on the off days, but its not necessary. **Your horse's bone is very green and young at this point. Don't push him. He will over do easily, if you're not tuned in and sensitive to what is good for him.** If your horse doesn't eat the night after you've done the three miles, you have over stressed him. Wait until his appetite returns, before you stress him again. Monitor his body frequently, as discussed in the previous Section. Be especially religious about the leg checks and make sure any ankle or knee congestion is down, before you stress him again. The morning after your ride is the best time to see how his body is tolerating the stress. It will not be unusual to find edema or congestion around the ankles, both front and rear. After being turned out loose in his paddock overnight, the filling should spontaneously be down by morning.

Make it a habit of feeling his legs daily to see how long it takes him to rebound from stress. You will see a pattern. Don't worry about ankle congestion after rides. Remember, this is a sign that you have stressed tissue and tendon and that they are reacting and rebuilding to tolerate work. If your horse becomes lame or has heat or more swelling on one side than the other, you must address the problem. This could be a muscle strain or pulled tendon, which require therapeutic rest. Always remember to observe your horse as he moves freely in the paddock. Notice if he seems sore, lame or stiff. He should walk out of the soreness from his work within a day or two, and be ready to ride again. If he doesn't seem quite right after three days, give him another day off. You have plenty of time. **The horse needs time to grow and time to just be a horse. If you rush, you will regret it.**

Another training process deals with starting gates. Diagrams of "pretend starting gates" are included. Have the foresight to build these gates at the very beginning of your training program. Ride him up to the gate and stop him. Let him look. Ride him through the gate. Do nothing more. Every time you go out, which is every third or fourth day, if he is calm and you have his attention, ride up to the gate, stop, walk in, stop and walk him out. Don't ask for any speed. Just get the horse comfortable. One of your goals for the 28th month is to have your horse walk into the gate, stop, back out, stop, walk in, stop and walk out of the gate. No speed. No jumping. We only want the horse to be familiar and completely relaxed around the gates.

If you have gates for two or three horses, it is better. You can walk them all in, stand them all together and walk them out. They may get a little nervous. Do not let

them get frightened or upset, when they walk into the gates. This is a very important and crucial time. It will become part of their routine. By the time you send the horse to a trainer at the racetrack, you want him to be able to break out of the gate at a gallop, from a flatfooted stop. In Phase Two, when the horse has more sense . . . and miles under him, you may try the "stand in gate, gallop out routine" . . . at this point, don't worry. The trainer at the track will teach him to break out of real gates with other horses.

In this first phase, you're teaching your horse to go forward for a sustained period, to obey, to learn about the big world, to go over various terrains, to go on uneven footing and to carry weight for a sustained period in the middle of his back. By the end of Phase I, your horse should be able to go three miles at a slow, perhaps slightly erratic gallop and have recovered a normal breathing rate, after a period of warm down, before reaching the barn.

Practice gates — preferably
angled up a hill !

Goals-Phase I
(Trail Riding Phase)

By end of Phase I, your horse should be able
To be ridden a <u>minimum</u> of <u>Three</u> miles
He should be able to gallop more or less -
    <u>Full</u> <u>three</u> <u>miles</u> - <u>even</u> <u>if</u> <u>erratically</u>

He should be <u>recovered</u> and <u>breathing</u> normally
    when he returns to the Barn
He should be ridden only every <u>third</u> or <u>fourth</u> day
    Turn <u>out</u> and <u>Rest</u> in Between days
Ideally he should be 25-27 months of age
    (if broken at 24 months)
<u>Continually</u> <u>check</u> <u>legs</u> - Charting <u>congestion</u> - if any

He Should not be ridden until his legs are
    <u>normal</u> and <u>recovered</u> from his
previous ride

Encourage
  <u>Confidence</u>
    <u>Steadiness</u>
  and <u>Sense</u>

WeLcoME !

Let The GAMES

Begin !

When is your Horse Ready?

AEROBIC PHASE

PHASE II

PHASE II-AEROBIC FITNESS

As you enter Phase II training, your horse should be able to get through three miles at a gallop. Perhaps he gallops erratically, but he does it. Now, we will work toward **Aerobic Efficiency**. We will begin to gallop three miles, always keeping a steady open pace, only slowing down for sharp turns or steep inclines. We are learning to gallop and turn at the same time, trying to help the horse get his legs under himself. Remember, as a rider you are trying to go with the animal.

While sitting flat on his back, not up high in stirrups, look for a comfortable "settling in" on the horse's part. He should recognize that he has a three mile trip in front of him. You want to help him get through this in a workman like fashion. The horse may be a little aggressive the first mile or so. Relax and steady him. You have lots of time.

His ears should start to relax as you progress in aerobic work. He should be familiar with the route and, as he becomes more comfortable, there should be a steady rhythm to his gallops. His head and neck should flow and rock without tension. His ears should flop forward and back as his head goes up and down.

Get the horse to do three miles aerobically. This means he is breathing "within" himself. Hopefully, you will start hearing a relaxed fluttering sound in his nostrils as he gallops. This shows good relaxation, and implies the horse understands he is going to gallop for awhile. The noise is similar to that made by gently closing your mouth and expelling air in a "Burrrrr" or "Purrrrr" sound. Your lips will tickle a little if you're doing it right. I make this noise, when I am galloping the horses. Remarkably, it encourages them to do the same. They mimic the sound.

Horses that fight and are not relaxed will breathe differently. They make a firmer and more determined noise. You must work on relaxing this type horse. Often, they fret and fuss, in the first mile. They begin to relax and settle in, during the second, and finally even out and concentrate to finish the third.

Developing a fit, aerobic horse takes about three months. You should still ride no more frequently than every third day. **If the horse seems dull, has persistent congestion in his joints, or has any other problem, wait until the fourth or fifth day.** Always turn him out every day and free roundpen him on the third or fourth day until you feel he can do three miles again. There should be steady improvement in strength, ability, and agility as he progresses. There will be a ride or two that make you think you've gone backwards, instead of forward. Don't get upset! It's only natural.

Keep your exercise chart current. When you get off the horse, record all your impressions. The horse is: dull today, bright, sore, cantankerous, he did not eat, etc. Make notes. Tell about your horse's personality and attitude. Later on, these notes will help you evolve a training program that suits your horse.

Fillies tend to overdo. They try to give too much and have a tendency to be off their feed, after a gallop. Some will need more time off between exercises.

If you stable your horse at night, you will notice, in the morning when you turn him out, that on some days he is more sedate than on other days. Usually by the third or fourth day he will bound out. Some horses are so stout they can use another mile

beyond the basic three. If they're holding up structurally and they want to keep galloping, let them go another mile. It's good for them to come home tired. **Not over-tired, or anxious, but relaxed.**

During this approximate three month period, **we are looking for long steady relaxed gallops and a good mental attitude.** There should be an evolution to a strong three miles, with an eventual mile warm-up in front, and a mile warm-down after. The horse shouldn't be breathing hard, when he gets back to the barn. As he becomes

more efficient, the three miles will take less time. You can **encourage the horse to pick up the rate of his gallop, as he progresses.** Encourage more efficiency of movement in the gallop. At this point, **NEVER LOOK FOR HIGH SPEED.**

Try to gallop in company. If you have a pleasure horse, a friend or spouse can ride him beside you. This will "steady" your horse. Soon, your horse will leave them behind, as he learns to gallop relaxed and with a

ground eating stride. If you and a friend are doing the same program, it is a great experience for the two of you to gallop side by side. Take turns going in front and behind each other...bumping each other. Learning to pass horses and learning to listen to the rider are important lesson for the youngsters. Teaching your horses maneuverability will help them to be agile, when they go to the track. This is a good time to experience dirt in the face, and some of the other indignities that might happen at the races.

Continue going to the pretend gates. Stand inside, back out, go forward, and gallop out from a flatfooted stance. If there are two riders and two horses, all the better. No speed. . . just gallop out side by side. It may be better to do this after your long gallops, when the horses are "settled". Don't try to "hustle" them out of the gates. . . that will make them **too high, too soon. Gallop them out quietly encouraging them to go straight.**

By now you have both become more confident in your route and in the horse's ability to handle it. You will now find that you have more contact with your horse's mouth. As you increase your speed you want to increase control, or "steering". You'll lean with him around curves and pick him up, if he starts carrying his head too low. You'll start guiding more with reins. At the end of Phase II you will want to start "pushing him into the bit" more.

Racehorses are helped and "held together" by the jockey's control of the head via bit contact. Horses evolve their own way of going. Some like to pull and have you hold them. Others gallop kindly with a loose rein. **When you "pick up the bit" and take a tight hold, they know it's time to start going faster.** You and your horse learn how to get along together to achieve your goals. **YOU MUST ALWAYS**

HAVE CONTROL. The horse must obey and respond to your guidance. You learn what he likes . Develop together.

Keep your eye on his ears. Remember they are a good barometer of how he is handling the work you have given him. At first, when he was younger and less experienced, his ears were straight up and forward, looking, with trepidation, at all of the new sights. The ears were his "radar". Now his ears should be relaxed, showing a more confident animal.

You may need more equipment now. Your horse probably began with a "D" bit and nose band. You can graduate up to all levels of control with your equipment. This should be addressed as individual horses present individual problems.

The Ears !

The horse is relaxed and listening!

At the end of Phase II we should have achieved the following goals: **The horse has developed an ability to go longer distances more efficiently, with a gradual stacking of stress to the system. There has been a slow progressive building of strong bone, tendon and aerobic air. There has been good healthy mental growth and a desire to run without fear or hurt. You are galloping a strong steady three mile gallop with a mile warm up and a mile jog warm down**.

In the 28 to 30 something month period of training, you **start to stall your horse for a least part of the day.** The reasons are to help him adjust to being in the stall, and to protect him from burning up so much energy. **We want him to direct and concentrate his energy into his rides.** Find a routine you are comfortable with and stall him either all night or all day. He will learn to be in a stall and act like a "good boy". Remember, at the end of his training period, when he is 30 to 36 months old, he will have to go to the track and will probably be confined in a stall for 23 hours a day. This is a very hard adjustment for horses who have never been asked to be in a stall at all. If you want a horse to be a racehorse, he must spend time at the racetrack! Unless you are able to race off the farm.

Continue to reinforce trailer loading and unloading. We discussed loading and taking him for little rides, when he was a weanling. This is important for the horse. When he actually starts being hauled, it shouldn't be traumatic. He should enjoy it. My horses have been good haulers. They didn't necessarily start out that way, but they became seasoned, happy, travelers.

Goals- Phase II
(Aerobic Phase)

By end of this phase, Your horse should gallop a Steady Strong Three miles with one mile warmup and at least one mile warm down

Gallops should get progressively stronger and faster as he grows more mature (but not red-line full speed)

He should be relaxed and breathing rhythmically

He should cool out by the time he is back to Barn

He should have been ridden at least half an hour tho The real gallop doesn't take that Long

Trail ride and enjoy the scenery while he cools with a rider on his back Carrying weight in the middle of his back is strengthening his whole structure!

You are riding only every third or fourth day

You are constantly monitoring Legs and Joints for Filling and Heat

No galloping with a rider until his structure is normal from the Last gallop!

Hopefully he is still turned out for at least a few hours (or all day — or all night)

He should be stalled for a portion of day or night To accustom him To Partial Stall Life!

Frolicing is Fun!
Make sure your
Horse is still Turned
out To play!

SPEED

PHASE III - SPEED DEVELOPMENT - BREEZING

Early in my training days, I wondered how to best train a racehorse. I wondered how do you make the transition from a fairly fit useful horse to a race horse? What were the methods? I searched for answers in training manuals and trainer's notes, but no one seemed to explain the **transition to speed, in a safe, logical manner**.

First of all, you must remember, SPEED KILLS. A horse can gallop six miles over hill and dale, jump 20 fences and come out feeling fine. But, ask him to go full speed, for six furlongs to one mile and you will encounter many problems, if he hasn't been properly prepared.

As I mentioned before, compare speed stress, in a horse, to a car with everything mechanically perfect, except a bald tire. You might be able to go forever at 50 m.p.h., but try to go 90 and the tire will blow! The horse's weakest points, legs, heart, or lungs is equivalent to the bald tire when we go to sheer speed.

Phase III is the transition to speed. In Phase II, we have developed a sound, fit horse able to do reasonable work, for a sustained distance. Now we want to hone his speed. **If you are not an extremely skillful**, strong and confident rider, or your terrain is dangerous and you don't have a few straight aways on your route, **now is the time to send your horse to the track with a trainer.**

Speed in a horse is the equivalent of all out sprinting in the human athlete. Anaerobic muscular fitness is required. This involves developing and conditioning the "fast twitch" muscles. These muscles operate under conditions of high lactic acid production, for very short periods, producing an "oxygen debt". This muscular conditioning is best done gradually, by asking the horse to extend into bursts of full speed, followed by aerobic recoveries.

Fast twitch muscles are recruited, developed and physiologically primed by speed bursts. In a relatively short time, the horse can be honed to a fine tuned, powerful sprinting machine. **All the previous months of slower gallops provide the necessary structural and cardiovascular basis for this transition.** After building bone, joint, and lung fitness, we turn to speed gallops, called "breezes", to achieve peak muscle fitness.

Once you start breezes and are kissing or clucking to the horse and letting him extend out, you can get in trouble. **When a horse tastes speed, you open a Pandora's box.** If at any point along the way, you cannot control the horse, **STOP RIGHT THERE!** Send him to the track. **It is very dangerous not to be in control of a horse that is starting to run full speed,** particularly on uneven terrain. **Speed makes horses both stronger and stronger willed.** This is good for the racehorse, but is dangerous when tearing through trees. The horse tells you when he is ready to go to the track and when he is, let him go.

As we move from speed theory to practical application, we take our Phase II horse who gallops steadily for three to five miles, and **allow him to breeze along the safest portions of the route.**

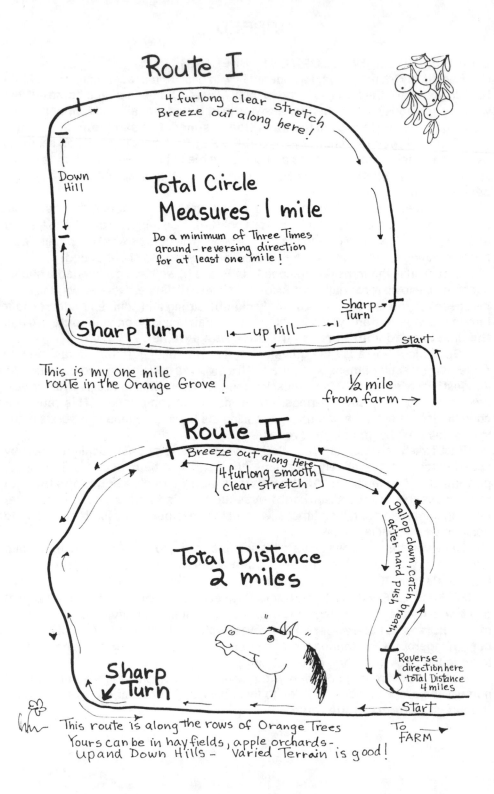

Route I

4 furlong clear stretch
Breeze out along here!

Down Hill

Total Circle
Measures 1 mile

Do a minimum of Three Times
around - reversing direction
for at least one mile!

Sharp Turn

←— up hill —→

Sharp Turn

Start

This is my one mile
route in the Orange Grove!

½ mile
from farm →

Route II

Breeze out along Here
4 furlong smooth
clear stretch

Gallop down, catch breath
after hard push

Total Distance
2 miles

Sharp Turn

Reverse
direction here
total Distance
4 miles

Start

To
FARM

This route is along the rows of Orange Trees
Yours can be in hay fields, apple orchards -
up and Down Hills - Varied Terrain is good!

My galloping area is in an orange grove. (See Route I drawings.) It is a circular route, approximately one mile long, with very sharp curves on two sides and a long, straight stretch that provides a four furlong (one half mile) breeze area. Your route could include wooded trails, be more hilly, involve flat desert, or be a 100 acre pasture. Adapt your route to provide safe breezing for your horses.

My route is multiple laps around a circular route. There is about a mile ride to get to and return from the route. The first mile of the route is done at an open full gallop. The second mile, I **kiss to the horse and let him extend or breeze in the safe part of the mile, if he wants to.** The third mile, I let him do what he wants, not pushing him or asking him for more. If you are fortunate enough to have safe three to four furlong sections, in your training route, and you feel competent in what you are doing, you can kiss to him and have him breeze in these sections, if he wants to. Remember, you are always going three to five miles, but kiss to him only in the second mile of the route. Allow him to ease into full speed. Never, never whip or push the horse to run. **Let him breeze in a natural manner.** Let the horse "come back to you" after the breeze. Don't ever pull him up sharply. Let him develop without having his natural desire to stretch out impaired. Just make sure you have room to do this. Only ride him every fourth or fifth day. Turn him out in the pasture or free roundpen him between breezes. For the first month or two, allow him to breeze slightly every time you ride him.

As you progress with speed work, the secret is to **let the horse extend out to his own capabilities.** You don't want to push him to the edge too soon. **Fillies may try to run too hard, too soon.** They will be a lot more honest, in this respect,

Fillies are
More honest
and Try
    Harder!

than colts. You have to learn to be cautious about how much you allow the animal to do. This is where the "art" of training comes in. If you are at all insecure about how much to allow your horse to do, or if you are not tuned in to how much your horse can handle, it's time to turn the horse over to a racetrack trainer.

At this point in training, **all the horses expect to gallop at least three miles, no matter what.** They do adapt differently to speed stress. Some will be "finished" by the third mile and take themselves back to a walk or trot. If they do, let them slow down. Never push them. Others, even when tired, will maintain a gallop and try to extend out more on the breezing stretches, in their route. It depends on the personality of the horse. If you find that your horse wants to go fast for the first mile, but slows down the second mile, even though you kiss to him, do not force him to do a third mile fast. The horse is probably trying to tell you that, by nature, he is going to be a sprinter. He is going to run early and then get pooped out. During these last few months of training you have to key in to what your horse wants and is capable of doing. On the other hand, if your horse cruises the first mile, hits the second mile fast, when you kiss to him, then slows down some before running the third mile, you probably have a "distance" horse. He will need a certain amount of time to gear-up to full speed. This type of horse will need warm up time before a race.

As you go into this last phase of fitness, **you should be using an English saddle, because it is much lighter.** You will notice, as you start to gallop or breeze out, that you naturally tend to lean a little bit forward, stand up in your stirrups and put your weight over to the horse's withers. When the horse levels into high speed galloping, it helps him, if you are slightly up off the saddle and not sitting on his back. At this point, it is better to shorten your stirrups a little. Shorten the stirrups, does not mean shorten them to jockey length. Just shorten them to a length that makes them comfortable, so you can pick up your weight and rock on top of the horse, rather than sit flat on his back, when he goes into his breezes. In other words, you evolve from sitting flat on the back to a more forward seat, with the concept of trying to hinder the horse as little as possible with your weight.

If you can imagine walking along carrying a loosely tied knapsack which bounces and flops every time you start to run, you can understand what a horse feels, with a loose rider going thump, thump, thump on his back. You want to be in as tight a position and in as tight a package as you can. **Leaning forward and standing slightly, in the stirrups, as you allow him to rock under you and extend out, is a very natural, wonderful feeling.** You should grow and ease into this...just as the horse is growing and easing into his breezes. Between the breezes, you should still sit flat on his back. You have already developed his muscles to carry your full weight. When he goes to the track he will be ridden by a jockey who is substantially lighter than most of the people doing this training. **When he graduates to a light weight person, over a shorter distance, on a faster surface, he will have great power and endurance**. The logic behind the program comes together beautifully.

As you progress, in this speed work, you will notice that the horse is no longer carrying his head in a relaxed manner. He will lean more against the bit. You will

have to take a tighter hold on him. You want the horse to respond to your signals and believe me, you want his mouth to get somewhat harder and firmer at this point. Always use two hands. Grab a handful of mane, hold the horse very firmly with **mane and rein in each hand**.

The more you extend into speed, the firmer the contact you need with his mouth. I equate it to a tighter and well connected steering wheel. When you are driving a car slowly you can have a rather relaxed hold, with a certain amount of play in the wheel. **When you are going at a high speed with a car, or a horse, you must have complete control.**

Encourage the horse to lean against the bit and have very firm contact with him as he is breezing out. This will help him when he goes to the racetrack.. . jockeys want horses to lean against the bit. They hold the reins rather tightly to keep control in a race.

Watch his ears as he rolls into breezes. As he tries to run harder, he will concentrate more. Instead of having his ears "scoping" and looking at things on the trail, he will now have them cocked back listening to the rider and eventually straining with all of his body to run his hardest. His ears will be back, not flattened as in anger, but showing the concentration necessary to pull together to run hard, carry the rider over the terrain and obey to him! Observe horses in the stretch during a race. Most are concentrating and have their ears back. When a trainer says his horse galloped across the finish line, with his ears perked up, he means that his horse didn't have to work hard to win the race.

Any time your horse misbehaves, give him a sharp whack. Use the whip to guide and discipline him. You don't have to beat him, unless he deserves to be beaten.

Mane and
Rein in
each hand!

74

The horse experiences the whip as an aid to discipline. . . not something for punishment. Always have your whip handy. If he goes into his gallop and wants to buck rather than gallop like a gentleman, crack him and say, "No", in a very firm voice. Also, give him a firm yank on his mouth. Let him know that negative behavior is not acceptable.

As long as there is a good turnout pasture for the horses on days when they aren't working, they can exercise on their own. If you want to ride your horse on the off days, or if you don't have a proper place to turn him out, very specifically take a different route and direction where you never, ever gallop. Take him for a nice trail ride of some kind. The point is, that when you do a particular route, a horse learns exactly where he is allowed into speed. **You must change the pattern on rest days or you will fight him the whole way.** If you insist on riding him on these off days, you don't want to fight him or confuse him,

You should not over train. This can not be over emphasized. Be very careful to not over work the horse. If you ride the horse any more frequently than every fourth or fifth day, or push him too hard, he will start loosing weight. **The minute you hit the higher speeds, excess fat will start melting off him.** If you work him too much, he will come back trembling and highly agitated. He might have a loose, watery manure. You must use your skills as a trainer now. Look at your horse very carefully. He might seem dehydrated the day after a speed work. Always monitor his legs. Be careful to check the suspensory and cup your hands under the fetlocks to feel for swelling. Remember, if there is any kind of swelling, edema or heat, you must turn the horse out, swim him, free roundpen him, or walk him. **Do not work with the horse until all swelling has completely disappeared.** This refers to normal stress swelling, not the twist of a leg or trauma swelling. The little areas of congestion you have found all along are normal, as he adapts to the harder training. Do not worry about it. **By not wrapping his legs and observing him carefully every day, you will perceive a recovery period for the horse.** Each day his structure will toughen as he adapts to the work you are putting him through.

If you do feel that the horse has strained something, twisted a leg, has different kinds of swelling or has a pull on a leg and is not evenly stocked up, check with your vet. You might have to do some bandaging.

As you gradually hone into progressively more speed, you start to stress every fiber of the horse's body. It is believed that it takes at least four days for a horse to recuperate from a hard anaerobic push. **He needs rest, free movement and more time to recuperate between breezes**, when bridging to high speed. You will eventually back off his breezes to every fifth day, then every sixth day, with turnout and free roundpenning in between. A**s he gets fitter, he will start thinking speed.** If you find he gets too "speed-crazy" you should be looking for a trainer. You have to be making your target date for the racetrack.

Remember, no more long slow gallops. **You are now flying through three miles**. Your horse is anticipating the run. You are probably doing the equivalent of a two minute mile, with speed spurts on your three mile route. You are only slowing enough to turn safely and maintain control of the animal. My mare needed two full

miles more to gallop down, after she did her hardest push in the third mile. Never inhibit the horse if he wants to continue to gallop down, even if it takes 3 miles. **Let the horse come back to you!**

He is **working out the lactic acid build up from the oxygen debt created by a hard gallop! SLOW GALLOPS IN BETWEEN ARE NOW CONTRA-INDICATED.** From here on out, **we are honing for speed with open gallops easing into breezes.**

Remember, at this point, you are targeting dates on which you will take your horse to the track. All racehorses are considered three year olds in January, regardless of the month of their birth. Since I do not race the horse until he is nearly three, I try to hone the horse into race condition by the time the track opens near me. You should be doing the same thing.

The horse tells you how much he can do
But you must learn how to Listen!
How he eats — how he acts —
How he responds to increments of Stress in Training —
This is how the horse tells You!

76

Goals- Phase III
(Speed Phase)

Start speed spurts within Three mile route
    Always ask for Speed in second mile
    Repeat in third mile if horse wants
He may eventually want to run hard at same spot in
   first mile — that's okay- But always ask for speed
in second mile   Soon you have three stretches
with speed spurts within three miles   You slow for turns
and uneven areas— Your horse tells you NOW how he
wants to run- Early speed- Late speed- Steady speed
      Discuss with a Trainer when your horse should go
To try track-   Your horse should only be ridden
                  every fourth or fifth day—
He is now starting to go full speed for the spurts in the
three mile route   He needs REBUILDING — RECOVERY time
Always have free choice hay- good grain and augment feed
if he looks "sucked up"   On rest days- TURN OUT and
OBSERVE MOVEMENT   He may be quiet the day following
gallop- He may be Bounding and full of energy by third
or fourth day   FREE ROUNDPEN horse if he feels great
and it's not time for a gallop!   AIM for TRACK!
Start BREEZES at track about every seven days
with free round pen in between!   MONITOR LEGS!

Adjust this schedule to what
you perceive as appropriate
for your horse and Terrain!

To Race TRACK !

Don't Overtrain!

THE Transition

TO TRACK

Race Track or Bust!

Introduction

First Method - Weekend Haulers

Second Method To the Track to stay

THE TRANSITION - FARM TO RACETRACK

First, congratulations! If you have gotten this far, you have achieved a great deal. You have a horse that you have been nurturing and developing into a running machine. He should like to run and should be chomping at the bit at the threshold of pure speed for a prolonged distance. How do we bridge the spurts that we have been doing within our three to five mile route into a speed machine?

I am going to discuss two ways of handling the transition form farm to racetrack. Though the basic training theory is the same, the lifestyle of the horse is distinct. I find it necessary to repeat each step of training, in each set of circumstances, so that there will be no misunderstanding as to how the horse is handled.

The first option is presented to those of you who live close enough to the track to haul your horse in and have found an astute trainer willing to work with you. The second option is for those of you who must keep your horse at the track. You want the trainer to understand what your horse is ready for and how to cope with him on the days when he should not be tracked.

A Cooperative Track Trainer is worth His Weight in Gold!!

Ideally, the first method is preferable. It is the best for you and the horse. I realize that it is not always possible for you to keep the horse at home and haul him. Remember though, there are many backyard racehorse advocates. You can contact each other when you are working with the logistics of track training. Cooperation between people with the same mind set works. . . even though we frequently feel we can do things better by ourselves.

I am compiling a list of trainers and farms that are working with my style of program. I will soon start a newsletter. As the newsletter grows, we will network our information and have a solid base of backyard trainers.

First Method-
Weekend Haulers

FIRST METHOD-WEEKEND HAULERS

If you live in the North, you should plan to start trying your horses on the track in the spring. It's no fun to be hauling or aggressively riding in cold, dangerous weather. Always accommodate the weather in your training schedule. Training in snowy country will be more erratic than in kinder climates. If you are in the last phase of training and can still ride every fifth or sixth day and free roundpen in between, the horse will be ready to go to the track.

Those of you in the West, or where weather is not a factor, can aim to breeze your horse at the track in November or December of the two-year old year.

Here in Florida, I start them when the track opens in December. Northern horses will be a little older when they visit the racetrack, as they will be in their three-year old year. This is fine. We want our horses to last, so we give them growing time. We are not in a rush. We want our horses to run as three, four and five year olds. **We forego the early two year old money and the early two year old break down.**

When your horse is doing three aggressive breezes within the three mile route, he can go to the track. It is time to begin the official breezes and works. **To work and to breeze, are specific track terms**, they are almost interchangeable . . . but a breeze is slightly less aggressive than a work. A work should be challenging but not as hard as the ultimate test, the race. **To breeze the horse means to let him run as fast as he can**, kissing to him and encouraging him, **but not hitting him.** He should be a tad under his absolute top speed. The horse is truly honest, so he should try. **To work the horse means to ask and "drive" or hit him.** A trainer will have his horse work with another horse in a pretend race. Many horses are redlined in their works and are tuckered out for the race. If it looks like the rider is asking for everything the horse has, that is a hard work. Fillies tend to give you everything they have even in a breeze. They are eager to please unless they have had a bad experience while running...then they may hold back and refuse to try at all. That is why I like the animal **to grow into his or her speed.**

Works are done at the track. At **such high speed it is dangerous to try a work at home. You may be breezing your horse at home as long as you have the safe, clear stretches on your route.** Works are generally picked up by the official track clocker . He can tell when a rider is "setting" a horse down and will "pick him up at the poles" . . .time the speed of the horse for each furlong. Some trainers don't want the clocker to pick up the time. They try to sneak a horse in very early when it is dark or the track is very busy. It doesn't usually work. The clockers in Florida are astute. They can recognize a horse by the way it goes and they don't miss many works. The clocker then asks the rider the name of the horse as he heads back to the barn. If the rider or trainer purposely give the wrong name, he can be fined. The clocker turns in the sheet of timed works to the office. The times are then printed in the *Daily Racing Form* so the public has access to the information. You need at least two official works in order to start your horse the first time. This rule may vary from state to state. Check the rules in your area.

The track trainer will tell you the ground rules at his track. You need guidance

with the logistics...when you can arrive to work out in the morning...how long you can stay in the receiving barn...whether he has an open stall that you can use over night and so on. **You must establish your relationship with the track trainer.** Most of them are used to having complete control of the horse and charging you day money. A track trainer, willing to work with you as a ship in, is invaluable. When you ship your horse in and out, you are interrupting the trainer's schedule. But, if you are willing to pay, the trainer will find the time to work with you. You can offer him a flat fee for the mornings you come in. He will co-ordinate getting a rider and will help you with logistical problems that arise. If he is interested and willing to run your horse, he should automatically get ten percent of win money. **A good trainer's co-operation will help you greatly.** Listen to him, learn all you can from him. Hopefully, he will establish a good working relationship with you. You can't even get into the backside of the racetrack without the trainer signing in you and your horse. He carries insurance and is responsible for your horse while he is at the track. **The trainer's overhead is high.** Take this into consideration when negotiating the relationship.

By hook or by crook, you now have a trainer who has agreed to work with you and your ship in. The first time your horse visits the track, it should be a getting acquainted type trip. Your trainer will have arranged for a rider with plenty of time. Pay the rider double the going rate and he will take the extra time necessary to familiarize your horse with all the new experiences at the track. As the rider takes a few turns around the shedrow, your horse will see the everyday hustle and bustle. **With stirrups long, he should then take the horse to the track and jog him the wrong way on the outer rail for the circumference of the track.** During the ride the horse sees horses gallop

How much <u>Water</u> does your Horse drink <u>after</u> a <u>WORK</u>?

by . . . all he is expected to do is look around at everything. If the horse is agitated or nervous during this first mile, then have him do it again. He needs to be comfortable with his new surroundings. **When the jog has been completed in an acceptable manner, the rider should turn the horse around to the right direction, and collectedly gallop him the full mile of the track.** If the horse gallops well, and the rider finds him capable, the rider will kiss to him and allow him to "breeze down the lane" (Home Stretch) during this full mile gallop.

Stress to the rider that he should not pull the horse up sharply after the finish line. He must let the horse gallop out as far as he wants to go. If the horse wants to gallop out another full mile, allow him to. **The horse will slow down on his own when he is tired and "come back to the rider"** (my term for allowing the horse to slow down when he is ready...we should have been doing this all along in our build up gallops.)

The way your horse handles this first trip, tells you if he is fit. He should want to run since you have been galloping him a strong three miles. This first work out should have allowed the horse to expend enough energy to slightly stress his system. When he comes back to the barn, watch how long it takes for him to get his breath back and observe how he drinks water, while he is cooling out. If he takes too few sips, you probably didn't stress him too much. If he sticks his head in the bucket and tries to guzzle the water, then you know he wasn't fit enough for the work he did and might be over stressed.

It is common for the horse to **cord up** with his first works. Actually, anytime he tries too hard and is not fit enough, this can happen. **Cording up** means that his back muscles are over strained and as you cool him out after the breeze or work, you will see a tightness along his back. Ask your trainer or groom to show you what to look for so that you will understand. Make sure you note in the chart that he **corded up**. **Do not increase** the distance of breeze until he comes back with a normal back. As far as treatment goes . . . I again say, turn out and movement until he is bright and bounding again. I have never had to give any medications for this. Allow rest and then try again!

Listen to the rider. He may say, the horse tired fast or was very strong and didn't seem tired at all by the experience. Remember what the rider says and when you get home dutifully note the information on the horse's chart.

Monitor his legs the next morning, as you have done throughout this program. It should not surprise you if you find some congestion around the ankles. It is very typical the first time the horse is on a hard surface. Observe everything about your horse...how he eats..what his attitude is...how his limbs are. Turn him out as you usually do and record everything. On each successive day, observe, check, and note. By the fourth day, he should be eating normally and his legs should be fine. If they are not, wait until they are. At this time, he should be feeling good and have a desire to frolic. The stress of this work should have triggered his endorphins and he should be rebounding and feeling high on himself.

During this time, free roundpenning for 15 or 20 minutes and getting him in a good sweat should be enough on the off days. Continue to turn out and monitor.

Six or seven days later, go back to the track. Have the rider jog the horse or walk him backwards around the track again...the full mile so he can again see everything. **Then have him turn the horse around at the finish line and let him gallop strongly and openly a full mile, breezing him down the lane. He must allow the horse to continue past the finish line until he slows down and "comes back to the rider."** We are trying to bridge the speed spurts from phrase three into solid five and six furlong works.

The horse must always be allowed to gallop out until he wants to slow down. This will help him eliminate the lactic acid that has developed from the work.

Horses should not be pulled up hard after the finish line, when they are really rolling. Pulling up hard is very dangerous, it causes a great deal of tying up, as the body doesn't have time to eliminate the lactic acid normally. **Always allow the horse to keep moving until he settles down.** Think about the Olympic Sprinter. When he crosses the finish line, he doesn't just stop. He jogs beyond the finish line and continues to move so he avoids severe leg cramps. A similar phenomena happens in your horse, when he does a hard push. Lactic acid builds up in his muscles, due to oxygen debt.

This introduction to the track is very logical. **It teaches your horse that he will always be asked to run down the lane.** He learns that the finish line never **changes and that the starting gates do**. (The gates are moved around the track so that no matter where the race starts, **it always finishes in the same place...in front of the grandstand.) You learn how fit your horse is by how far beyond the finish line he carries out the work.** You see whether he really needs a lot of warm up before a race (by observing whether he is running faster in his work or breeze down the lane or whether he runs early and is tired by the time he hits the home stretch). The pattern of an early run or a late run will start to emerge.

The rider will tell you, if your horse is stronger after the finish line and wants to run long, or whether he wants to run early and not be rated. The track trainers observations are very important to you. He can give you his candid opinion.

After this second trip to the race track, you repeat the same routine as after the first trip. Consider sending him to the gates on the third trip. You can begin to get him used to the process. The first time send him to the gates, after he has done his breezes. His energy will be tapped some then and he might be more willing to listen. He can also be cooling down as he walks from the track to the gates. The crew will have the rider stand the horse and gallop, or walk him out. This depends on what the horse is capable of doing. After a few trips to the gate, the horse should be ready to break from the gates. When the Starter (head of the gate crew) thinks the horse breaks well, he will give you a gate card. Put your confidence in the gate crew and heed their advice. They have had tremendous experience and should know how to handle your horse.

One thing to watch out for at the gate! Some jockeys just hold the reins, when the horse lunges out they can fall back and maintain their balance with the reins. The bit **jerks the horse's mouth** just when we are trying to teach him to leap out efficiently. If the poorly trained jockey does this a few times, the horse will learn to connect leaping out of the gate with a hard yank on his mouth. Soon, even if the jockey doesn't yank, the horse will throw his head up in anticipation of the yank. This will distract him and keep him from a good efficient break. Much better to tell the jockey to **hang on to mane as well as rein** when breaking. That way the pull on the mane in no way inhibits the horse's head from breaking properly. Watch your exercise boy or jockey at the gates. **Don't start bad habits!**

As you progress you will see a change in the horse. He will start anticipating the track and the breezing. **Have him learn to put his energy into the gallop at the track, if he gets over-anxious.** By the third or fourth trip, when the horse knows what the race track is all about, it is probably not necessary to do the mile jog backwards. **Tell the rider to back up to the wire (finish line), turn around and immediately go into a strong gallop and breeze four furlongs down the lane.** Have him continue out as previously explained. If the horse comes out of breezes well and recovers well, on the next trip ask for five furlongs. If he does this well, have him breeze out of the gates the next time. If he handles each challenge well, continue to increase the distance and/or speed until you get a good five or six furlongs, in a time acceptable to race with. The trainer will tell you about times and conditions on the track. He will tell you about your horse's work, as compared to others at the track.

To get an idea of whether your horse is breezing or working viably, look at the clocker's sheet or racing form on the date you last worked your horse. Compare your horse's time and distance to the other horses on the list. If your horse is two seconds slower than average, you know he needs to be tighter. Work the same distance next week and see if he can go faster. If he improves, step up his distance.

At this point, you have shipped in to the track once a week for approximately six to eight weeks and free roundpenned for 15 to 20 minutes every third or fourth day at home. **Do not turn out your horse the day before a race or a work.** Stall him day and night, it will give him an edge.

You should now have a gate card and be doing fairly tight works. **(A gate card is the official permission from the Starter, stating that your horse has been schooled and has broken from the gate in an acceptable manner.) If your horse's shins are going to be sore, they may start now.** Don't get upset if they do. Look at the Section on Bucked Shins and proceed from there. Remember, this is common, not the end of the world. **Treat him cautiously and then continue training.**

Once you have a strong, five furlong work, with a strong gallop after the finish line, look for a race. Many trainers like to work a horse until he's perfect before they enter in a race. Not me. **I use the first four races as part of the training process. I consider them the last four works.** Accept that it may take about four races for the horse to learn to break well, run straight and begin the concentration necessary to become a useful race horse.

After four races, the horse should be well fit and running as honestly as he can. You will have to judge whether he got a good break and had a good position, before you can determine what kind of horse he is. There is some fine tuning that goes on at this point. Your trainer will help you with these things. He might feel that the horse needs blinkers. Many trainers put them on automatically. I personally wait to see if there is a need. Let the horse go with as little equipment as possible. **Aids like blinkers, stronger bits, and tongue ties should be used only if necessary.** Rely on the advice of your track trainer, if the advice makes sense to you. If it doesn't make sense, question it. Ask why he recommends things and try to think from the horse's point of view. Always try and help your horse. Read the Section on Setbacks.

Remember to **continue to monitor your horse**. See how he is the day after works and races. Check his legs, see how he's eating, observe his attitude and write it all down in his chart. Know your horse.

A list of good trainers in your area, who will work with our program will be in our Newsletter.

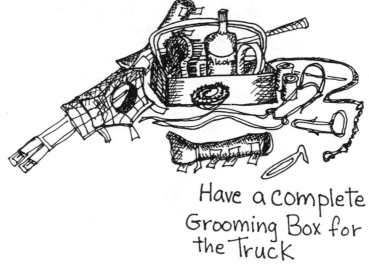

Have a complete
Grooming Box for
the Truck

Track Breezes

The first time or two, go the wrong way a full mile so
That horse can see all activity before galloping
Have rider with long stirrups!

At finish line (after wrong way mile), gallop horse
in right direction –
At top of Stretch, kiss to horse
and Breeze to finish line
DON'T PULL UP AT Finish Line!
LeT Horse continue Breeze
and COME BACK to rider
(This way you don't inhibit fit horse
from getting the exercise he needs!)
He may breeze a furlong or two beyond
finish Line – Keep timing and see where
the horse slows down.

Observe: where horse tires –
How long it takes to cool –
How much water he drinks

NEXT trip to track
Begin the same – Then Breeze 3 furlong from finish
Let horse continue Breeze beyond finish (if he can)
EACH Successive Work or Breeze extend the
length of the Breeze
and Tighten the speed

Only go further – faster
if horse is healthy
and sound!

trip # 1 breezed 2 furlong in 24
trip # 2 breezed 3 furlong in 39
Trip # 3 breezed 3 furlong in 37
Trip # 4 breezed 4 furlong in 52
Trip # 5 breezed 4 furlong in 50
continue until you have 6 in 1:18
or so

Second Method -
To the <u>Track</u> to <u>Stay</u>

SECOND METHOD - TO THE TRACK TO STAY

When a horse is sent to the track to stay, after having been trained by the methods in this manual, the transition can be hard. The horse is feeling good and has been allowed to jump and frolic for a few hours every day. Now, **in the race track routine, his every movement is restricted.** The amount of time he is ridden and exercised is decreased. There is no outside time.

When I first started training, my horses went to the track after having undergone a more aggressive training schedule. They had been galloped five to ten miles everyday. When I turned them over to the trainer the first thing he said was, "What's wrong with these horses? They just stand there. They're so quiet." I, of course, was offended. My "children" were just being good. I had turned them out every day and galloped them hard. When they went into a stall they were tired and well mannered.

A week later I came back to the track. As I walked by my sweet horses in their stalls, they lunged at me or anyone who walked by. They were like all the other unhappy, bored horses who are not allowed to frolic. They were full of pent up energy they couldn't release.

Bad habits can develop in horses who live at the track. They evolve over a period of time, because the animal can't cope. He is not allowed normal living and is bored, nervous, frustrated, in pain, or all of the above.

When you go down a typical shedrow at the track you'll see animals bite at you, lunge at you and weave back and forth. Others are cribbers. They bite the stall door, or fence, and suck air in through their mouths. **These traits are manifestations of the frustration of being in an unnatural environment.** They help to alleviate the horse's boredom. **Most of these vices will disappear when the horse is living at home and turned out.** However, some are high strung and are always nervous.

My horses soon were cranky like all the rest. Then they began having a great deal of trouble with tie-ups. I asked the trainer what the horses were doing. He told me they were being sent to the track to gallop one mile. As they came back, they all seemed to have tie-up problems. It was manifested by a shortness of stride, generally in the rear, and an inability, in severe cases, to even walk. The horse may paw the ground with his front feet and have spasms in his rump muscles. Trembling, sweating and obvious stress accompanied these symptoms.

After galloping one mile they were being pulled up, turned around and brought back to the barn. The problem was obvious to me. They were used to galloping five to ten miles. A one mile gallop was like a warm-up to them. No wonder they were tied-up. They were full of energy, had a one mile warmup...and were told, "That's it." They surely headed back to the barn bouncing and full of desire to run, with fuel in their system...pumped up and ready.

Tie-up is a phenomenon seen a great deal in the last century. At that time horses were worked everyday but Sunday. On that day they didn't move. Their metabolism had to adjust to the different Sunday routine. When they went to work on Monday, their muscles were "locked". Feed had to be adjusted and the horses needed some kind of movement on Sunday to avoid this problem.

When my horses had the problem at the track, it was because they were galloping way too much. **They were too fit and had too much of the wrong kind of work. I was galloping them too long and making it more difficult for them to adjust to the confinement of the track.** So, I took them all home and developed the program that I am teaching you.

No matter how it is approached, **it is difficult for a horse to adjust to being stalled 23 hours a day. The younger they are the more difficult it is.** They want to bound out of the stall in the morning. This intimidates the groom and he will over shank the horse unless he is really tuned in and realizes the horse just feels great. We don't want the horse to be punished because he feels good. We can only hope your trainer has good help. These are things for you to be aware of, that should be discussed with your trainer. When the trainer takes your horse on the track for the first time, he must allow the rider to ride with longer stirrups than usual. He should have the rider take the horse around the wrong way, completing the circumference of the track while allowing the horse to walk and jog and look at everything. If the horse is nervous and is still over reacting to the environment, do a second mile while trying to relax and accustom him to the activity of the other horses around him. Since the horse has had a lot of under saddle experience and mental growth with you, he should not be too over reactive.

When the horse has settled down, have the rider turn him around and gallop the full mile in a relaxed manner, allowing the horse to breeze down the lane and gallop out as far as he want after the finish line. If this means going a whole extra mile, assure the rider that it is all right. **Always allow the horse to "come back" to the rider. It is very important for the horse to be allowed to gallop and slow down when**

Young Horses can find Confinement Difficult !

Standing in a stall for 23 hours out of every day, does not develop a resilient athlete

he wants. **If he doesn't get comfortably tired, you'll have an animal that builds up energy. He will start fighting the rider.** These animals are fit. **They just need speed honing. They do not need miles of drilling, slow gallop or hobby horsing. They do need to accustom themselves to the track routine.**

For the next three days your horse should not go to the track. **Continual trips to the track on a daily basis and the stacking of stress to the bone, used in conventional training, tend to break down young horses.** Ask the trainer to have someone hack the horse around the backside of the track for half an hour. **If there is no other choice, have him ponied for a least a mile.** At some tracks, a paddock may be rented and you can turn the horse out to frolic for a least an hour a day. **Again, I stress that daily pounding on unnatural surfaces eventually breaks down a horse. In allowing your horse time to rebuild in between the track gallops or works, you keep him from many track breakdowns.**

Standing for 23 hours, which causes a lack of blood circulation, and then running hard is the scenario which makes horses more prone to break down. Your trainer may not like to hear your methods, they interfere with established routine and demand more from his help. But, you want to make the situation healthy for your horse. It is your purpose, as a trainer, to get the best for and from your horse. You and your track trainer can reach compromises that suit both you and the horse.

Now we are into our fifth day at the track. The horse breezed out, after a mile or two backwards to see everything on the first day. Then, hopefully, he had two or three days without track pounding. If all was well, he could have been sent to the gates to stand and gallop out on those off days. If he did, he will only need a few times at the gate before you start incorporating every fourth day breezes with breezing out of the gates.

Do not fool yourself into thinking Horse is fine if you have been <u>masking symptoms</u> with medications!

Now you must give the trainer some leeway with your horse. He may do every fourth or fifth day breezes. As the horse tightens and becomes more efficient and honest, he may need more time in between breezes and works to recover.

The recovery time should be equivalent to an hour or more of turnout, or some kind of off track trail riding or ponying, no pounding, but lots of movement, a couple of times around the track the wrong way, if you have no other alternative. The idea is movement without hard pounding. After a month or six weeks of training at the track, you should be getting a handle on the horse. **He'll be trying harder down the lane and be more willing to quit after the finish line, as the works lengthen to racing distance.**

At this point, **if there is swelling, sore shins or lameness, do not give Bute and continue running. Allow the horse to rest and recuperate from soreness. Tell the trainer you don't want jugs. You don't want Bute every night and you don't want pain masking medication. If there is pain, it is for a reason. A young three year old should not have pain.** If he does, he should be allowed to walk out of his soreness. **Don't get into the habit of ignoring pain on young unruined horses by masking it.** I am not opposed to helping an older horse, who has soreness and stiffness, and needs Bute to run.

Avoiding pain killers helps the trainer observe what is brewing in the young horse. In traditional training, if the pounding on the track surface causes soreness and filling then the trainer gives Bute. Then he poultices and wraps. This inhibits the swelling. The next day it is impossible to determine the status of the legs. The horse is sent out again and the process is repeated. **The horse's problems are masked by all the wrapping, poulticing, and medication.** When the horse goes bad, they are all sorry and just can't imagine why this happened. They were giving such up to date care. This is where over use of systemic corticosteroids may begin.

You can now understand why I prefer shipping in. **It really is life at the track that wears horses down. It's too little work, too fast a speed, and too young an age.** The horse stacks the stress of trauma from the track surface and over periods of time problems appear. **Turn-outs and free galloping are very important parts of training. IF YOU CAN KEEP THEIR TIME ON THE TRACK DOWN TO LEGITIMATE GALLOPS, BREEZES OR WORKS, YOU WILL DEFEND YOUR HORSE FROM MANY OF THE TRACK BREAKDOWNS. EXTRA TIME FOR GROWTH AND REBUILDING IS IMPORTANT.** Remember, these are the equivalent of the horse's teen years. **We want him to survive training and grow into a useful mature horse.** Beware of trainers who want to use a lot of drugs and vet help on your horse. The horse should be sound, healthy and young enough to handle the work without any chemical enhancement.

At this point in training, you should read and follow the instructions given to week-end haulers. Let the trainer work or breeze the horse every five or six days depending on how the horse holds up. **When he shows the fitness to go a strong five furlong work and gallops out strongly, put him in a race.** There is nothing like a race to find out whether or not the horse wants to be a runner. After four races, you should be able to tell if he is a cost effective race horse. These are suggestions. Your trainer may have a different approach. Respect and listen to him. He may want the horse tighter and ready to win the first time out.

If your horse appears to be trying hard in the races and has no legitimate excuse for losing, his best is probably not enough to justify the expense of the race track. Try not to be pulled into putting more and more into a horse that doesn't have the talent. It is not cost effective. If you are training at home, the expenses are not as bad and you can afford to be more patient. You must realize that you can't give a horse talent he doesn't possess.

Hauling

Hauling
and Shipping

A few suggestions
for the road

Loading the Horse

Equipment

HAULING

HAULING AND SHIPPING INTO RACE TRACKS

Not everyone should consider training their own racehorse when it is time to go to the track. The racetrack is another world; **a whole new set of rules**. Trainers at the track are very adept at entering horses and appraising chances for a particular horse in a particular field. If you find a trainer willing to listen to how you want your horse started at the track, he is worth his weight in gold.

When you are going to do the hauling yourself, you must be aware of the many pitfalls along the road. I have trucked over three hundred thousand miles and have learned a few things along the way.

Rule number one and most important...**maintain your equipment.** Make sure your truck or hauling vehicle is large enough and strong enough for the load. Be sure your hitch is properly attached to the frame of the vehicle. We had real bumpers when I started. Some hitches were attached to the bumper. Very bad, because the bumper was only attached to the car by bolts. Heavy duty hauling is done with a variety of hitches attached to the frame of the vehicle by bolts or welding.) **Make sure your hitch dealer is reputable and installs the recommended size hitch for the weight involved.** There are charts indicating the proper ratio of hauling vehicle wheel base to the trailer length.

Never exceed the recommended limits. When hauling a four horse bumper hitch trailer with one or two horses, never put both horses in the rear of the trailer. **Always put more weight on the tongue to avoid fish-tailing.** If you have ever experienced the horror of fish-tailing, you know the sheer terror of having no control whatsoever over your vehicle. It is a hard way to learn about weight distribution. If you are hauling a two horse trailer with one horse in it, it is advisable to put the horse on the left. No, not so you can look at him in your mirror, though that's an added benefit, but because on two lane roads it keeps the trailer more stable when there is no shoulder on the right. The horse's weight could cause the trailer to pull and fall on the right side. **Think stability!**

Always have rubber mats on the floor of the trailer. Never have the horse struggle to keep his balance because of poor footing. Horses seem to prefer having something to prop themselves against while traveling. Think of yourself. If you were standing in the middle of a trailer rolling down the highway, and had no use of your arms, how would you maintain your balance? Maybe by wedging yourself against something. My horses seem to travel better when they have bars or walls to brace against. If you watch a lone horse rolling by you in a stock trailer, you'll notice that even though he has the whole trailer, he'll be braced against one side and corner to balance himself. If you are hauling one horse, put up the center bar to give him some support.

Any dividers between horses should have rug or rubber padding all the way down to the floor. My very expensive trailer did not have this. Once a horse stepped on the coronet band of another. We cannot afford this kind of injury. Examine your trailer and install the necessary safeguards. The black rubber bungee type straps

used by truckers are excellent tie downs in the trailer. They allow the horse movement but stretch and pull the horse's head back to where it should be. Put snaps on either end and clip one end to the halter and one to the trailer. A hay bag or a hay bin (the only place to use one,) should be in front of the horse so that he can nibble during the trip. Have extra lead ropes handy in case of emergencies.

If you are traveling in hot country, remember how much heat a horse's body creates. Always keep the windows open. Have you ever seen very closed in trailers with no air circulation, rolling down the road in the summer? Did you wonder if the owners opened the trailer to find a horse with heat stroke? In hot weather keep the trailer open for breezes. If your windows are in the front of the trailer, make sure your horse is tied loosely enough to move his head out of the wind, if he wants. Never tie him so tightly that he can't drop his head, cough, sneeze and generally make himself comfortable. He can get a crick in his back if he must carry his head in an awkward position.

The question of whether horses are better off facing front or back is often discussed. My horses seem to like the equipment I have. Why look for trouble? Horses are pretty adaptable. They even stand sideways in some vans. The fashion in new vans and trailers seems to be at an angle, a slant load, which is okay, too. Don't worry unless you have a problem with a particular horse. **As long as the horse has good air circulation, and is not too hot or too cold, he should be all right.**

A FEW SUGGESTIONS FROM AN EXPERIENCED HAULER

When my teenaged sons were entrusted with the horses and equipment, they were told, "**Drive as if you have no brakes!**" Of course, this was a typical worried mother, forced to depend on the reliability of a seventeen year old. (My God, how could I?) But, actually, that is very good advice. **You must never think, even if you have super electric brakes, that you can haul a trailer with a horse in it driving the way you drive a car**. Zooming up to lights and having to stop quickly, just won't do with a horse in the back. He'll be sitting beside you before you know it. Remember, his body mass is high. If you throw it around, it can be very unstablizing to the towing vehicle, and very hard on the horse.

If you drive as if you have no brakes, you'll shift cautiously up to speed, and try to coast down when coming to stop lights, downshifting if you have a manual transmission. This is better on your equipment and the horse. No sudden jerks to start; and no hard braking to stop.

When you get into the vehicle to haul, take a moment to think. **Under no circumstances feel pressured or rushed.** If you are running late, accept that you will arrive late, and let it go. There is nothing more horrible than a trailer wreck with live animals.

Initially, hauling was very perturbing. Driving my horses and children down the turnpike in a torrential rainstorms, or trying to stay on a tiny two lane road with giant semi-trailers breathing down my neck having no place to pull over, was terrifying. I would imagine a horrible twisted wreck featuring my trailer in a mangled mess. It was necessary to make a conscious effort to block that image out of my mind and imagine

myself arriving safely at the race track. Over the years, I have had to force myself to concentrate on this kind of positive imagery. Don't disregard the dangers, control them as best you can, by driving safely and soberly with proper equipment. Will yourself to arrive alive.

It is impossible to avoid the summer rains here in Florida. Go slowly and cautiously when you're caught in inclement weather. You can listen to good tapes for amusement. In the North, plan your racing and track training to coincide with the good weather. You probably don't want to be hauling on icy roads and in terrible snow storms. Plan to train at home or lay up in the bad weather and run when the snow and ice is gone. **Work with the environment, not against it.**

A CB radio is a big help when you are traveling in unfamiliar areas. Truckers give good advice on routes, traffic and conditions. The radio was essential, especially when I was broken down on the side of the road. Yes, this does happen, even with the best of plans.

In my ten years of shipping into races, a race was never missed due to hauling problems. Being a female, and training from the farm, I was acutely aware of how bad it would be to miss a race because of a breakdown. There have been close calls, a wheel falling off the four horse trailer in the middle of the cane fields at ten o'clock at night. Luckily, a trailer repair-man made the mistake of answering his phone at eleven p.m. He gave in to my pleas and worked on the axle, with the three horses in the van. We were back on the road by two a.m. The horses made the races in plenty of time. (We had to make the races, one of the horses was owned by a syndicate of five lawyers. All they needed was some kind of silly excuse such as a wheel falling off...ha!)

Both of my trucks are capable of hauling either trailer at all times. You don't have to have back-up equipment if you are only training for yourself. **If you are a professional, you must have back-ups . . . the worst possible things happen at the worst possible times.**

One truck broke down three hours into the Miami trip. A call home and the other was on its way. Fortunately, I have great kids and wonderful neighbors willing to help me in a pinch. Another time, an engine, five thousand miles beyond the 50,000 mile warranty, blew because of a faulty water pump. (On a   diesel, this is a common occurrence every fifty thousand miles.) Rather than arranging a tow home, the truck and horses were towed to the racetrack, a hundred miles away. The time to worry about the truck after the race. . . the horses come first.

Never, never unload a horse on the side of the road! If the horse is having a fit in the trailer, that's where it will have to be. It would be worse to unload him and risk having him get away from you. He might run into the traffic and cause havoc. No matter what, keep the horse in the trailer until you are in a safe place or a farm where you can handle the problem.

Years ago, Rompun, a tranquilizer, was kept in my glove compartment. It was for emergencies, but, there are very stringent rules about needles on the backside of the race track. I was afraid of entering the racetrack with anything like that. I have discussed this problem at length with the track vets, but found no solution. I just haul and pray. If you have problems with a hysterical horse, go to the nearest policeman,

98

police station or fire station. They will help you find a vet in emergency circumstances.

Never feed a horse heavy grain before a trip. Give them hay along the way. If it is a long trip, give them a handful of grain every now and then so they don't think they are starving to death. Always offer water when you stop. Generally, on a three to six hour trip, you'll only need to stop for gas and water. Feed them when they are settled at the track, the night before the race. I go to Miami the night before the race as the trip is five to six hours. The trip to Tampa is an hour and a half, so we go the day of the race. Birmingham is 12 hours away. We stop and water them, but never unload them. It is handy to have two water buckets and one feed bucket for each horse. In Miami they drink a lot of water. You might just have one bucket of each, if you are staying close enough to check and water them. Take their food already mixed with vitamins, etc., and tied in plastic bags, along with a couple of bales of hay.

All my racing equipment, bridles, blinkers, etc., is kept in the truck, hanging on hooks in the back seat. An exercise saddle with extra girths and saddlecloths also lives permanently in the truck. Everything is ready to use. There is a complete grooming kit with brushes, tape, alcohol, and Vick's for the nose, tongue ties, and various little items. A complete set of equipment is necessary so you are not unprepared at the track. Separate equipment is at the farm. **If you don't have enough equipment to have two full sets, make a list. Check it twice before you leave to be sure you are prepared at the receiving barn.**

Have all the paperwork necessary to get through the stable gates; Coggins, health certificate, and registration papers. Try to be respectful and courteous to the track personnel. Not always an easy task, especially if you have been braving storms, bad traffic or crazy horses. When you get to the barn, unload your horse as efficiently as possible. My routine is down to a science. It takes me fifteen minutes to unload, feed, tuck in four horses and hose out the trailer. Always clean the trailer. Calder ants are attracted by the manure. They taught me the hard way to hose out the trailer immediately.

Once, after a long day at the races, the four horses were loaded one by one in the big trailer. I was so eager to get on the road back home, that the swarm of red ants devouring manure went unnoticed. Because of the perfunctory manner in which the trailer had been cleaned the night previous, the manure had not been completely removed. While pulling out of Calder there was a great deal of kicking and stomping in the trailer. I knew better than to ignore it and pulled over. The horses were in a frenzy with ants crawling up their legs, stinging as they went. After an immediate return to the receiving barn, all four horses were unloaded and the trailer was hosed and scrubbed. An hour later we departed again and arrived home very late that night.

When you embark on your travels, be calm, cool and collected. Keep a few rousing tapes in your truck. "This Land Is Your Land, This Land Is My Land", is a great song to sing as you cruise across beautiful expanses of open countryside on your way to the track. Visitors accompanying me in the truck mumble about my off key singing and archaic music, but that's okay. "Michael, Row Your Boat Ashore" always gets my blood pumping. It can keep me awake for another ten miles at the end of a long haul. Friends tell stories about trips from hell when referring to escapades where they

are trapped for six hours in my truck enduring the gamut of music, from "If I Had A Hammer" to the "1812 Overture". (Played loudly, the cannons sound like they are being shot from the back seat..guaranteed to wake you up if you are drowsy). These friends also complain about getting grease or a little dirt on their clothes when they help me load the horses. What are good friends for but to share exciting times; so what if they get a little sweaty or dirty along the way.

Just think of the fun you and your friends will have when you all begin *your* GREAT ADVENTURE!

Prepare to HAUL HORSES !

Have the <u>correct</u> <u>equipment</u> for the job!

Have the <u>Vehicles</u> <u>well</u> <u>maintained</u>

Have the Trailer <u>well-padded</u> and <u>safe</u>

Have <u>good</u> <u>air</u> <u>circulation</u> for the horses

Drive as if <u>you</u> <u>have</u> <u>no</u> <u>Brakes</u>!

NEVER DRIVE UNDER STRESS or in a RUSH!

<u>Be</u> <u>prepared</u>- Have <u>plenty</u> of <u>gas</u>

Have the Horses' Traveling Papers

<u>Read</u> the <u>Map</u>!

Happy Trails !

SUGGESTIONS ON HOW TO LOAD

I have just come in from struggling with a horse that was not taught to load when she was young. Perhaps this is the best time to discuss loading techniques. **You must have obedient horses that load with no problems, in order to successfully train off the farm.** When you buy a horse, the first thing to do is take him home and teach him to load. Horses purchased at sales usually have not had much experience in loading. Ten strong men and a vet with a tranquilizer may be needed to get the animal into a small trailer.

Don't start something you can't finish. The ideal way to teach a horse to load is when he is very young and you can shove him around. By letting him eat in the trailer, follow you in with a bucket of feed, or by putting mama horse in the trailer to eat, he learns naturally not to fear the "'DARK BOX". Unfortunately, I seem to receive horses that have been galloped free for two years, pulled in, run through the sale (with the help of mood altering drugs) and then sent to me as the fuzzy haze wears off. By this time they are frightened of the new environment and react appropriately. This is why it is good to have two, or preferably three, strong men. **Start out with no prejudice toward the horse.** I actually act as if I expect the animal to docilely enter the trailer with a slight tug on the shank. Have the trailer parked and attached to the truck in an enclosed field. If the animal gets loose, he will not be able to go far. The ramp should be easy to step onto and at a gentle angle. My first trailer did not have a ramp. The horse had to step up and into it. If your trailer doesn't have a ramp, don't worry. Teach him to step into it.

Horses apparently perceive the ramp as a bottomless pit. Their general reaction is, "Oh, boy, I'm not stepping on that!" The horse will throw up his head and yank back hard (body language, for, "No.") Have a shank with a chain on the horse for these lessons. Put the chain over the nose, never under the chin. That would encourage him to throw up his head further and rear on you. Yank hard on the shank at this point and let him know you don't want negative behavior...(yanking back and refusing to do as you bid.)

Use a twenty foot long shank when loading. If a horse does pull it out of your hands, you can still grab it fast. Be very vocal with naughty horses. Say, "No!" very sharply. If the horse continues to pull back, I'm of the school that says, "You want to pull back, then go back!" Yank, and if he continues to back up, continue to yank sharply on the chain. At this point it is probably better to put the chain over the teeth, under the lip. You don't want to do any damage, but you want this animal to respect you when you say, "No." **The minute he stops pulling back, praise him and gently lead him forward.** If he baulks and pulls his head back again, yank hard. It is imperative not to allow the horse to get in the habit of pulling back and rearing to fight you. You must be firm about unacceptable behavior. **A horse that rears is a terrible danger.** When he stops pulling back, your helper can tap him on the rump to encourage the horse to go forward. When he does, he is praised and there is no pressure on his head. Never yank on the horse unfairly or in unfounded anger. It must always be clear that the punishment is for negative behavior, not because you are having a temper tantrum.

It may take just five minutes, or a couple of hours for the horse to realize that if he goes with you there is no pain, and when he fights you, he is punished. When we get back to the ramp, and he still refuses to step on, go inside the trailer and pull and control his head while the two strong helpers lock hands and literally shove the horse inside. Once in, the doors are closed quickly and the animal is praised, fed and maybe taken for a short ride. Then we open the door and back him out, allowing him to turn his head to see what he is stepping onto. We walk him around for a minute and ask him to go back on the trailer. If he refuses, we again go back to step one and shank and yank until he is again willing to obey. Usually, the fight is not as long or as difficult the second time around. Every day, for a week or two at feeding time, lead him to the trailer and have him follow you in. Give him a few bits of feed, praise him and lead him out. At other times, lead him on without any enticement. He must load under all conditions.

This system usually works. Remember, **if you are going to start the process, plan to spend the whole day, if necessary, until you finish with the horse in the trailer**. If you give up before he is in, **you'll have double the trouble next time**. You may have the same situation getting them into water to swim. Generally experiencing a big fight the first time, then a few mini fights, then getting easier, until they find that the trailer or the water isn't so bad.

Whenever it was time to work with a difficult horse, he was told, **it's the trailer or DIE**. Hopefully, he would get the message early, before we're both exhausted. The best time for loading lessons was when my sons, the six foot three cowboy type and the six foot four wrestler, were handy. One horse, Street Beat, knew how to load when he came to me. He was not afraid of the trailer. But he had a "Maybe I will, maybe I won't!" attitude. The horse pulled his trick one day in Miami, when it was time to load up and start the long trip home. Since I usually handled loading myself, I didn't expect a problem. He baulked and became difficult. He acted like a horse's ass, backing into cars and doing all sorts of dangerous things. He seemed to know that I couldn't wale the tar out of him there. Finally, various strong men had to help me load him. I made up my mind he wouldn't pull that on me again.

The next afternoon, I called my son out and we began **THE GREAT STRUGGLE**. It was June in Florida. The humidity was easily equal to the temperature of 101 degrees. We started the loading process and the horse baulked. We did my "if you want to back up, back up" routine. He backed all the way to the fences before he would stop and come forward. My son, Nando, was driving him from behind. Every time he got near the ramp, he would baulk. Again and again, we struggled. After an hour and a half, my son, the horse and I were standing there panting glowering at each other. The sweat was pouring off of us in buckets. Nando said, "Mom, do you think he could die in this heat?" I figured the horse was at least as sturdy as we were..and we weren't dead yet. I said, "Nando, I don't think so...but if he is going to die, he is going to die in the trailer!" Street Beat must have heard me, or decided that today, we were not going to give up. He acquiesced, strolled into the trailer, and never baulked again.

There is a mental game going on here. Horses are animals. They respect those who command respect. If they can dominate you, they will. **You must dominate them mentally and convince them that you are physically dominant also.** You may need help from equipment to prove your point. Use what you have, but always be fair to the animal. **Many times they are legitimately frightened**....other times they remind me of my children between fourteen and twenty one...**stubborn and willing to test you every way they can!**

Suggestions on Loading

Don't start unless you have the Time
to finish the job.

Assume the horse will cooperate
        Praise and Reward him when
he obeys
        Punish him when he is bad
"Yank and Shank" if necessary

        Get him in the Trailer
          feed him, Pet him
            Praise him

Unload him   Have a helper behind.
Reload him   the horse – to drive him
                  forward

Snort! Snort!

EQUIPMENT FOR THE HORSE WHILE BEING HAULED

Various types of wrapping and bandaging exist for horses during travel. Personally, I prefer the neophrene boots that cover the leg from below the knee to over the hoof. They are attached with velcro, fit nicely, and protect the coronet band as well as the lower leg. Using fleece and bandages is very time consuming if you ship horses frequently. You can put the shipping boots on in a few minutes and the horse will be ready to go. I use boots on the front legs only. Horses tend to fuss and kick, trying to get them off their hind legs. (That's my excuse...if you prefer, put them on all four legs.) They cost around sixty-five dollars a set, and are well worth the investment. They can be washed and wear well. (A company called Tuffy Products Bighorn, Inc., makes them).

Beware, many horses have what are called "bandage bows". Bandages can slip or are put on too tightly and cause damage to the tendon. On a long trip, **someone must continuously check the wraps or the horse is better off without them**. One of the worst stories is about a trainer who wrapped his horses' tails so they wouldn't be rubbed raw on the trip. The van hauling the horses from Florida to the North broke down for several days. The horses were given food and water and were cared for, but no one thought about the tail wraps. When the horses arrived and the wraps were taken off their tails, it was too late. The blood supply to their tails had been inhibited and all the horses lost their tails. The trainer lost his job. He surely never expected such a delay. Be very suspicious of wrapping for any period of time, unless there is a medical reason. Don't look for problems. If the trip is long, some trainers pull the shoes and leave them barefoot. Be sure your horse has competent supervision when he travels. Shipping boots, bell boots and leg wraps all contribute to the safety and comfort of the animal if they are competently utilized.

Happy Trails!

Happy Hauling

I Don't want to !

Training Aids

Heart Rate
Monitor- Interval
Training

Swimming

Treadmills

Chart Keeping

TRAINING AIDS

Heart Rate Monitor and Interval Training

Early in my training endeavors, I read everything possible and attended seminars. One seminar, held in Philadelphia, was on sports medicine. Tom Ivers was the main speaker and he was teaching "Interval Training." The program touts workouts every fourth day and miles of galloping on the other days. The horse is not given time off to rebuild. Nevertheless, as a beginner, it sounded like a good program. I used the heart rate monitor, but allowed for track "variations". My horses were galloping in heavy sand and hills. His were galloping on a flat predictable surface.

The interval training method encourages long slow miles, up to a point and then many speed works within the galloping program. It contains very specific instructions on how to build up speed. The program emphasizes high tech monitoring and is quite structured. It depends on equipment, which separates the trainer from his animal. **He may focus on interpreting the numbers and ignore the physical signs the animal may be showing.** The program is very aggressive, physically, for the young animal. It requires many miles of galloping on a daily basis, at a track. It is also very demanding for the trainers and exercise people. **Too grueling for man and beast**.

I was able to do the speed intervals with the proper distance, follow the spiking of the heart rate in full speed, observe how long it took to recover, etc. The most important information the heart rate monitor told me was that my training route certainly did "fit" the horses. Their recovery from sustained high heart rate was well within the recommendations. They were working harder and going slightly slower than they would on the race track, because they were carrying more weight and galloping in heavy sand. That was fine with me. Pure speed could be honed at the track. The monitor taught me they were cardiovascularly fit.

However, we must keep in mind that we are training a complete body, not just the heart and lungs. My horses lost tremendous amounts of weight, even though they consumed huge quantities of feed. They also developed swelling in the fetlocks if they did the recommended speed works and gallops. If they rested a day or two, they came back with a better attitude and were much fresher. During the third stage of the Iver's program, they seemed to be over drilled and would go off their feed. **The problem with the program stems from demanding too much speed too frequently**. This holds for racing, also.

In the third stage of interval training, you are giving tremendous amounts of feed and galloping many, many miles. I believe my methods are kinder to the horse and trainer. Tom says that a horse in his program will be doing five eights of a mile with faster and faster works, honing into five furlongs in a minute two, a minute one,

a minute, fifty nine seconds, etc. There are horses that, on their best day, with the best training in the world, can't deliver five eighths of a mile in a minute flat, or a minute one or two, etc. If his training were that consistent, every horse Tom put through the program should become a champion. There are many basically untalented horses that show good conformation, heart rate, etc. Unfortunately or fortunately, talent and other undefined qualities come into the picture .

Before trying Tom's methods, my horses were galloping about ten miles a day, and I'm not light. I have never been under 160 lbs. (God, what an admission!) I had been a recreation director and felt drilling and pushing, etc., would work on horses as well as it did on humans. This was a mistake. **Horses and humans do not develop equivalently.** One of the most important differences is that **the horse has a built in overdrive system.** When he needs a surge of power, his spleen kicks in and he is given an extra shot of red blood cells. The horse is unique, in that his innate built in "fight" or "flight" ability has been honed through the centuries. He can increase his oxygen intake nearly 35 times from rest to run. By comparison, human athletes are highly trained to develop their oxygen delivery capacity. At the height of their training, they can only increase their oxygen intake about 10 times. Therefore, the horse is a natural runner and his training is to enable him to sustain his gift of speed. Based on my observations from galloping my own sets of horses for about ten years, I do not believe that works or races every four days, with miles of galloping in between, make the horse stronger or more fit. They wear him down. **He doesn't have time to rebuild from the trauma of an honest work or race.**

When I had sets of four or six horses, they were "insulted" (stressed), and then rested two to four days , depending on the phase of training. As explained in the training chapters, **the rest days are vital for the rebuilding process**. The turn out and free roundpenning is my way of allowing them free, but loosening up time.

Tom Ivers' interval training is highly intense, and remember, we're working with animals that have brains, personalities, various likes, dislikes, and tendencies. None fit into the heavy training schedule completely. **Controlling to the second, every work on a given day is asking a lot from horse and rider.**

I hate to tell you some of my predicaments, while trying to read the heart rate monitor, strapped to my thigh, control the horse and keep the electronic leads underneath the girth, where they would give an accurate reading. It must have looked hilarious. We barely missed the trees many times, when I was concentrating on the numbers, instead of watching where I was going.

Tom says each horse is slightly different and that his training should be adjusted accordingly. I agree. There are many ways to train. **The monitoring did help me assess and understand the horse's cardiovascular system.** However, the horse's physical signs provide the same information, if you know how to observe them. **The horse's attitude and body will indicate to you his readiness to do another round.** Horses brought up, with a solid foundation, ease very nicely into speed logically and naturally. Let them tell you what they are physically able to do.

The heart rate monitor is a good device to measure an individual's recovery time. It teaches you about cardiopulmonary function. However, you can train quite well without

it. There are subtle changes going on in the horse that don't register on the monitor until it is too late like fractures, etc.

One thing I learned with the heart rate monitor, was that on extremely hot days, after the works, the horses would continue panting, although the monitor showed the heart rate was back to normal. Why? The horses were trying to cool off. The panting was lowering their body heat.

A group of horses that I had trained, following Tom's methods, were sent to Chicago. They were two and a half years old and were honed. Not an ounce of fat on them from miles of galloping. When they arrived in Chicago, the track trainer was upset. He felt they looked gaunt. (The stress of the trip probably made them a little dehydrated.) I told him to allow them a few days to recover from the trip and to gallop them. He followed the instructions, then called and said, "They certainly are the most fit horses I've ever received." I learned that having a horse that honed was not appreciated. I had done three times as much work as any other trainer and the track trainers weren't really happy. The trainer told the owner the horse needed more weight (fat) before he would continue training.

All the galloping in the world does not make a horse run faster than he is able to run. Therefore, it is imperative that as a trainer, **we seek the way to allow the horse to develop his own natural speed without breaking him down**. Our main job is to do no harm along the way.

My overall view of interval training as taught by Tom Ivers in "The Fit Race Horse", is that it is entirely too much work, too much stress on the limbs, too much feed being passed through the horse. Over all, it is **too intense a program for a young horse**.

Although I don't agree with all of Tom's methods, there is a great deal of extremely valuable information for both owners and trainers in his books. They are fun to read and were invaluable to me. My program evolved from a combination of training programs and experiences. It is interval training and track training interspersed with rest, common sense and hands on monitoring.

Don't Overtrain!

SWIMMING

Swimming is excellent. It takes all the weight off the horse's joints and makes him feel good. Just mulching in the water is therapeutic. However, swimming should not be used instead of galloping to train a healthy horse. Galloping prepares a horse to be a runner.

Swimming is good for an injured horse, under certain circumstances. When a horse is recovering from bone trauma and the injury is still too compromised to allow him to be turned out to frolic and feel good, **swimming will help him get his blood circulating without the bone concussion** that would cause more injury. Having an injured horse jog in the water is good, too. The water deflects the concussion of the hoof striking the ground and he starts using his muscles sooner than in complete confinement.   It's excellent if the horse has had a temporary strain.

However, if your horse has open, festering wounds, it may be better to allow some degree of healing before you allow him to swim. These wounds should be hosed on a daily basis. Use your own judgement, as to the severity of the wound, in relationship to water. Salt water might be helpful. You should also avoid swimming "bleeders". It stresses their lungs so intensely, they may start bleeding immediately.

Horses that have foundered will get great relief walking, floating and **moving around in the water.** If the founder is severe, this might be the only relief they get from the pain. When First Prediction foundered, we put her on a 20 ft. shank and let her float, while we sat on the dock reading or contemplating life. Doubtless, this water therapy helped her recover from the severe founder.

Use swimming the same way you use free roundpenning. It keeps a horse supple and allows cardiovascular exercise between gallops. It is especially useful in the summer, when it is a convenient way to cool the horses.

Between races, when a horse is "dead fit" and competing, he could swim every other day and be free roundpenned on alternate days. This keeps the horse fresh for races and relieves any soreness from the last race. In this sense, it is a good maintenance tool.

Never use swimming as the only form of exercise. The horse must always be turned out and allowed to move. Some farms religiously swim horses. They take them from the stalls, walk them to the pool or lake, swim them and put them back in the stall. This is not good. The horses' bodies are only developing the swim movement patterns. Their bodies must also develop regular running movements. Therefore, **galloping, interspersed with free roundpenning and swimming is the recommended exercise program**.

If you have an old class horse with lots of aches and pains, swimming is probably good for him between races. This kind of horse needs to be kept healthy and comfortable. The races keep him fit and **he needs recovery time after the races to rebuild from the trauma.**

If you don't have access to water, don't worry. If the horse is sound, he can live without swimming. Fortunately, my farm is on a lake. Our wooden dock was lined with conveyer belting, in areas that might be dangerous. A floating dock was attached

at the end of the stationary dock. To swim a horse, a shank is put on, and he is forced to swim around me. Some people swim horses out of small boats. I have no experience with this. If you have easy access to a body of water, enjoy it.

Swimming can be used as a treat for the horses, as a therapy for injuries, as a part of the training program, but never as their only source of exercise.

Swimming is Refreshing!

TREADMILLS

My experience with treadmills is limited. According to what one reads, they are very useful for gathering data on heart function and general physical conditioning. Much information has been compiled about exercise physiology, by having horses train on the treadmill. It has also been used to study horses with paralyzed flaps. It has been possible to film the actual flap movement, during aerobic and anaerobic exercise. This information has enable the veterinary community to understand how the flap actually works. Treadmills are a comfortable way to study blood chemistry, while the animal is actually performing. In cold and snowy areas, when there are no other alternatives, they can be useful to keep horses exercised. A certain amount of muscle development can be maintained using a treadmill.

However, be leery of using a treadmill for fitness training a racehorse. When a horse is taken out and ridden, he develops various sets of muscles. He also learns skills for coping with the environment mentally and physically. All the hours in the world, on a treadmill, will not help a horse walk out boldly in a field, or not be frightened by a covey of quail, a rabbit scampering or a dog showing an interest in him. All elements must be dealt with in training. This means taking the young horse out and having him learn from experience.

Show people use the treadmill to develop certain muscles. Since our goal is to develop a useful, strong, resilient horse, real galloping is our best tool. Try and combine logic and common sense with scientific knowledge. A great deal of damage can be inflicted utilizing mechanical aids that are supposed to help. Think of a horse galloping on a treadmill. Can the break over of the hoof can be the same as on a natural surface? This alone could change his gait pattern.

Under certain conditions, the treadmill could be useful. A real gallop is preferable, but be flexible. Use your common sense and choose what will work for you!

CHART KEEPING

Charts are very important. You must write down all your observations. When you return from handling your horse, write down whether he was lethargic, pissy or extremely bright. A pattern will emerge indicating how your horse reacts to his training. **Your observations tell you how durable he will be** and how frequently he can race.

Since you are galloping or working every third or fourth day, your comments will start to tell a great deal about how he is responding physiologically to the insult and stress. Your comments will provide a baseline reference as to the level of filling the horse has after work...slight amount on front and back...just a little in one joint only (beware). **Note any and every change.**

Your horse might have needed five days to recuperate from the first few three mile gallops. As you monitor, you might find he starts recouping after three or four days. As his body becomes more efficient and competent with the training, he may soon recover the next day. Some light fillies are tuckered out for five or six days after a race. They only need to be turned out with a kiss on the nose and

Write down Everything!

some nurturing between races. These are examples of the type of information you should put on the chart.

A sample of one of my charts is included. I use a common large size poster board and line up the days of the month across it. Any comments that don't fit into the squares are put down below. Write down any work done on the horses; teeth, shoes, and worming, etc. Different treatments may be highlighted with different colors.

These charts get pretty messy. However, they enable you to review past years and see how the horse evolved, whether there were signs early on that were missed. The chart shows this because notes about filling and heat are carefully kept. Your notes will show that some horses are consistently off their feed for a day or two after a work or race. You will note that others bolt out of the stall leaping and carrying on the day after the race. Put it all down, and act accordingly. Be very, very specific in your observations about eating, attitude, soreness, edema or heat. Knowledge about your animals is the key to keeping them sound and happy. **Good trainers are observant trainers!**

JUNE 1991

	1	2	3	4	5	6	7	8	9	10	whole month
Pregnant mare		Trim		Bathe					Bathe ③	W	Bathe
Mineola Gold	Raced - Colder	Shoes Reset	Quiet when Turned out		Better Bouncing - HAPPY	R.P. - Good	Swim Feels good		Hard fast gallop here	W	Never for Race? / Race? Miami?
2 yr old Colt	R. Pen	trim	Swim R. Pen	Ride ① 3 Miles	Legs OK	R.P. No saddle	Ride 3 Miles	No. Filling Legs good	No. Filling Legs good	W	Ride 3 Miles Better / R. Pen Legs good / ② Ride
2 yr old Filly	④ Runny Nose Fever green cough Mucus!	No cough	cough	Mucus clearing -	ND cough		R.P. No cough good	R.P. No feels good cough	Trail Ride 3 miles 2nd	W	good No cough No snot / Bouncing / Trail ride 3 miles / good! clear!

Very hot - horses in 10 AM - 4 pm - Out at night! MANY Baths!

① He is silly - Looks at everything over reacts - very skitterish!

W = wormed with ivermectin on June 10th

② acting better - goofy 1st mile but then settles in - some galloping and trotting!

③ watch out - itch Starting on Back - Bathe after each Rain!

④ Filly Has Bad cold + cough - green Mucus - put Vics - cleaned Nose - Turned out in small pen - not near any other Horses - a little off feed!

Put any notes or Special Treatments here - identify what was done - why

Your charts will show Trends!

USE Tot Colors! Hi!

Why do we have more **BREAKDOWN** and **BLEEDING** in Racing Today?

Could it be Because we have more Potent Medications That give the Horse, The Trainer, and The Owner the **ILLUSION** of Soundness!

You DECIDE!

Medications

MEDICATIONS

My opinions here may cause me some trouble. Perhaps this section should be called "Ethics in Racing": Medications, when to use, when not to use. I must share a little background information with you here. My father worked for the Federal Government, the Bureau of Narcotics, while I was growing up in San Francisco. The "evil" of drugs was indoctrinated in me at a very young age. Perhaps this early training has made me more reactionary than most when certain options are offered by some veterinarians, to get a few more races out of a horse.

I am constantly interested in the cause and effect of whatever is being done to the animals. I was married to a physician for 18 years and have great respect for the tremendous benefit science and medicine have provided for us.

The problem in racing is an attempt to "fool Mother Nature", when often rest and time off from the pounding and speed will alleviate a problem before it becomes chronic or irreversible. At the track, the trainer is reluctant to stop a horse close to racing time, for a slight problem. So he asks the vet for something to "help" the horse get through the race. "You know Doc, he's been training so good. Our race is next Tuesday and now he has this heat in his tendon." Red Alert! Now is not the time to stress that tendon by running the horse.

Many trainers don't or can't stop at this point. There is tremendous pressure from the owner who doesn't want another darn excuse. The owner may even insinuate he will look for another trainer. The trainer, in desperation looks for a quick fix which unfortunately may "fix' the horse for the rest of his career. The horse runs, with chemical help and strong bandages, and bows his tendon. Now he is compromised for life. The trainer shakes his head and tells the owner, "What a shame. He was doing just fine until that misstep on the track. Just bad luck...but, hey, there's another sale coming up and we'll throw this horse out for a year and see how he does next year". This scenario is simplistic, but very similar skits are being played all too frequently at the track.

In similar situations, I have felt pushed into a corner. What to do? Use chemical help for a few more races to indulge an owner, or lose the owner and watch the horse run well for a few more races with another trainer. Afterwards, the horse is never seen again since you can "only go to the well" so many times.

The following story is typical of the problems trainers have. At the end of a meet at Tampa, my friend told me he had a three-year-old filly he was sending to the killers unless he could find someone who wanted her. She had won a few races and was very game. "She's got a knee," he said, without elaboration. I knew better than to ask if cortisone had been injected in her knee, or how often she was injected until he couldn't

get anything more out of her. I looked at her...she had a powerful behind and was a muscular horse. Her knee looked "rough" but not puffy and full of fluid, though it was hot to touch. (Cortisone can eliminate heat and swelling, leaving the horse to think his joint is healthy even when it isn't.) I agreed to pay $250 for her and decided to throw her out to pasture for the summer and see how she was in the fall.

Since she was running at thirty-five hundred dollar claiming races when she was right, she was certainly not worth spending any money on, even for X-rays. Surgery wasn't feasible, because she probably had joint deterioration at this point.

It wouldn't cost too much to carry her. If she wasn't lame next season, I'd try galloping her. I loaded her and took her home.

A friend from the track heard about my purchase and asked to buy half of her for $125 and agreed to help pay her upkeep. This was fine with me. Trainers become "horse poor" very quickly in this business and it was great to have someone to help pay for feed.

In the fall, she started training (my third and fourth day ride) and she tuned right up. She showed nervousness in the gates and had to be hauled back many times since she was left at the gate in a few of the first races.

She would become slightly lame out of the race, walk out of it, and be ready eight or ten days later. She was given Bute before the race but that was the extent of her medication. She had been on the Bleeders List, but I took her off as no signs of bleeding appeared and the Lasix seemed to do more harm than help. After an injection of Lasix, she would break into a sweat, have runny diarrhea and start urinating. She was running with a hard knocking gang of fillies and mares and did run viably in most of her races, once we solved the gate problem. To our great joy and astonishment she won a very game race where she was left last out of 12 horses. She did a tremendous stretch run and won by a nose. What joy!

Her next race was a lackluster performance. The jockey got off, and said, "You know she's not pushing off her left leg the way she used to. I think her knee is starting to bother her again". In view of that, I turned to my partner and said, "It's time to give her away." "Wait a minute," he said, " You know there are ways to keep her going." Enter the horns of a dilemma. The money would be useful. By injecting the knee with cortisone, the mare would feel no pain and could continue running with the illusion of a sound joint. I knew we could get a few more races out of her before the ultimate break down. Just thinking about this, my own knees and ankles started to hurt. As close as I have been to financial ruin, I have not been able to condemn a horse to this kind of finish. I realized, in this case, the decision was not mine alone to make. My partner

accused me of being naive. Ridiculous, since I knew as well as anyone various ways to keep the horse running. Unfortunately, I was also aware of the consequences of those methods. I said, "Listen, if you want, I'll give you my half of the horse. Take her to another trainer, camouflage the pain and have her run full speed with a compromised knee."

"Are you willing to be responsible for the injury that might result to a jockey, or the damage to the horse?" I asked. "If that's what you want, my half is yours. I can't even sell her the way she is. My choice would be to give her to a good home."

He looked at me. This was heresy. Something not too many smart trainers would admit is that what you do today can cause breakdown tomorrow. This is never presented as a cause and effect situation to owners. Few trainers are going to inform an owner that the horse could be incapacitated by trying to get a few more races. But, that is exactly what happens. Some trainers cleverly wash their hands of the responsibility. They just say they will "help" the horse feel better. The vet does his part by indulging the trainer and doing what the trainer wants. The vet might cau-tion the trainer that when certain drugs are given, the horse should rest. The reality is, maybe if the medication can't be traced and the horse can move, he will run. This is a great way for everyone in-volved to avoid respon-sibility when the in-evitable happens. They can all com-miserate about the bad luck.

Back to the filly and my predica-ment. My partner got my message and agreed to give the horse away. She is now herding cattle in Central Florida. I will not train a horse that I know is in pain. Nor will I train a horse that is unaware of the pain he has. If the owner feels otherwise, the horse goes to another trainer. But I prefer that to the fear of someone being harmed or the horse breaking down. Obviously, I have lost owners and am not considered a sharp trainer when I refuse to use the best medical science has to offer. I'm in this business for the long run. I spend the time necessary to properly prepare the horse to run. That extra three to six months in the training program is costly, but worth it if the horse has talent. If he doesn't, it was very expensive.

This is why we need **new people in the business who can do much of the early work themselves**. Their horses will hold up better and if they don't have talent, they will have another life as a hunter or riding horse. **Horses are not disposable items.** I will not turn them over quickly in search of the good one. Now I train one or two a year hoping they will pay off, but recognizing the odds against it. I am happy and I can live with myself.

Back to medications. Anytime you give a horse a painkiller so he can run, you are in trouble. Pain is a warning sign. Being over forty, I have a lot of aches and pains.

I know that aspirin helps when my bones ache. Bute is probably the same for horses, helpful for slight problems. This doesn't mean mega doses. Some trainers say, "I love running that track; there are no limits on Bute." Too much of anything can be dangerous. Vets see many horses with perforated stomachs caused by Bute abuse. One filly suddenly died on me two weeks after arriving from the track. The necropsy disclosed purple discolorations on the wall of the stomach...ulcers...where large amounts of Bute had eaten away the lining. Other horses on long term Bute develop anemia or other blood disorders.

Many people don't worry about this, because the horses go to the killers when they're finished at the track anyway. Again, I can't, knowingly, set up animals for a short life. But in the racing business, where the owners pay a lot of money and want quick results, trainers push horses until they produce or break down. There are always more coming up. Wouldn't it be more cost effective to rest a few days and race many years?

Beware, any time a trainer says to you ,"He had a little filling in his left ankle, but he is not lame." Next comes, "I don't understand. He never took a lame step." Could be true, but if you are astute, the horse generally tells you that problems are coming. He gets filling, or heat. He favors or paws and digs holes in his stall, or he stands and holds his feet in a particular way to alleviate pain. The way he walks out after he has been stationary tells you something. Listen and observe the signs. Figure out the reason for his actions. Don't simply mask the signs with drugs and carry on. This is what I like about my methods. **When the horse is off, turn him out every day and observe. When he starts frolicking and feeling sound, go back to galloping. No vet bills** and, if you are observant, **you should not have catastrophic breakdowns.**

"He NEVER Took a Lame Step!"

Race day, for most owners, is very expensive. The vet gives most horses a "cocktail" the day of the race. Usually it consists of a combination of vitamins (B-12 or multi-vitamins, possibly various kinds of corticosteroids that are supposed to help with inflammation (Azium or Vetalog). If allowed, nervous horses may be given SoluDeltaCortef. This is supposed to help a hyper horse. It is also a steroid. Many trainers swear by these injections. I avoid their use and only capitulated under duress from an owner. At the time, I didn't realize they were corticosteroids. I can't say that I have never seen them produce dramatic results on my horses. But then, my horses were always sound. One hyper filly dropped her head when given SoluDeltaCortef and almost snoozed in the gate. She didn't run well half asleep. Others trainers feel this really helps their animals. Do your homework and make your own informed decisions.

Certain medications definitely make a dramatic difference on sore horses. Banamine is sometimes used a few days before a race. One owner claimed a horse from a very aggressive leading trainer...famous for how hard he was on a horse. Indeed, the horse won the race the day we claimed him, and I went to the spit box to pick him up. As he cooled out of the race he was getting progressively more lame. By the time I went to lead him to my barn, he could scarcely walk, he was in such pain. When the owner came back to admire his horse, I said, "Watch," and led him out. The horse was very sore. The owner agreed for me to take the horse home, turn him out and observe how well he walked out of his stiffness.

At home he was turned out in a grassy paddock. It should have been heaven to a horse just off the track. Most animals frolic and trot around from the sheer joy of being able to roll and have free movement after the confinement of track life. This horse just stood in the middle of the pasture and didn't move. When he did walk, it was very painfully. I watched him for days, waiting for any desire on his part to move without being prodded. He never had any. I called a friend who worked in the barn where the horse had been claimed and asked if there was anything they did with this horse to get him to train. He said that the horse never went to the track without Bute every night. I tried it and he at least moved, but did not appear to be free of pain. He still seemed quite sore, when he galloped.

Another phone call revealed that if I wanted a good gallop he would need to have 10cc of Banamine..a non-steroidal anti-inflammatory. It acts like a Super Bute and is a potent pain killer. The former vet advised me to give this medication two days before running or working him. This horse could only move with Bute. He could not move at all without help. I was so uncomfortable with the situation that I tried swimming him, but there was no way this horse could perform without the medications. He would go into races walking sound but come out lame. We had the vet try to pin point the problem but we were never successful. The owner tried acupuncture and massage without much luck. He wanted to see his horse run.

It became more and more frustrating. I hated using medications, but knew he couldn't move without them. I was acutely aware that the owner figured he claimed the horse when he won, why couldn't he win with me? The vet tried injecting stifles which seemed to make matters worse. At the same time, the owner decided to send the horse to Maryland. He became very sore on the trip as standing in a van right after getting his stifles injected is contra-indicated. The owner and trainer both complained about his condition when he arrived. I vowed never to accommodate an owner against my own principles. Trying for results because the owner spent money and wanted action with the horse not lay up, was not my game. After the trip, this horse was laid up for six months and then started to run without much success. Horses trained my way don't have these problems. They run frequently and I don't ache because I'm asking a sore horse to run. Turnout time and exercise every fourth day when racing really works.

I can't leave this subject without mentioning anabolic steroids. A friend of mine, an orthopedic surgeon, has seen the results of using these kinds of steroids on human athletes. He sees a lot of tearing of the muscle insertion on the bone, because a muscle that develops beyond the size it is meant to be is too powerful for the "framework". It is like putting a huge engine on a small chassis. Nature has devised a beautiful balance with form and function. If larger muscle were needed, stronger

insertion ligaments and tendons would develop, along with the framework.

We come along and hyper develop one component (the muscle) while disregarding the rest of the system. This is very dangerous. **Many horses are on anabolic steroids.** They are not illegal. They tend to create very "pissy" personalities. Fillies appear to be in a permanent "PMS" syndrome. Anabolic steroids can make some horses dangerously aggressive! It is questionable if anabolic steroids do enable a horse to run faster. There is no proof that larger muscle mass enhances intrinsic speed. Many gifted runners are not heavily muscled. Heart, lungs , conformation and every other component must blend together to have a great horse. **My lovely mare ran four years without any kind of chemical enhancement. She ran on solid training against some super stars.** She came back again and again and was clean legged. **If you have a talented horse, you can run without all the junk**. If the horse isn't talented, nothing will help. Since most of you are doing proper training with good foundation, remember my mare. She was born with a little more speed than average and she ran and won. No cheap shot, no gimmicks.

Try to run and win the right way. You will feel good about what you are doing with your animals. I've had so many other horses not nearly as talented but they run persistently for years because they had time to grow and develop.

A Talented Horse can run CLEAN! And will Last!

INFORMED OWNER

These opinions are very personal and are approached cautiously. Experience has taught me that most owners have no idea of exactly how their horse is being trained. They are often intimidated by the backside environment and terminology, a very dangerous and costly position.

This manual discusses the purchase of a horse and the typical training routine at the racetrack. When your horse goes to the track, there may be variations in training, between what I describe and what may or may not be happening to your horse.

If your horse was purchased at a two year old in training sale, he was "cautiously" trained to breeze two furlongs. Many farms break their horses at 18 months and teach them to walk, trot, slow gallop and do figure eights. Depending on the date of the sale, the horse will be turned back out or begin his training, galloping every day or so. If his training begins, he will usually gallop no more than a mile and will be kept in a stall.

Think of what it might do physiologically to a young animal, with green unformed bone, when he is confined in a 12 x 12 ft. stall for as much as twenty-three and a half hours a day. Is this a natural way to raise an athlete?

If your horse came from a farm where he was turned out most of the time during early training, he has a big advantage over the typical racehorse. When you drive through farm country you see rolling hills with mares and foals grazing in pastures. Unfortunately, once horses go into training or sales preparation many are stalled. Sales people don't want the horse to get any scratches or injuries that might make him look less attractive in the sale ring. They believe there is risk of injury if the horse is allowed to frolic and zoom around the pasture. Farm managers feel an obligation to protect the animals from such "dangers".

Short-term the horse is coddled and protected. Long term, he is not learning to be comfortable with other animals. He is missing the natural exercise and growth necessary to be a resilient race horse.

On large farms, when breaking yearlings and two-year olds, long term tranquilizing drugs are sometimes used to make them docile. The breaking process is easier and less time consuming. Many believe this is the only way to break and train fractious Thoroughbreds. I am not comfortable with this idea. The well adjusted, well trained horse will cope better with the racing environment, if he has been allowed to develop and learn normally.

A day or two before the sale when these horses are asked to breeze for the first time, usually at the sale site, they will be pushed to get a good timed work. This is when many buck their shins. If you want a horse that has bucked shins, buy him, but allow him time to grow and develop. It is too early to ask him to run fast, especially with so little foundation. Don't let him go directly to the race track. (See Sections Two-year old, and Bucked shins)

Most horses bought at two year old in training sales are sent directly to the track. They are confined in their stalls. Only let out once a day to learn to gallop on the real track. Galloping on the real track allows speed that could never be attained on your

farm. Speed that is unnecessary so early. Since they are not allowed to move naturally, this kind of training starts making them sore. They are only getting a mile or two a day, but they get it every day. Because they are running intensely on the track surface everyday, with virtually no real warm up or warm down, the soreness compounds. Drugs are given to allow them to continue training. Usually it is Bute, every night.

No two year old should be medicated for that kind of soreness. It is much better to rest him and observe the soreness. When it disappears, continue his training. If asked to run without the needed rest and gentle movement required to adjust to their work load, these undamaged horses will become damaged.

At the track as the animal becomes more muscularly fit, he is able to go faster. Typically, this is when bone chips start to appear. Then it is green bone, with chips, running on a hard surface. The trainer will sometimes X-ray and allow the horse to continue training, if he feels the chip won't interfere with the speed. The horse can only continue with the help of painkillers, corticosteroids and wraps. The trainer will wrap, give support therapy, and continue until the horse is injured.

The usual training will continue to be one or two miles daily, interspersed with a day or so of walking around the shedrow or on the hotwalker. As a new owner, I vividly recall going to the racetrack for the first time. I saw this type training and asked if this was all they did. I actually said, "15 to 45 minutes out of the stall and you charge $35 a day. No afternoon exercise?"

Some trainers, sensitive to their animals, see the problems coming and allow turn-out time back at the farm. Others capitulate, pressured by the owner, who wants his horse running until he wins, or breaks down.

The breakdown inevitably comes, when the vets try to help the horse continue training. He has to tell the trainer that there are medications that will enable the horse to continue running short term, but that it will be damaging long term. Corticosteroids, in the joints, alleviate symptoms. The horse continues running unaware of the damage he is doing to himself, because he feels no pain. It is a medication that has an unhealthy but effective short term effect, but if misused has a very damaging long term effect.

In conventional training, even when the horse is sore, training continues. To continue training, when problems appear, may cause long term disaster. Tendons are bowed, knee and ankle joints are injected, and the process just goes on.

As owners, informed or uninformed, you should know how to read the vet bill you receive from the track. They may tell you more about how your horse is doing, than your weekly talks with the trainer, If you see X-rays on the bill Redalert! Immediately ask why they were taken . If your trainers says, "Well, he was a little lame" or "There is some heat in..." a particular area, tell him to **stop the horse until physical signs are gone.**

What usually happens is, if the X-ray shows nothing, the trainer continues training.

He may not realize that some kinds of damage don't show up in an X-ray. By continuing his training program, he compounds the damage.

Once a filly was sent to me from the track who supposedly had bucked shins. They had continued training her and she had won a race, but the trainer told the owner that she just didn't want to be a race horse. When I looked at the horse, she had very rough looking shins. I had her X-rayed before we went home.

When we got home, I noticed that she didn't want to go into her left lead and that she was slightly lame. Later, the vet called with the results of her X-rays. She showed a very clear crack on her cannon in the vicinity of the rough shin. Previous X-rays had not shown the crack, though the horse certainly had physical signs of problems more serious than bucked shins. The lesson here is never ignore your own observations. X-rays and tests only help with diagnosis.

This filly was in training, lame and even won a race. Because the X-rays didn't show a break, she was pushed until damage could be seen. Had she been stopped a few days, when the shin problem started and allowed to heal, she would not have needed six to nine months of rest to heal a fracture. The fact is that there must have been some physical sign in her leg to trigger this X-ray. Until a physical sign disappears, whether the X-ray shows a problem or not, the horse should be turned out and rested. Any use of anti-inflammatory medications (corticosteroids) or painkillers at this point will only mask the problem and permit the horse to further damage himself. If the horse needs pain relief, while he recuperates, by all means keep him comfortable. However, do no resume his training program until the medication has been suspended and the horse has no further physical signs. Please be observant with your animals. This program is designed to teach you how to recognize problems.

The background on what might happen at the track should help you to understand that keeping the horse out and loose most of the time in his formative growth period, will allow him to withstand the track pounding. Many breakdowns in young horses, could be avoided with a variation in the training regime.

The series of events that lead to the breakdown can sometimes be charted by reading between the lines of vet bills. Some vet bills from a leading trainer are included. They were received by a friend, when her horse was under the trainer's care at a major race track. The filly ran in stakes and was a fairly decent allowance horse. She was sent to this trainer by another trainer who told the owner the mare was fine except for a windpuff on her left front. A run down of the bills is also included. Try to reconstruct what happened to the horse while being trained at the racetrack.

We will walk through this bill and pretend we are "Columbo". Let's see if we can reconstruct the scenario of the final breakdown of this filly.

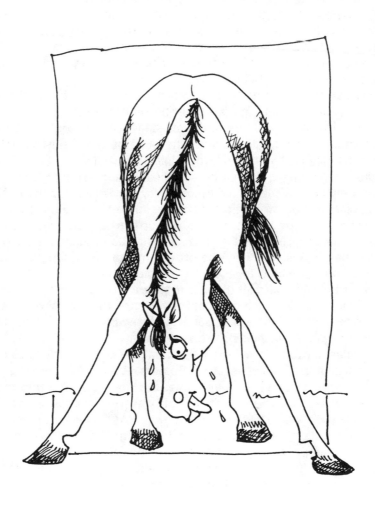

VET BILLS

THE FOLLOWING VET BILLS ARE FROM AN ACTUAL LEADING TRAINER AT A MAJOR TRACK

TRAINING THROUGHOUT THE EIGHT MONTHS IS $45 a day...vet bills, shoes, ponies, are all extra.

The horse was at the track a total of eight months. I am going to walk you through those months. This filly had placed in a Stakes and was a solid Allowance horse. She definitely had ability.

MONTH ONE

Upon arriving at the track, the horse
was visited by the vet.
1/4 Wormed
1/5 X-ray left ankle
1/6 Tube oil
1/8 CBC Blood Chemistry

TOTAL VET COSTS $155

We see the trainer observed something as he had the left ankle X-rayed. The oiling of the horse on day six suggests perhaps a colic. A CBC would not be unusual for a new horse coming into a trainer's barn. There are no further vet bills this month. Perhaps the horse is getting used to the track.

Say Ah!

MONTH TWO

2/13	Electrolyte Vitamin JUG
2/13	Banamine Injection
2/14	Adequan Injection
2/15	Pre Race Treatment
2/15	Pre Race Injection
2/15	Post Race Endoscopic Exam
2/19	Liver and Vitamin Injection
2/20	Bronchial Injection
2/21	Bronchial Injection
2/21	Inject Right and Left Stifles
2/22	Bronchial Injection
2/23	Electolyte Vitamin JUG
2/23	Banamine Injection
2/24	Adequan Injection
2/25	Pre Race Injection
2/25	Pre Race Treatment

HORSE RACED ON 2/25

Electrolyte jug - IV fluids mixed with electrolyes and vitamins and perhaps other additives. Expensive and unnecessary.

Banamine - A very POTENT PAINKILLER! Lame and sore horses under the influence of this medication appear sound. That definitely means pain was masked! Notice Banamine is given two days before every single race that this horse runs! If administered less than forty-eight hours before the race, it might show up in the drug test!

Adequan - This medication is helpful to joint repair. It seems to enhance the healing process. Unlike cortisone, it is not destructive to the joints.

Pre Race Treatment - Perhaps an inhalant of some type to open the lungs.

Pre Race Injection - Probably a mixture of short acting steroids or pain killers, such as SoluDeltaCortef, ACTH Adenazine, Medicorten and Prednisone.

Liver and Iron Injections - Maybe the horse had low blood count.

Bronchial Injections - Throughout the horse's time at the track, she is given this medication the three days preceding every race. No one can give me a clear answer as to what it is. It might be a medication from Canada called Clenbuteral (a steroidlike product) that has been used as a lung medication.

Injection of right and left stifles - This tells us that the horse is going sore in her stifles. The problems may be in the front legs. We see a manifestation in the rear, because the horse compensates by putting excess weight on the hind legs. Usually, the stifles are injected with a caustic substance, possibly an iodine type product that causes scar tissue in the area. This is called an "internal blister". The best cure for sore stifles is rest, long trots and slow gallops on a kind surface. The track this horse runs on is noted for causing soreness. (Horses show the soreness in the stifles when they don't stride normally with their rear legs and they are short strided. They will have trouble backing up or turning in small circles.) Stopping this horse and allowing her soreness to heal would be preferable to medicating.

The Post Race endoscopic exam suggests that the horse quit in the race and didn't run well. The trainer was looking to see if she bled.

THE VET BILLS THIS MONTH WERE $435. THE TRAINING CONTINUES AT **$45 PER DAY.**

MONTH THREE

3/1	Wormed
3/1	Flu rhino vaccine
3/8	Bronchial Injection
3/9	Bronchial Injection
3/10	Bronchial Injection
3/12	Electrolyte Vitamin Jug
3/12	Banamine Injection
3/13	Adequan Injection
3/14	Pre Race Injection
3/14	Pre Race Treatment

HORSE RACED 3/14

3/14	Another scoping . . . perhaps bleeding after this race?
3/22	Bronchial Injection
3/22	Equipose Injection
3/22	Injection of Right and Left Stifles . . . again
3/24	Electrolyte Vitamin Jug
3/24	Banamine Injection
3/26	Pre Race Injection
3/26	Pre Race Treatment

HORSE RACES 3/26

3/29	Bronchial Injection
3/30	Bronchial Injection

The new injection this month is Equipoise, an anobolic steroid, consisting of male hormones. This is the same medication that caused such problems when used by the Olympic Athletes.

Note that the horse has had her stifles injected again. They are bothering her, but she may not know it in a race, as all the medication she is given may mask the problem. She'll be sore, when the medications wear off!

She was scoped again. They must be expecting her to bleed. It is just a matter of time with all of these drugs.

<u>TOTAL VET BILLS $400</u>

Anabolic Steroids!

MONTH FOUR

4/1	Electrolyte Vitamin Jug
4/1	Banamine Injection
4/2	Adequan Injection
4/2	Injection-Right and Left Ankles
4/3	Pre Race Injection
4/3	Pre Race Treatment

HORSE RACES 4/3

4/8	Electrolyte Vitamin Jug
4/8	Banamine Injection
4/10	Pre Race Injection
4/10	Pre Race Treatment

HORSE RACES...HORSE WINS 4/10

4/21	Bronchial Injection
4/22	Bronchial Injection
4/24	Electrolyte Vitamin Jug
4/24	Banamine Injection
4/29	Bronchial Injection
4/30	Bronchial Injection
4/31	Electrolyte Vitamin Jug
4/31	Banamine Injection

The worst thing we see this month is the injection for the ankles. The price, $50, tells us it may have been cortisone, the first step toward the destruction of the ankles. Remember, cortisone is used for pain. When given to a human, it is stressed that the person must not use or stress the injury. The horses are injected and asked to run hard, starting the cycle of destruction discussed in Drs. Krook and Maylin's Book, *Race Horses at Risk*. BEWARE WHEN YOU SEE INJECTION IN JOINTS ON YOUR VET BILL. YOUR HORSE WILL NOT LAST! (The exception seems to be using hyaluronic acid, a substance that is similar to joint fluid. It seems to cushion rough joints and enhance healing, but horses should always rest after these injections!)

The rest of the medications are as previously explained. In spite of all the stuff, the horse does win! Many of these drugs are not necessary. However, some definitely "help" the horse run. Others, of course, are destroying the horse because she is able to run when she should really be resting and healing. Continuing with the animal in this manner is counter productive long term. **As an owner, it is up to you to decide how you want your horse to be handled.** Trainers that are not leading trainers might work more closely with you as they will have time to get to know your horse rather than give him all the medications they can get away with. (This is not to condemn every leading trainer. It is just that leading trainers have large stables and may not be as willing to work with interested, involved owners.)

THE VET BILL FOR THE FOURTH MONTH IS $377

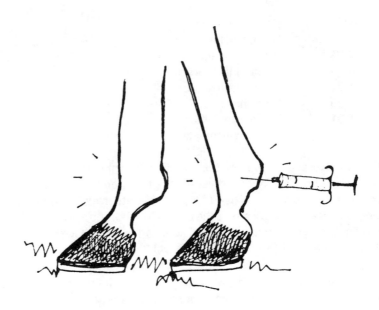

Injection of Ankles !

MONTH FIVE

5/2	Pre Race Injection
5/2	Pre Race Treatment
5/6	Encelphalitis Vaccine
5/19	Bronchial Injection
5/20	Bronchial Injection
5/21	Banamine Injection
5/22	Adequan Injection
5/23	Lasix Injection
5/23	Pre Race Injection
5/23	Pre Race Treatment

HORSE RACED 5/23

5/25	Bronchial Injection
5/26	Bronchial Injection
5/27	Electrolyte Vitamin Jug
5/27	Banamine Injection
5/28	Adequan Injection
5/29	Lasix
5/29	Pre Race Injection
5/29	Pre Race Treatment

HORSE RACES 5/29

This month the filly is put on Lasix. One more stress to an already stressed system. She did win another race this month. With all of the drugs and Lasix on top of it, it is admirable that the filly manages to finish races...let alone wins them. This filly has been put in claiming races since her first start with this trainer. She has been progressively dropped in class with each subsequent race.

THE VET BILLS WERE $435 THIS MONTH

MONTH SIX

6/2	Bronchial Injection
6/3	Bronchial Injection
6/3	Inject right and left hocks
6/4	Bronchial Injection
6/9	Electrolyte Vitamin Jug
6/9	Banamine Injection
6/10	Adequan Injection
6/11	Lasix
6/11	Pre Race Injection
6/11	Pre Race Treatment

HORSE RACES 6/11

6/15	Bronchial Injection
6/16	Bronchial Injection
6/19	Electrolyte Vitamin Jug
6/19	Banamine Injection
6/20	Adequan Injection
6/21	Pre Race Injection
6/21	Pre Race Treaatment
6/21	Lasix

HORSE RACES 6/21

6/28	Bronchial Treatment
6/29	Bronchial Treatment
6/30	Bronchial Treatment

In one of the races, the filly ran second. We see that this month the hocks have been injected, probably with cortisone. Now she has been treated for sore stifles, sore ankles, and sore hocks. She still runs because she has "heart" and is not aware of her deterioration.

<u>**THE VET BILLS FOR THIS MONTH ARE $342**</u>

INJECTION of HOCKS!

MONTH SEVEN

7/1	Electrolyte Vitamin Jug
7/1	Banamine Injection
7/2	Adequan Injection
7/3	Lasix Injection
7/3	Pre Race Injection
7/3	Pre Race Treatment

HORSE RACES AND WINS! 7/3

7/12	Bronchial Injection
7/13	Bronchial Injection
7/14	Electrolyte Vitamin Jug
7/14	Banamine Injection
7/15	Adequan Injection
7/16	Pre Race Injection
7/16	Pre Race Treatment
7/16	Lasix

HORSE RACES AND WINS! 7/16

7/17	Worming
7/25	Bronchial Injection
7/26	Bronchial Injection
7/27	Bronchial Injection
7/28	Bronchial Injection

Lasix!

Bronchial Injections!

Banamine!

This month the horse has won two races. Incidentally, one of the purses in one of the races was taken back three months later. The DRUG TEST CAME BACK POSITIVE! Perhaps the buildup of so many medications finally showed through in spite of the fact that the horse was on Lasix, a drug that can mask the results. The trainer's comment when he found out, was, "I don't understand. I gave her the same stuff I give all my horses!"

I will agree with that. Sometimes the vet bills of other horses in his barn were on the same page as those of this filly. I could see that every horse got the same stuff. The horse had been progressively dropped in price with each race and that is how she was able to win.

TOTAL VET BILLS FOR THIS MONTH ARE $420.00.

Drug Test Positive! Purse Taken Back 3 months Later!

MONTH EIGHT

8/1	Bronchial Injection
8/2	Bronchial Injection
8/3	Bronchial Injection
8/4	Bronchial Injection
8/5	Adequan Injection
8/6	Pre Race Injection
8/6	Pre Race Treatment
8/6	Estro IV (Premarin...used for bleeders)
8/6	Lasix

HORSE RACES HER LAST RACE 8/6

8/7 Eye Medication
8/13 Ultra Sound Tendon

    Did you notice something different in this bill? The horse has been given Bronchial Injections for a more persistent period of time. These injections could be Prednisone, a steroid that is used a great deal in lung disease. It has many side effects, one of which is aggression. It is used very cautiously in humans, as the illusion of well-being can fool you into thinking that your lungs are well. At this point, the horse has an accumulation of problems manifesting themselves. The bronchial injections may help get one more race. Since this trainer certainly knows the signs of distress, he took a final shot. The Estro IV also implies that there might be a problem with her breathing and/ or, her lungs. I'm not sure the horse even finished the race. I saw her five months after that last race and her ankles were still swollen and misshapen. She had bowed the left front tendon down low and who knows what other damage had been done. It looked like the suspenensory ligaments might also have been torn bilaterally. Unfortunately, there was so much disfigurement it was hard to tell. With time the ankles should start healing, but they will never be sound.
    Had this horse been handled differently, she could have run for years. She did not have a bad step or bad luck at the track. **This is a text book case of abuse and poor management...all done in the name of Horse Training by a leading trainer.** This owner actually paid forty five dollars a day to have a decent, talented horse ruined. He also paid enormous vet bills. Her bow may eventually heal, but she will never run again. She is only four years old. My recommendation to the owner is to breed her, if she can be bred. Steroids are known to cause fertility problems in horses.
    As I reviewed this horse's history, I felt ill. Seeing the progression and use of medications, there is no doubt to the outcome. I hope you question what is being done to your horse...and then maybe he will have a chance!

Last Race!
Bowed Tendon!
Torn Suspensories!

ANOTHER REAL VET BILL

A horse arrived at my farm in December. The owner had called me and asked if I would be willing to take it. The trainer had said there was nothing wrong with the horse. He had just tailed off. His form deteriorated with each race after he won his maiden race.

This horse, a colt, had been purchased in the March Two Year Old Training Sale and had gone directly from that sale to the race track. So, at the ripe old age of twenty four months, NJ (the colt) found himself at the track. Keep in mind he was probably stalled and in training from the age of 18 to 20 months.

When he arrived, he really didn't look too bad. His joints weren't swollen or loggy appearing. It was obvious they had been fired, but he looked reasonably sound. He was very well balanced and proportioned. His legs didn't turn in or out. He conformation was correct. He was turned out in a small paddock. He didn't move when turned loose. He stood in the paddock and showed little interest in his surroundings. At the time this was attributed to the fact he might had been given a tranquillizer.

Upon my request, the owner to sent me a copy of the vet bills so that I could try and reconstruct his experience and performance at the track. Let me share the bill with you.

3/ 3	Fecal exam
3/14	Tying up powder
3/24	Firing of shins
3/24	Kling bag
3/24	Tetanus toxoid vaccination
3/24	Firing paint
3/29	Kling bag

We may surmise from the treatment, that the horse was put into training, had a tying up problem, and was given a powder for it. He then bucked his shins. The trainer wanted to keep him going, had him fired and kept him at the race track. It appears that he was probably walked and hosed until his shins were better as there are no bills for April. Remember, this is a twenty five month old animal, confined to a twelve by twelve stall and walked once or twice a day for maybe half an hour.

5/ 9	Electrolytes and Vitamins
5/27	Fecal exam

Since there are no other bills for April and May, we may assume that NJ is training uneventfully. Probably galloping a mile to a mile and a half with gradual increments of speed at the end of the gallops every few days. He may have gone to the gates on occasion. The actual time he spent on the track would have been about 15 minutes a day.

HORSE RACED 6/7

6/20	Electrolytes and vitamins
6/23	Butazolidin
6/23	Medicorten
6/24	ACTH
6/24	Adenosine

Can this medication enable him to run when he is sore?

HORSE RACED 6/24

These bills seemed tame compared to the bills we just examined. But why would a young healthy horse need painkillers and steroids every time he ran? Medicorten is a corticosteroid. Medicorten and ACTH are very potent anti-inflammatory medications. They are effective in treating chronic inflammation but have potential side effects that can leave horses seriously crippled. This combination of medications were the pattern throughout NJ's time at the track. It appeared that the trainer and vet were giving these medications just in case, since there were no X-rays or other signs of joint problems.

THE VET BILLS FOR JUNE WERE $130

7/11	Medicorten
7/11	Butazolidin
7/12	Adenosine
7/12	ACTH

I'm not a pincushion!

HORSE RACED 7/12

7/16	Electrolytes and Vitamins
7/22	Butazolidin
7/22	Medicorten
7/23	ACTH
7/23	Adenosine

HORSE RACED 7/23

At least no Lasix or other breathing medication have been given.

THE VET BILLS WERE $136

8/22	Electrolytes and Vitamins
8/22	Equipoise
8/27	Butazolidin and Medicorten
8/28	ACTH
8/28	Adenosine

HORSE RACED 8/28

I didn't like seeing that he was given Equipoise (an anabolic steroid) usually contra indicated in colts. He might have been off his feed, depressed or unagressive.

THE VET BILLS WERE $113

The vet bills were identical for August, September, October and November. He raced an average of twice a month in October and won his maiden race. He ran poorly after that. He arrived at my farm in December. I told the owner the horse was quite depressed and moving very slowly. He was probably body sore and needed time to heal. He had a little heat in his left knee, but showed no lameness at this time. The vet came out and checked the left cannon bone to rule out fracture from the bucked shins. The X-ray showed no fracture, and at the time the vet noted that he was not lame.

In the middle of January the vet had to return. The horse had become progressively more lame. He was only being turned out and fed. He moved very little but appeared to be in pain and manifested much more heat and swelling in all the joints. He looked very poor. I now wondered if he had chips in joints, as his overall movement had deteriorated. The vet again checked the horse, noting that he was lame in both front legs. The knees and ankles were X-rayed to check for chips. The X-rays showed no boney lesions and rest was recommended.

It was at this point that I started calling vets asking questions about the medications used on the horse. I was told that ACTH suppresses the normal function of the adrenal glands when used long term with corticosteroids and that two to three treatments a month in the horse's formative growth period was excessive. I also learned these medications could explain why the horse was so depressed and why he showed no colt-like interest in any other animal. It could take months for his adrenal glands to start functioning again.

Please understand that I do not claim to be a Ph. D. in Pharmacology or Veterinary Science. However, I felt the need to try and understand the basics of this very complex field. Some may accuse me of over simplification. The information I gleaned from veterinarians and pharmacologist is shared with you concisely and in laymans terms, because it is vital that we have a basic understanding of the contents of medications given to our horses.

During my inquiries, I saw the following article by Laura Hillenbrand in *Equus*

Magazine (Vol. 166). I feel it is worthy of our attention and have included part of it for you. "Corticosteroids...synthetically replicate the basic structure of the hormone cortisol, which regulates many functions within the body, including reducing inflammation . . . Some forms have up to **700 times the suppressive power of natural cortisol**. Corticosteroids have proved to be the least expensive, fastest acting, and most effective anti-inflammatory medications ever used in veterinary practice."

Inflammation is a part of the healing process. When you inhibit inflammation, you are also inhibiting healing. Inflammation is also a sign that there is a problem. . . . if ignored and suppressed, you enable the damage to continue, while the problem continues.

The article states, "Along with the benefits, these substances carry potential side effects that can leave horses permanently, or even fatally, crippled. . . All forms of corticosteroid administration carry potentially harmful side effects. Repeated use of these drugs has been shown to handicap the adrenal gland, causing a drop in levels of several other key hormones as well as cortisol and creating hormonal imbalance. . . . Because they suppress the immune system and the inflammatory healing reaction, the drugs may also leave a horse vulnerable to undiscovered infection. **The greatest risk in corticosteroid therapy,** however, involves the possibility that the medication will so prevent the body's protective and restorative mechanisms that progressive structural damage occurs. This can happen in two basic ways. First, **corticosteroids can thwart or delay healing to such a degree that supporting capacity is never restored to injured tendons and ligaments, and essential structures such as the cartilage cushions between bones within joints are not regenerated.** Cartilage, which is naturally worn away with use, is slow to heal. **In horses repeatedly given corticosteroids** (especially when the drug is injected intra-articularly), **not only does the natural replacement of old cartilage stop, but the current wear greatly accelerates**. Eventually, **the cartilage is completely worn away and bone rubs against bone, leaving the joint crippled.** Secondly, the pain relief provided by corticosteroids, while doing nothing to cure injuries or inflammatory conditions, can **encourage a horse to use a damaged limb as if it were sound**, unknowingly risking catastrophe with each stride. . . all experts agree that high, frequent doses of the drug can inflict serious damage." The article suggests circumstances when the drug could be helpful. Usually short term, small doses, locally targeted.

This information is shared with you because, at first glance, the medications NJ received are not alarming. They were only given when he raced. However, I soon realized that NJ was going through a "drying out" of the medications he had been given. He was now a mere thirty months of age and moved and acted like a thirty year old horse.

He lost weight and muscle tone and looked like the kind of horse the Humane Society would fine me for starving. He was self destructing in front of my eyes. By early March the horse was looking worse. I took him to the University of Florida Veterinary Teaching Hospital. They examined and X-rayed him and listened to his history. Their diagnosis was Degenerative Joint Disease. It was possible that the cartilage was

had no idea whether he could ever be useful racing again or even sound. At this point, the horse was thirty three months of age and had been physically on the track only six months.

After much discussion with vets, he was given Adaquan*-four injections and then the oral equivalent Flexfree. (GAG-Glycosamimoglycan- It helps cartilage growth. If the cartilage has been completely destroyed nothing will help).

In early May NJ had acute swelling in his hind legs. I thought he might be going into renal shutdown or some other kind of metabolic problem. He was hauled back to the vet. The vet found the blood tests to be normal. Since then, NJ seems to be recovering. He is starting to develop a little muscle tone and began light exercise in July. If he continues, he might be able to train in October.

The point is, this vet bill didn't appear to be excessive and the horse didn't appear to be in bad shape. It was when he had withdrawal from the medications that his real state of health became apparent. He may not hold up to racing and the owner's investment will be lost. Why start this process? Train with common sense and leave medications for ill horses . . . not young healthy horses that only need a little time. Horses treated this way may never make it to a second season of racing. So many horses have a similar history. Many have not been able to return to racing.

One day I ran into this horse's trainer at the track. He asked me about the horse. I told him how the horse had seemed okay when he arrived, but had gone bad in about two to three weeks. The trainer rolled his eyes heavenward, kissed his fingers and said, "Thank You, Jesus!! Can you believe it? While I have the horses, they're fine and then two to three weeks later with others . . . they go bad! And you know what? I know why they are so good with me! It's the medicine! I know what to use . . . thank you God for such good stuff!" This man truly didn't make equate the medicine to the disintegration of the horses. He believed the medicine helped them. The fact that anyone can be so ignorant about the cause and effect frightens me. This is a horse trainer. He makes a living in the racing industry and he has not figured out why his horses only last on season.

So many of us are not aware of what is in medications we are giving our horses. I was not aware that SoluDeltaCortef*, Prednisone*, Vetalog*, and Medicorten* are all corticosteroids. Since various medications are given persistently over long periods of time, it is not surprising that so many horses suffer the weakening of bone, suppression of normal hormonal function and the lowering of the immune system. Think of minor colds and flues that normal horses should recover from in a week. Steroids suppress the symptoms and the horse keeps going. Then when lung problems do show up, they are more acute, because the horse has continued to preform when not well. Clenbuteral*, another steroid like medication, again enables the horse to preform when he should be resting. Is there any wonder that there is more bleeding today? Horses are running with a false sense of health because of the potent qualities of the medications.

A list of a few brand names for steroids is included. Study your vet bills. Find out what the medications contain. "Something to make him feel good at the gate." is not an explanation. Remember, you have a right to know, you are paying for them.

COMMON MEDICATIONS AND THEIR USES
AT THE RACETRACK

Pre Race "Feel Good" Medications
Adenosine
ACTH
B-12
Azium (Dexamethasone, a steroid)
B-Complex
Testostrone B-12
Triple A (a combination of Azium,
Adenazine and ACTH)

Muscle Soreness
Adenosine
Azium (a steroid)
E-SE (Vitamin E and Selenium)
Lactonase
Robaxin
Prednisone (a steroid)
Prednisolone (a sterod)

Pain Medication
Aspirin
Azium (a steroid)
Banamine
Bute (Phenyl Butazone)
Betamethasone (a steroid)
DMSO
DEPO MEDROL
Prednisone (a steroid)

Circulation
Aspirin
DMSO

Antiinflamatory
DMSO
Vetalog
Medicorten (a steroid)
Bute
Banamine
Prednisone (a steroid)
Azium (a steroid)

Respiratory Problems
A-H Injections or granules
Azium (a steroid)
DMSO
Glycopyronate (Robinal)
Prednisone (a steroid)

Calm Down Medication
Calcium and B-12

Bleeder Medications
Amicar
Estro IV
Lasix (a diuretic)
Naquasone (a diuretic)
Intal-(intra-Tracheal)

Some of these medications are long acting steroids. Others are simply vitamin mixtures. Others are mood elevating drugs. Still others are potent pain killers. **This is not a complete list**. It is to familiarize you with names you will encounter frequentlly on the backside.

143

In order to simplify reading, the following list contains the registered trademark names for some of the medications referred to in the text. Those products not mentioned are generic names or do not appear in the *Compendium of Veterinary Products, 1st Edition 1991,* published by North American Compendiums, Inc., Port Huron, MI. All references to these medications are the compilation of information provided by professionals. My interpretation of this material is presented to you in layman's terminology. The cause and effect observations are based on my hands on experience and are not to be construed as scientific evidence. These medications are extremely beneficial if used therapeutically. However, they must be used in accordance with the recommendations of the manufacturing company. If you have doubts about their use refer to the product insert.

THE OWNER PAYS THE BILLS. HE HAS THE RIGHT TO KNOW WHAT HE IS PAYING FOR. DON'T BE AFRAID TO ASK!

Adequan®	Luitpolp
Azium®	Schering Plough
Banamine®	Schering Plough
Depomedrol®	Upjohn
Equipoise®	Solvay
Lasix®	Hoechst Roussel
Naquasone®	Schering Plough
Robaxin®	Fort Dodge
SoluDeltaCortef®	Upjohn
Vetalog®	Solvay

144

EQUIPMENT

Equipment
    for Riding

Helmet
Saddle
Bridle

EQUIPMENT FOR RIDING

The Helmet

This section will briefly cover typical equipment used in training an average racehorse with no known quirks or problems. Before you get on a horse, it is mandatory that you automatically put on your riding helmet. There are many varieties available. You may purchase them at tack shops and racetracks. I have a special fondness for the Jofa hockey helmet but any of the approved safety helmets you choose will be acceptable.

The Lead

Whenever you handle a horse, use a chain shank. Never hurt the horse or yank on him unless his actions demand it. When his behavior is unacceptable, punish him immediately . It will swiftly teach him you won't put up with dangerous comportment.

The Bridle

For the training stages any style leather or nylon head stall with a nose band and chin strap will be suitable. When your horse is ready for the track, you may want to purchase some fancy racing tack.

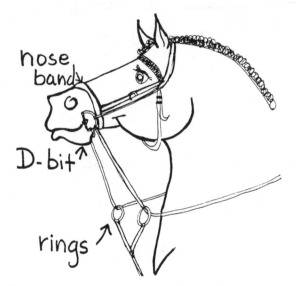

The Bit

Start training with a simple "D" bit snaffle. It is not too severe and allows decent control of the horse. A nose band will help teach the horse to keep his mouth shut and to keep his tongue under the bit.

In the second stage of training, as the horse grows stronger, you may find you need more control when the horse goes into more speed, or when he shows a harder mouth. Generally, it isn't necessary to go to severe bits. Sense how the horse likes to be ridden and decide what is most suitable. Be aware that all horses act differently. Some like to lean against the bit...others like it barely in contact...fillys tend to be more sensitive. Each horse will evolve his own way of going.

The Reins

Use reins that do not slip through your fingers. When the horse is in a lather, this can be a real problem. Braided leather or rubber padded reins are good choices to help you keep steady contact with your horse's mouth, especially when you get into the Speed Phase of training. Leather or suede gloves also may be helpful.

The Martingale

Use a set of "rings" or a running martingale in the early stages of training. It discourages a horse when he tosses his head or rears. It also teaches him to "give at the poll" when you rein in, rather than allowing him to stick out his nose and try to fight. Martingales should not be used at the track for speed works or races.

The Saddle

When you are breaking your horse, you will have to decide what to put on his back. Whether it is a western or english saddle is not crucial. A western saddle is good to accustom the horse to something flopping around on his back. When I start riding, I go to an english exercise saddle, because it has nothing more than a "tree" type structure covered by leather with stirrups attached to it. It allows me to feel how the horse is moving. Since I recommend long stirrups, the early riding style is almost like being bareback with stirrups.

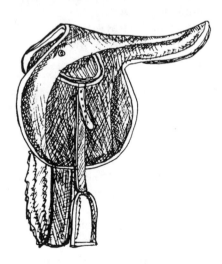

If you can't afford to buy an exercise saddle, use any saddle you possess for Phase I training. When you begin Phase II training, a western saddle may be too structured for you, the horse, and the style of riding you will be doing. I recommend you buy an exercise saddle at this point, so the horse will not be inhibited and can move easily.

Washable nylon girths covered with fleece are easy to clean and don't rot when you use a lot of water and have humid weather. Leather girths mold or rot quickly with use unless they are oiled frequently. Frequent oiling is a lot of work for the do-it-yourselfer.

My preference in stirrup "leathers" is also nylon. One has never broken on me

without warning. Something I can't say about leather.

Always use a good thick pad between the saddle and the horse. If you are riding various horses, use a saddle cloth of washable cotton under the saddle pad to avoid the sweat and bacteria being carried from one horse to another.

The Whip

You or your rider should always take a riding crop or whip, when riding young horses. This is to accustom them to it as a **training aid**. The jockey is **expected to carry a whip and use it as needed** in the race. If the horse has not been accustomed to it at home, valuable time may be lost while teaching him about it at the racetrack.

Always Wear Your Helmet when you Ride !

Try to have 2 Complete
sets of Tack So that
your Truck is Race Track Ready!

EQUIPMENT FOR THE TRACK

Specific problems tend to show up when you go into track training. Then you will decide whether to use blinkers, more complex bits, tongue ties, etc. **Your trainer and rider will be able to tell you what equipment will help solve specific problems.** Always analyze whether the horse needs a change in equipment, or whether something you are doing is causing problems in his behavior.

Some trainers put on all sorts of equipment "just in case", right from the beginning...much of the equipment may hinder the horse rather than help him. This can be confusing to the animal. Add one item at a time.

Be aware, if your horse is racing, that any change of equipment, such as blinkers, must be declared when entering the horse in a race. The less equipment necessary to do the job, the less chance for confusion or mistakes. Keep it simple.

Blinkers

Blinkers are used to make the horse concentrate on his business. They keep him from veering or bolting. They are also used on timid horses who don't want to pass others or on horses who are distracted by the crowd. Sometimes one eye will be covered, the other open. Sometimes half blinkers are used. There are endless blinker configurations. Trainers will try anything to get a good run out of the horse! Remember Gate Dancer? He had blinkers with ear muffs attached so he wouldn't hear the crowd. Don't laugh, he won a lot of races that way!

Shadow Rolls

Shadow rolls may be used to encourage a horse to carry his head lower. The lambswool band blocks the horse from seeing his shadow and shying at it.

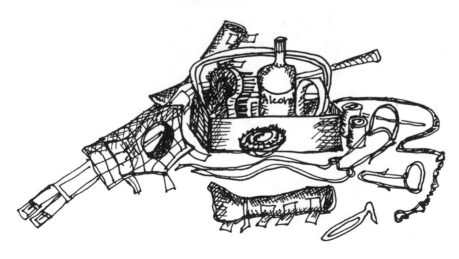

LEGS AND BANDAGES

Bandaging and
Leg Support

Tricks for
Special
problems

Shoeing
The Duck Foot

LEGS AND BANDAGES

Walking down the shedrow is like walking along a horse hospital ward. Nearly every horse has some kind of bandage, poultice, plastic wrap or scabby paint on his legs.

Years ago, I thought there had to be a lot to learn in this business, terms like blistering, firing, poulticing, were a foreign language to me. All the trainers and grooms seemed to know what they were talking about. With time and experience, I learned that was not necessarily so.

I have mentioned my opinion about firing and blistering in other chapters. Briefly, the theory is to insult the area with a chemical or physical burn, causing the body to supply blood to the injured area and to create scar tissue. Doesn't the actual problem do that? Don't fractures, bucked shins and other injuries cause swelling, heat, and therefore blood supply to the injured area while the body is trying to heal?

In any case, I'm told a good blister (i.e. huge swelling and scabbing of skin caused by a caustic agent) will straighten things right up. Some trainers recommend training during the healing process - others may stall the horses...many theories...not much concrete evidence that any of this voodoo is more valid than rest and good massages. Don't massages stimulate heat and blood flow? Think about the animal's problem from a competent horseman's point of view and see if the solution offered makes any kind of sense at all. An experienced veterinarian who knows horses...not just race horses...can give you an answer. Racetrack veterinarians are very good at keeping compromised horses going. Do any of you want such a horse? If you explain your philosophy to the racetrack veterinarian, he can advise you accordingly.

There are reasons for using bandages. They are good support for an animal trying to defend his injured leg. He puts so much weight on his good leg that it can stock up from the added stress. Both legs should be bandaged, under those conditions. A horse that has a cut or wound should be bandaged and medicated for a few days to get the healing started. When the wound is set and no longer oozing or fragile, usually after three or four days, the area should be exposed to the air. Gentle irrigation (hosing) encourages blood flow to the area. It helps the body form new scabs, which enhance the healing process.

Horses that are forced to stand in their stall a great deal of the day tend to stock up. Standing bandages are put on them to keep the filling down. Isn't **walking them twice a day or turning them out preferable to having them bandaged all the time?**

There are a few things to remember about bandages.

Don't leave them on while the horse is turned out. As he moves, they can slip and bow a tendon from the constriction.

Never leave the bandages on for twenty four hours without rewrapping them.

Never put a bandaged horse in a van and assume that he will be checked. Send the horse with a groom or don't wrap his legs.

Most importantly-don't fool yourself into thinking your horse has healed from an injury because his leg is tight after removing the bandages. Leave him unbandaged and moving, in order to properly asses his injury. **TRAINERS GET A FALSE SECURITY BECAUSE BANDAGES SUPPRESS SWELLING. SUPPRESSED SWELLING DOES NOT MEAN HEALING HAS TAKEN PLACE OVER NIGHT!** Bandages do have their place...be sensible when you use them.

Bandaging and Leg Support in the Race

Vetwrap is a support wrap commonly used all over the country. Some trainers I highly respect, use vetwrap on all four legs of every horse, in every race. This can be expensive...about ten dollars a throw...dangerous if the groom is not completely competent. Many a horse has been injured by incorrectly applied bandages. Unless you know that a horse has a tendency to hurt himself or get into trouble, don't wrap him.

Once in a while, a horse will get into a scuffle coming out of the gates or in the heat of the race. Vetwrap protects tendons that might be cut or injured, in such instances. Statistically, the chances of injury are slim. If you are a super cautious person or your horse tends to hurt itself, be safe rather than sorry. Keep in mind the damage which maybe caused by incorrectly wrapped bandages and always supervise the wrapping or do it yourself.

There are new bandages on the market every day. Like the supplements, they promise miracle results. Some are supposed to keep a horse from bowing...hard to believe. There are many variations on the theme of support and strength. Some tests suggest a decrease in leg concussion with particular types of wraps. They could be very beneficial to a horse with tendencies toward leg problems. Wraps may also decrease the amount of damage done if a horse does break down in a race. There are times when one might want to wrap a horse for racing. Let your horse sense tell you when to do so.

"Polos" are the soft cushioned bandages, in bright colors, seen on horses, during their early morning workouts. They protect the animal from hitting himself during the workout, but are never used for races.

If you have a horse that is compromised or has bad ankles, by all means give him the extra support. It might be helpful under racing conditions. Remember, use your own judgment and horse sense.

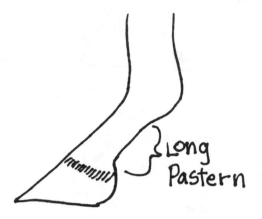

Long
Pastern

Tricks to Help Specific Leg Problems While Racing

Horses with long pasterns have a tendency to run down during a race, even with the best conditioning. As the fatigue sets in, the fetlock drops lower and lower. Eventually, it can hit the track, causing a burn or worse injury. Trainers try to avoid this problem by using run down patches. Run down patches are pieces of material that are placed at the point of impact and wrapped with vetwrap. Patches of plastic, rubber, or leather are available for the same purpose.

If your horse comes back from a work at the track with a burn on his fetlocks... on either the front or rear leg or legs...make sure he has protection the next time he goes to the track--after he is healed. **Don't allow the burn to become a chronic problem.** It could hamper the animal's desire to run.

A protector made from a motorcycle inner tube has worked on some of my animals . Motorcycle inner tubes are smaller than automobile inner tubes and larger than bicycle inner tubes. I have created various types of leg, heel, and fetlock protectors using these inner tubes. Someone showed me one of the styles and the others have been devised as the need arose. They can be left on the horse all of the time and are accepted as a second skin. After a few minutes of stomping their feet, the horse forgets them.

Illustrations on how to make them are included. They work very well for some of the horses and eliminate hitting problems in certain cases. Horses can be raced wearing these protectors.

Style #1 - Is to protect the fetlock area from rundown...either front or back legs. You might wrap vetwrap over it in a race, so it doesn't twist around.

This style is useful to protect the hind hooves from hitting the front ankles, if your horse has that tendency.

Style #2 - Is to protect the balls or heels of the front feet. You might have a horse that consistently catches himself while galloping and running. Make sure his feet are well balanced, the toes aren't too long and try this.

Style #3 - This is to protect the front of the rear ankles and coronet band from being hit by the front feet. A horse that brings his rear legs up and under and interferes with his front action will show hitting and cuts around the coronet band and ankles. One rear hoof movement may hit the other in this area. If you see persistent random cuts around the rear ankles and coronet band, try this design.

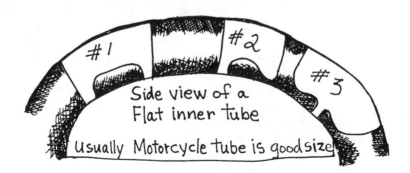

Side view of a Flat inner tube
Usually Motorcycle tube is good size!

SHOEING

To shoe or not to shoe. It is easy for me. I never use shoes until the horse is nearly ready for track works. But, this is Florida. **If the horse is well trimmed, he has little use for shoes.**

However, if his white line is splitting or he has a specific need, shoeing should be considered. . **Keep horses in training on a good trimming schedule.** Use a simple trim...the line of the pastern running straight through the hoof. You take each foot individually and trim or shoe to its own characteristics. Some very simple drawings are included that encourage you to consider the horse, not an abstract angle someone has deemed as the perfect angle. Horse's feet are as individual as ours. Horses may have skinny "muley" feet, very shallow and platter- like feet , a great hoof wall or weak hoof wall. Some are white (the "lore" being a white foot is a soft foot) and some are dark.

Feed supplements may help strengthen the hoof wall. Biotin with methionine is deemed excellent. Making sure your horse has all his trace minerals is a must.

Have your horse jog barefoot on the road to see the natural wear down pattern of his hooves. A little concussion is good for the bones. It seems to be tradition to put training plates on the front of the horses and sometimes all the way around. If your area is rocky or hard or your horse is chipping, by all means protect the hoof. **If all is well, don't rush into it.**

Decide to put shoes on after a work or two at the race track. My track is heavy and sand covered. Therefore, I have the farrier file down the toe grabs or put a rim shoe on. **Toe grabs can cause problems, especially on hard, unforgiving surfaces.**

If your track is very hard and you have toe grabs protruding, the way the horse breaks over is changed. This is not as much of a problem on a heavier track that has "give."

Aluminum racing plates are generally used for racing. They are light weight and easy for the farrier to shape. If you turn your horse out, with plates on, he'll sometimes catch himself while frolicking...the toe of the hind foot "grabs" the heel of the front foot. That is the price I'm willing to pay for his peace of mind. Make your farrier aware of this. Having him make sure that the shoe doesn't hang over the heel of the foot will help. Bell boots, on the front, might help too.

My horses rarely have foot problems. I believe a great many problems are started by the enforced inactivity of the animal. Walking, grazing, and moving are integral parts of being a horse. Being over fed and forced to stand in a tiny stall all day and then asked to run guts out is sure to set up the horse for problems. Thrush and fungus thrive in the dark, moist environment. Another section explains about dipping the feet in diluted bleach water or scrubbing the frog with a mixture of soap and bleach. This practice is a tremendous help in controlling these problems. A stall with an outside paddock allows the horse to choose where to drop manure. A horse raised with a paddock out back generally does not mess in his stall.

Many, many foot problems are started in the name of good training.

Initially, it seemed necessary to shoe. Then I wondered why? I tried going without shoes and found it was much better for the majority of horses. Many horses that have lived at the track for years have been sent to my farm. They often have very deformed feet. **The combination of poor shoeing, lack of legitimate exercise, standing all day and over eating puts great pressure on the feet.** Combine this with infrequent shoeing, coercing a long toe and no heel and you will probably make a complete mess of the feet.

One horse with persistent abscesses in his feet was sent to me. He had been on the track for three straight years. They apparently tried to fix the abscesses with the shoeing. He was a huge, beautiful, seventeen hand horse and arrived with bar shoes, of which his feet were falling out . His feet wanted to be larger than the shoes. He was the equivalent of a Chinese women with bound feet.

It was obvious his feet had to be bothering him. The heels were so contorted and contracted they couldn't breath. When a horse moves, it is necessary for the hoof to flex. There was no way these hooves could flex with bar shoes. They were nailed in position and couldn't possibly relax and contract. His heels were malformed and "contracted." His frog and hoof shape were completely distorted. When I told the owner he had been improperly shod, he commented that he had paid over $2,000.00 for shoeing, in the last year or two.

The most important thing I did for this horse was pull off his shoes and have him constantly turned out and moving in deep sand. The sand was kind to his feet and the movement allowed blood supply to the feet. After about eight months, the heels had started to relax and we could clean them without too much trouble. (The abscesses formed in the folds of the heels, surely because filth was trapped there.) Aggressive hosing helped stimulate blood flow and clean the area. The same adage used for physicians should be used for trainers. "Above all, do no harm!". There are many good books out about shoeing. If you have specific problems, speak with the experts and read, read, read.

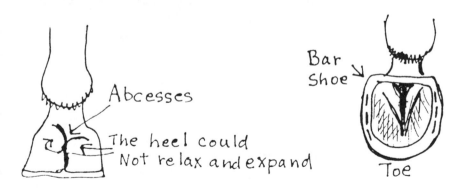

THE DUCK FOOT

In Florida we sometimes use the name "duck foot" for the way many horses' feet start to look after years of shoeing with the mistaken belief that a longer toe will allow the horse to have a longer stride. The theory is he'll strive to throw his foot out further, enhancing the length of his stride. (Obviously, if he doesn't fling the toe forward, he'll fall over it.) Making the toe longer puts more pressure on the tendons. Mechanically, this is a perfect set up for bowing tendons.

With all the stress we put on the horse, let's not do more damage by fooling with the natural angle of the hoof. Long toes, high speed and hard surfaces are the perfect combination for breakdown. Stand back and look at your horse. He should be on a level surface. Trim to allow the healthy logical angle that keeps the hoof and pastern on the same line, as shown. Thoroughbreds tend to have very little heel anyway, so usually we are working on toes and maintaining whatever heel we have.

There is a very easy to read article on hoof angles in *Equus Magazine,* Volume 170, page 26. It is entitled "Balanced Hooves," by Barbara Robbins.

The logic of good shoeing is discussed. Once again...use your horse sense.

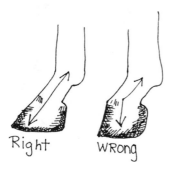

Right   WRong

WRONG

Toe grabs on a hard surface may change the break over action

Young Horses can find Confinement
Difficult !

FEEDS and SUPPLEMENTS

FEEDS AND SUPPLEMENTS

In various parts of the world, people use different basic foods as their mainstay. Whether it is potatoes, rice, wheat, or corn, supplemented with meat, fish, or combined proteins, there is a tremendous diversity in the diet.

When it comes to feeding horses you will find a multitude of opinions. Owners have come to me with charts, scales and very intricate instructions on how their dear little horse must be fed. They assure me that they have calculated exactly how much he needs because he burns X amount of calories per work. I marvel at their precision. How can they know so precisely?

It is extremely impractical to have different feeding menus on large farms. (There are exceptions for a horse with a specific problem.) The more complicated the feeding program, the more opportunity for mistakes and accidents. Too many steps may confuse your help.

All of my animals receive the same basic feed mixture. Everyone on the farm is fed half cracked corn and half sweet feed. The sweet feed is 14% protein and is mixed locally. The corn is 7% protein. Pound for pound, corn is much higher in energy than oats. University studies have shown that corn converts most efficiently into glycogen, which fuels cells during anaerobic stress. Between the two feeds, the animals get about 10% protein. The amount of feed given to each horse varies. Every animal gets free choice hay (usually fertilized coastal). The hay is about 10% protein and is locally grown. My basic feed measurement for Thoroughbreds-yearlings, two-year-olds and up - is about four quarts of the mix twice a day. Yearlings and two-year-olds are building and growing. The more mature horses are easing into racing and need to replace fuel that is burned. Quarterhorses are such easy keep. They seem to need less than half as much as the Thoroughbreds. When a new horse arrives, until he adjusts to the feed, he is given a third of the usual amount, gradually increasing it to the usual gallon, twice a day.

Observe and see who finishes and who leaves feed. Once your horses are stabilized on your feeding program, **augment the feed if an animal looks too thin.** Some large racing horses will need as much as eight quarts twice a day.

Since each metabolism varies greatly, it is imperative that you understand what kind of "keeper" each horse is. Personality can be a major factor in feed consumption, sending the charts right out the window. Is he high strung or laid back? What's his genetic background? Some bloodlines are historically easy to maintain and others are not. There may be other influences too subtle for us perceive.

Sometimes, horses appear high strung because they are given high protein feed which is not burned off with a reasonable training program. Fifteen minutes on the race track doesn't burn many calories.

My system allows horses to be turned out every day for a few hours. If they are being over-fed, they can run and frolic to burn off their excess energy. The point is, although charts may say a horse needs so many pounds for so much work, it is really a very subjective figure. **Look at your horse...is he carrying enough weight or does he look drawn?** Horses in the interval training program, where they are worked every four days and galloped miles in between, develop muscles with a "hard" look.

When I was trying to follow the interval training program, my horses looked drawn and over-trained. **The program was drilling out their speed and brilliance.** When the horses' muscle gets too hard a look in the interval training method, it is not usually because of lack of feed. Mine were eating huge and frightening amounts! **The look stems from overtraining.** It is important that you learn to **tell the difference between over training and under feeding.** If your horse is eating huge amounts of feed, is on a good worming schedule and still looks ribby, it may be that you are **over working** the animal. The problem can be high speed done frequently, without time off for the animal to rebuild in between the stresses, especially young animals. Learn to know your animal and feed accordingly.

Two, three and four-year-olds are really very much like teenagers. A tremendous amount of food energy goes into building bone, muscle and tissue. Just as teenagers get big hands and feet and skinny bodies before they fill out, horses go through adolescent growth spurts.

Good feed, good training and lots of turnout during this growing period is important. At five, the horse is considered mature in bone and body. If we race judiciously as they grow and develop, and allow time for rebuilding between races, we are forming a useful, strong animal that can last many years!

Some trainers, thinking that their horse needs more feed (when really he may be over-training), will add pure corn oil or other kinds of fats to the feed. Horses seem to be unable to metabolize fat and may develop pockets or globules of fat which constrict major vessels. This in turn may cause impairment of blood flow. An excess of anything can be dangerous!

WHEN AND HOW TO FEED

Did you notice that I mentioned giving grain twice a day? In the old days, while innocently imitating track procedures, I got up in the dark and woke up the horses to feed them. When they galloped two hours later, I worried, thinking it might be too close to a heavy meal. After much thought, it occurred to me that I never had breakfast until my work was done, so the horses could do the same.

Now, I get up at dawn, (the hours varies greatly from summer to winter) give all the horses hay and turn out those who go from stalls to paddocks. **The animals loosen up in the paddocks, frolic, and socialize while I pick out the stalls.** After their ride, roundpenning or swim, they go back to their turnout paddocks until feed time. They can still nibble on the hay that was given at dawn. At ten a.m. in the winter, and at nine a.m. in the summer, they are given their grain and supplements along with enough hay to last all day . Depending on their schedule, in the summer they are stalled during the day and turned out at night. They are fed hay and grain again at dusk. This system has worked well for me.

During the hot summer days they are fed in the cool of the evening. In the winter, they are fed while there is enough light to visually observe how they look, before they are tucked in for the night.

This program makes sense, because animals are sensitive to the rhythm of the earth. We tend to be more tied to the clock. If you work and must arrange your horses around your schedule, that is fine. Animals are adaptable and can live with many different situations. **The most useful animals are those that aren't ruffled by unpredictable circumstances.** Races and traveling schedules will break up their routine soon enough.

The racetrack routine is very restricting. The track is only open until ten o'clock. All the horses must be out and back by then. Doing most of the training at the farm, you are able to adapt the training program to suit your life-style and schedule. You can have horses and have another life, too.

Bran mash again? It must be Sunday!

Once a week, all of my horses are given bran. They are given four quarts of bran well saturated with water and perhaps a squirt of corn oil. My schedule is every Sunday morning, to avoid confusion. No supplements or other products are given. Some of the horses remind me of children, when they are fed healthy food. They say, "Yuk... bran again." Others horses devour the bran. Still others try to hold out and only finally choke it down, when there is no hope of real feed. Those that refuse to finish get it stirred into their night grain. We live in an area that has a great deal of sand. I constantly worry about the horses ingesting too much of it,

when grazing on short grass. The bran seems to control the problem. Keeping attractive, properly cured hay available to them helps also.

Speaking of hay... a few comments. People rave about how great alfalfa is for horses. Alfalfa is very high in protein. It is about 18 percent. To me, this is too rich to combine with the very high amount of grain the animals are being given. A lower percentage of protein in their roughage is preferable. Munching on hay or grazing is very soothing for the animal. When man gets too smart about feed, he forgets that the animal might find it comforting to eat a lower quality hay all day long, instead of a small amount of high protein hay, which is consumed in a short period. Why not let the animal fulfill his desire to chew? High protein pellets fill the animal's nutritional needs, but are consumed quickly. The horse may start chewing on boards, doors and other surfaces, out of boredom. Work with the animals' intrinsic needs. Remember, they are grazers.

Here are some general comments about feed. If your feed is from a reputable local feed mill or from a company that mixes the feed especially for your area, the fourteen percent sweet feed mix should be available. Read the guaranteed analysis. It should tell the crude protein, fat, fiber, etc. Trace minerals and vitamins should be mentioned. Ingredients such as folic acid, selenite, etc., either occur naturally in the feed or are added to the mix. This is mentioned so that you don't go overboard with supplements. When the horse is racing and you feel he needs help, you may want to add a little more of this and that, but too much supplement is dangerous. Doctors Krook and Maylin have stressed in their book, *Race Horses at Risk*, that many breakdowns are attributed to abusive overfeeding and supplementing to push early growth. This has resulted in animals with improperly developed bone. Cysts of cartilage form in the bone, which weaken overall strength. The bone caves in when put under the stress of racing. This type of breakdown happens time and time again. It is disheartening to think that a healthy looking animal can have serious internal faults. If you want to know more about his subject, read the book. It is an eye opener.

For questions about feed and problems to be aware of in your area, call your local extension office or nearest agricultural university.

My whole philosophy is this: Remember the natural life-style of the animal and try to keep him in a way that allows him to be a horse. Don't try to fool Mother Nature.

A local Feed Mill should have the proper mix for your area. It should be fresher than feed shipped in from far away. Check with the nearest Agricultural University for Specific Nutritional needs in your area!

SUPPLEMENTS

This subject could be debated forever. There are testimonials for all kinds of products. It is easy to fall into the vitamin and health food syndrome. True health food fanatics live restricted lives that revolve around strange diets that prompt some of us to think "death is preferable to eating that stuff!"

Go back to Mother Nature. Think about how horses were meant to be grazers, moving constantly. A bite of grass here, a few seed heads there, a lovely salad; all courtesy of their environment. I am instinctively frightened by the amount of grain we give these horses. They would have grazed for many, many hours, burning many calories to encounter that much protein in the wild. We stress our animals in ways that are not natural (sustained high speed, with weight on their back), so we assume that we must compensate.

Overall we have improved their life-style in relation to the dangers in the wild. We do stress their metabolism, especially if they are honest. The amount of weight a horse can lose in a race is amazing. **The one minute and twelve seconds of racing can take so much out of the animal that he needs days to recuperate.** I tell my horses that nothing in life is free and they must perform for me in exchange for the comfort I give them.

This is where supplements may be necessary. Being over stressed, the horse needs help to rebuild. A horse may be dehydrated for a few days after a hard race. In Florida, during the severe summer heat, this is especially true. I give a handful of electrolytes for a few days after the race, always checking his skin to see how he is doing. To judge how the horse is rehydrating, take a pinch of skin on his neck and see how long it takes for the skin to go back to normal from the pinch. The longer it takes the more dehydrated he is. **Remember that electrolytes are also assimilated from a good diet and a salt mineral block.**

The time a horse needs to rebuild himself is the best barometer of his overall ability to withstand the rigors of racing. I am opposed to jugging a horse after a race to speed his recovery. Jugging means having the veterinarian give the horse a solution of electrolytes and IV fluids intravenously. The whole structure of the horse is stressed in a hard race. . . the bone, muscle, and soft tissue. By jugging the horse you make him feel better than he really is. It is better to have the horse mope around a few days - self imposed rest. **His body tells him he needs rest and that in itself will make him rest. When he is recharged, he'll tell you by frolicking, when you turn him out.** Most horses I've trained show a definite pattern. If they have tried hard and raced honestly, they are a tad off their feed that night. They might be slightly off for another day or so. By the fourth or fifth day it seems that their own endorphins make them feel high off the race. They are on their way to rebuilding. When turned out they frolic and cavort.　Light free roundpenning and maybe one flying open gallop and they are ready to race again on the tenth day.

After a few races or hard works, you begin to discriminate between a robust horse that needs and wants to race frequently and a horse that is hard on himself in a race. Unlike many humans who can push themselves and come back stronger, when a horse is pushed too much, he is capable of doing himself real damage. When he has an adrenaline rush, he is capable of running on a fractured leg or doing other equally harmful things to himself. The rider on the horse urging him to go faster and faster may make the horse overexert. **Your role as a trainer is to know when enough is enough.**

The cost of training a horse at the track is so high that owners put too much emphasis on the horse's daily behavior. If he has one bad day or is slightly off his feed, there is a tendency to over react. "Call the vet. . . we are losing time." At home you can be more relaxed about letting him off a day or two. **We all have bad days. Horses are no exception.** They are not machines! Blood tests and X-rays for every minor bump get to be very expensive. At home you have another great advantage over the track; you can constantly observe and monitor your animal.

Time has been taken here to discuss the above because **there is a tendency to oversupplement and overdose the horse.** Rational rest is the best thing after a race. Legs that have a little edema after a race are normal. No need to give young horses Bute for that. Let them rebuild themselves.

Although horses should get all of their nutrition from well balanced feed, I do use a vitamin supplement. There are a great many out there. I will share my recipe with you, as an example. You can adapt your own program and preferences.

Pour a twenty five pound bag of Clovite into a large, clean container. Add five pounds of brewers yeast, which is high in vitamin B and amino acids. In view of the 50% corn diet my animals get, a nutritionist told me to balance the calcium phosphate ratio, so I add one pound of dicalcium phosphate. Add a three to five pound container of vitamin B powder and the same amount of vitamin E and Selinium. Check your soil; you may already be high in selinium. Add a three to five pound container of biotin (good for hooves). Stir this concoction thoroughly and give about two ounces (a handful) to each animal in his morning grain feed. I may give actively racing horses a squirt of Red Cell or the equivalent for good measure. You may think my attitude is a little cavalier. However, basically the metabolism will get its nutrition from well balanced feed. These are really just extra backups.

If your horse's gums aren't pink and healthy, check with your veterinarian. See if your horse is wormy . Have a blood chemistry run, if there is a problem. In a well fit and conditioned horse, the gums will flush up pink very quickly when asked for exercise, indicating an efficient cardiovascular system. When I swim horses, they curl their upper lip. It is easy to assess how long it takes for the animal to go from light pink gums to rich strong pink, as they exercise. It is a good gauge of their cardiovascular efficiency.

A huge amount of money is spent on feed supplements. Observe what works. Read the literature and judge whether it makes sense. If a talented horse is kept happy and healthy, he will run. **No magic powders will help a horse without talent.** If it makes you feel good, give your horse a pinch of this and a squirt of that. Try not to overdo as his kidneys will have to work overtime to strain the excess additives out of his system. One simple all around vitamin once a day should be adequate for his needs. Anything above and beyond that should be studied for real value and cost.

Del Castillo's Feed Schedule

Dawn Turn out horses to individual

Paddocks (after <u>feeling</u> and <u>checking Legs!</u>)
<u>Give Hay</u> * note whether
or not all grain was eaten!

9 or 10 AM Grain and Hay
and Vitamins –
Tuck back in stall – all (all feed
morning work done! supplements are
added at this feeding)

<u>Afternoon</u> – Turn out for
an hour or so ... depending
Sometimes I gallop, round pen or swim
in the afternoon – depending on schedule

<u>½ hour before Dark</u> Hay and Grain –
Tuck Horses in for night

Hay 3 Times a day
Grain 2 Times a day
Bran – Sunday A.M.

THE SCIENCE OF CARROTOLOGY

You might, indeed, ask, "What the heck is carrotology?" Early in my endeavors with horses and racing, a friend came to visit. She loved horses, but knew nothing about training. She was an expert in nurturing. For years, Claire has returned and taught the horses how to eat carrots. Yes, they sometimes need to learn this important skill. Claire's husband, George, is a sharp handicapper from way back. He also comes to see what the horses have to say. Sometimes Claire will come in and tell me, "You know, Aly says his shin is bothering him!", or give me some other piece of information. I dutifully go out and check the animal to find that she is instinctively right.

Over the years, she has befriended all of the horses on the farm. She does have her favorites-she brings gourmet carrots to First Prediction. She shares her carrots, kindness, and advice with all the horses. They know Claire and George by sight, and nicker to them when they arrive.

It is very special for the animals to have someone who does nothing but love and care for them. When I had quite a few horses, I assigned girl riders to specific horses so that they would take a personal interest in them.

George and Claire

You will be warned time and time again not to fall in love with the horses. It is a business...be pragmatic! You must realistically appraise the ability of the animals you are training, but that does not preclude caring and loving them. Some animals are so honest and noble that one can't help but admire them. There is nothing wrong with having feelings. It might help the racing industry tremendously to have more feeling and caring individuals involved. You all should have a support group like George and Claire. Find some "Grandparents" for your horses.

Go for it...give your horses a kiss on the nose and let them know you care!

SETBACKS

Coughs and Colds
Bucked Shins
Paralyzed flap
Bleeders
Bowed Tendons

SETBACKS

Every owner enters into the joy of owning a racehorse with the illusion that the horse will start training, run fast, run even faster and win lots of races. Unfortunately it rarely ever happens this way.

Training a horse to be a sound racehorse is very much like raising children. You put in a lot of foundation, and survive the childhood diseases and personality conflicts before you arrive at a whole and complete person. Most of the time, with a horse, we don't know whether training is cost effective, until we see how fast the horse can run. Sometimes we find we have spent too much money and effort on a slow horse.

No trainer can guarantee anything. In fact, it challenges the fates if the trainer is foolish enough to say something like, "This is a big winner." Disillusioned owners have told me many stories. They accuse their trainers of lying to them about horses. More than likely, the trainer was completely sincere. He believed the horse he recommended for $20,000 would win back his cost, even though statistically most horse will not pay their way, let alone the initial cost.

If it were so easy, trainers wouldn't have to work so hard and get up so early. A very clever trainer I knew told me my problem was not educating my owners properly. "Just tell them it's like owning a boat," he said. "The owner doesn't expect his boat to make him money. He has it for the pleasure it gives him." This might all sound good, until you realize a boat doesn't humiliate an owner by running last in front of friends who have bet the boat very heavily.

Most of my owners are self made men. The kind that can't relate to paying $20,000 for a horse, putting another $6,000 into training and being told the horse might be able to win in a field of $2,500 claimers. Who could really relate to that anyway? But, many times it is the scenario. What is possible, **is that the horse may be very useful at that level and steadily bring in enough money to justify his expenses.**

The joy of seeing your horse win at any level is a great experience. Of course, if the horse starts making money at a given level, he may be claimed. Other astute trainers or owners see that he is useful. They pick him up and make money from all your hard work. Nobody ever said life was fair.

I share this with you because many owners tell me they had bad luck..their horse got a cough...bucked his shins...popped a splint...Lord knows when he will run. This really isn't bad luck. It is very typical of a young horse going through normal experiences on his way to becoming a real race horse. Just as our children experience coughs and ear aches in the process of growing up, **horses must encounter and over come minor set backs.**

Down time is expensive to owners paying $45 a day for training. The trainer, who is aware of the owner's attitude, feels pressured to continue further training too soon.

If the horse gets a cold at the track, he will probably be treated with antibiotics..infections can bounce back and fourth in the shedrow...especially

among young horses. This is another reason I encourage taking more mature horses to the track. They have a higher resistance level. Coughs, colds and minor lameness are not as crucial at home as they are at the track. The horse at home has more room and nothing is as concentrated. They are given more time to recover when you're not paying expensive day money. Many times a few days or a week turned out will allow the horse to fight the common cold or cough.

The following Sections discuss common and predictable set backs, and how to treat them. Remember, my way of treatment is not the only way. These are solutions that work for me.

Until you have more experience, many of you will want to confer with a vet about these problems. *Lameness in Horses,* by O. R. Adams and *Equine Medicine and Surgery,* by American Veterinary Publications were my "Bibles" when faced with a set back.. There is also an excellent anatomy book, *Color Atlas of Veterinary Anatomy*, published by J.B. Lippincott Company, Gower Medical Publishing.

Do your homework and constantly learn from experience. **Never be afraid to ask questions if something doesn't make common sense to you.**

Be an informed Owner!

Read and learn!

COUGHS AND COLDS

When you start working your horse one day and you notice he coughs or is breathing funny, it may be a cough or a cold. There might be colored mucus, yellow or green, coming out of his nose. Stop working him immediately. Turn him out unless it's cold or inclement weather, or if he becomes nervous when he is out. If you must stall him, make sure he is walked or turned out briefly each day. He needs movement to help him cough and drain the mucus.

Never leave a horse in a stall 24 hours without some kind of exercise, even if he is ill. His legs can stock up and other problems can occur if we don't stir up his blood. Ten minutes of hand walking twice a day will help.

Three days. . . that is my magic number. If the horse doesn't show improvement in three days, I call the vet. Of course, if he has a high fever, is in acute stress or looks severely ill, call the vet immediately. He should be consulted before using any cough remedies or medications. Many of them have substances that must not be used within so many days of racing.

Don't load a horse with antibiotics for minor illnesses. Use your common sense. Remember your first child. The pediatrician was called incessantly until you learned to relax and not over react. After you handle horses enough, you'll learn not to over react.

Allow your horse rest and turn out until he no longer coughs or breathes funny. Then try free roundpenning him. If he starts coughing persistently, he needs more rest. If he cough a few minutes and then seems allright, continue with free roundpenning.

If your horse is stalled at the track in the winter, it is possible that the air he is breathing is more harmful inside than the cold air outside. Urine odors and concentrations of germs are trapped in tightly closed barns. The horses ping pong all kinds of viruses back and forth among themselves. It is possible that these chronic low grade respiratory infections may be a cause of bleeding. Single stalls with a half door open to the outside are better for the horses as the air is circulating.

Horses have ciliated epithelial cells in their nasal passages and upper airways. These cells are responsible for trapping dust, mold spores and other debris prior to their entry into the lungs. Drs. Jackson and Pagan of Kentucky Equine Research believe the ammonia from urine and manure in enclosed stalls damages these cells and therefore leaves the horse more susceptible to molds and other pathogens.

Remember, if your horse has been given the various systemic steroids which are so popular right now, his immune system is very weak and any kind of virus can knock him down. Medicorten, Prednisone, Prednisolone and Azium are all **steroids that will lower his immune system.** Don't start using them as short cuts to racing young horses!

Horses in general, seem to have less respiratory problems when kept outside with a good shelter as opposed to being in poorly ventilated barns.

Bucked Shins

Sore Shins

Usually 2 or 3 days after a hard work!

The horse doesn't want you to touch them!

BUCKED SHINS

If the worst problem your horse has is Bucked Shins, consider yourself lucky. If handled properly, they are a minor set back along the way to a mature horse.

The general consensus of opinion is that Bucked Shins are a tearing of the periosteum sheath caused by concussion and speed, generally found in immature horses. They can be considered a series of micro fractures. They usually occur when speed on a firm surface "insults" the bone. They can easily become a saucer fracture if not handled properly.

When the horses on my farm ran on a kind surface, even putting on speed, no shin problems appeared. When they started racetrack works, after about three works, spaced seven days apart, the horses would get sore or bucked shins. Since by this time the horse is working five to six furlongs, **I think the stress of high speed at a sustained distance helps cause Bucked Shins or soreness to occur.**

If your horse has sore shins he will be touchy when you run your hand down the front of the cannon bone. If the shins are really bucked, after two or three days, you will see a little knot or swelling on the front of the leg. If it is severe, the horse may stop in the middle of the track work and walk back in obvious distress. If you even point at the shin, the horse will pick it up quickly and very clearly tell you where it hurts.

If the shins get really sore, have them X-rayed to rule out a true fracture. If there is no fracture, follow your vet's advice, which will probably be poultice and rest. He

may suggest "cooling the shins out and firing" them. This is a thermal cautery...heat is applied to a series of needles that are pressed onto the front of the cannon bone. It reminds me of putting gun powder on a wound in order to sterilize it. Many trainers and vets swear by the method. I almost had it done to one of my horses, but at the last minute I canceled because it made no common sense to me.

Many trainers say, "Well, cooling the shins out and firing them forces you to rest the horse, because he is so inflamed that you couldn't possibly train him until the swelling and reaction subside." This is a very poor reason to administer the procedure. Must they incapacitate the horse in order to rest him? Some horses rebuck even with this treatment. So what is gained?

Chemical blistering is also a common remedy for sore shins. A very caustic solution is rubbed or painted on the horse's shins or completely around the front cannon bones. This causes a reaction like a terrible chemical burn. The legs swell up tremendously. The trainer then "works" on the legs until they come back to "normal" at which point he starts training again. Many trainers feel the blister and resulting scar tissue "toughen" the shins.

Over the years, I have found a solution that works for me. When your horse comes back sore or with bucked shins, check them every day and turn him out every day...all day if possible. Gently and lightly run your hand down the front of the shin. His reaction tells you how sore he is. That's how you monitor or check them. Observe how the horse walks. If the horse has been X-rayed to rule out fractures, don't give him Bute. Observe his movement from one day to the next.

If he is really inflamed, by all means poultice him, but don't wrap the shin with more than two turns of cellophane. That's all - no standing bandages! Cellophane can be put on so tightly and wrapped so many times it cooks the skin. After wrapping the horse's shins turn him out. The next morning pull off the cellophane wrap and let the poultice dry and flake off. The following day hose until the poultice comes off . Repeat the process if you feel it will help. Depending on the severity of the inflammation, your horse should not be as touchy on the shins after five days. Always monitor his shins no matter how you think he is feeling.

When your horse seem better and is moving freely on his own in the paddock, gently free roundpen him at a light gallop. If your surface is hard, he may show a little soreness. Check his shins the day after the round penning by running your hand

Learn to read the Horses' Body Language!

down the front of the cannon bone. You must do this every day and note his reactions on the chart. See if the horse has gotten sorer. If he has, let him go for two or three days before you free roundpen him again. If he is less sore, gently free roundpen him. If he is not sore, go back to training.

Work him again, no sooner than 14 days from the first day of soreness. He may come back sore. If he does, repeat the process from the beginning. He should heal more quickly this time because he is now starting to develop scar tissue on the front of the bone.

Never work him at the track more frequently than every ten days when he has had sore shins, even if he is not sore after five days. It takes ten days to replace the calcium lost in a hard work at the track. By allowing a certain amount of healing and not confining or stopping the horse, his body is allowed to repair, rebuild and toughen the shins. It may take two to six months for your horse to come out of the works, or races without being sore. If your horse is racing at this time, make sure he isn't sore going into the race. Don't give Bute and fool yourself into thinking he is not sore when he is. If he shows no soreness when you run your hand down the cannon ten days after his last soreness, put him in a race or rework him. The night before the race you can give him Bute, don't give it after a race, because you must know how sore he is.

We are trying to encourage new tissue to be laid across the bone. While we don't want to push the horse to overdo and fracture the bone, we do want to "judiciously insult" the bone. You get a feel for this as you go along. You must know and check your horse every day to have a good point of reference from which to judge.

None of my horses have rebucked after this treatment. Bucked shins must be "worked through." When your horse isn't sore, you will see that his shins have a thickness that makes them almost appear convex.

Your vet may have other ways of treating bucked shins. He may even turn the horse out for three months   which should not hurt him. I prefer my treat-   ment. The horse loses little conditioning   time and con- tinues to race, even as   he heals.

Bucked Shins

Sore shins probably appear after 3rd or 4th Speed Breeze at Track caused by High Speed at Sustained Distance

Horse will be very touchy when you go near shins! Check severity of soreness everyday!

Turn horse out! After 5 days or so, he should be able to free roundpen

Don't give Bute! His soreness keeps him from hurting self-

Check Shins on 6th day - if sorer, leave alone another 2 or 3 days - if less sore, free roundpen again

Each day that he is less sore than previous day, free roundpen again until you go back to a strong fast gallop with rider

Shin { a "bump" might appear 2 days or so after Speed Work

Work horse at Track no sooner than 14 days from 1st day of soreness

He may be sore again after Work- Turn out, free roundpen, and gallop again when not sore- You are "Working Through" BUCKED SHINS!

Xray horse to eliminate fractures!

PARALYZED FLAP

A paralyzed flap is a big setback for the horse. If you suspect this problem, your veterinarian will slip a long tube with a lens attached, into the horses throat. He will see whether or not the horse has Laryngeal Hemiplegia (Paralyzed Flap).

Simply put, because of a malfunctioning opening, the horse is unable to take in the air he needs, especially when he is under stress. This is a very frustrating problem and is most dramatic for race horses.

Many times you don't know your horse has this problem until you finally red line the horse. A young horse in training, may make a "roaring noise" or stop running hard for no apparent reason when pushed. An exam by the vet will confirm whether or not he has a lazy or paralyzed flap. Lazy flap is an early sign of the same problem. The flap is slow to open and close. Eventually it becomes paralyzed.

Surgery is available to correct this condition. I have not had very positive results with the procedure. In an informal survey of trainers, few felt it was worth the effort. Unless your horse shows real talent, don't invest time and money in the procedure. Before making any decisions, go to a large center where many of these procedures are preformed and talk with experts in the field. As in all medical procedures, they find better methods every day.

It is a tremendous frustration when you find a horse with potential who has this problem...it's all a part of being in the business. Now you see why it only looks easy.

open wide!

Paralyzed Flap

BLEEDERS-EPISTAXIS

EXERCISE INDUCED PULMONARY HEMORRHAGE

There are many theories about bleeding and what causes it, but there are no real proven answers. Typically, your horse is running and in the middle of the race or in the stretch, he throws his head up and stops running well. His big moves and hard drives stop and he just gallops in. By the time he gets to the finish line, the horse might manifest bleeding by having blood spattered over his body. The blood is coming out of his nostrils. This is upsetting to see. The track vet and stewards make official notice of it and put him on the "Bleeders List."

Another way bleeding might manifest itself in your horse is while in the race, and in the process of a strong drive, the horse seems to fade and gallops in. There is no visible problem...no blood...no lameness. You might be scratching your head as you go back to the barn wondering what went wrong. Then after you walk him a few rounds and let him drop his head to graze, you notice a trickle of blood coming from his nostrils. If so, he too is a bleeder. Until you have a bleeding problem, you're not really even aware of what it means.

Some horses gush, others show a trickle and some bleed so little you don't know it until you've seen them race a few times fading in the drive. In desperation, you ask to have the horse scoped to eliminate the possibility of bleeding.

When you have your horse scoped, the vet will meet you at the barn after the race or work. The horse must have been stressed enough to trigger the bleeding. The vet will pass a long tube with a lens he can look through, into the horses lungs to see if there is any bleeding that hasn't worked its way up and out yet. The horse will experience mild discomfort. If the vet verifies that there is bleeding, he will send you to the State Vet, who will observe the horse and put him on the Bleeders List. (These procedures vary from state to state - check the rules in your state!)

If your horse is put on the Bleeders List, it means that he must not run for two weeks and may be given Lasix four hours before his next race.

Once your horse is on the Lasix List, it is announced in the program and your horse must be on the grounds at least four hours before the race to have the Lasix administered by a vet. If your horse is observed bleeding with Lasix, he will be ruled off for six months. If he continues to bleed, he will not be allowed to run. There are trainers who fear the horse will bleed through the Lasix . They instruct their grooms to keep the horse's head high after the race. The groom will lead the horse off the track with the horse's head resting on his shoulder so that blood does not drip in front of the officials.

For some reason, when Lasix is given, a horse tends to run better the first time back. The betting public likes knowing about Lasix administration. They think, "if the horse was moving well before he started to bleed, then he might move really well with Lasix." There is also a belief that if a horse is on Lasix, other drugs can be given and the test results will be confused making it possible to give illegal or unproven substances.

I personally am very uncomfortable with a bleeder. If you have to give Lasix, be acutely aware of the diuretic effect it has on the horse's metabolism. I believe it is very dangerous to use Lasix, especially in heat and humidity. One hot afternoon at Calder two Lasix horses dropped dead after a race.

Think about the effect of Lasix on the horse's system. Four hours before a race you take away his water bucket and give him a shot of Lasix. Soon he starts urinating. Some horses react to the medication with trembling. Others pass a loose stool. They lose fluid. Theoretically, pressure against the wall of the capillaries is lessened, due to the lowering of fluid volume. In effect, the same amount of red blood cells are being circulated through the system but with less fluid. Maybe, because the blood volume is less, they don't bleed as easily?

Try and understand what is really going on physiologically. When you are running a horse in severe heat with chemically induced fluid loss and he is red-lining his system, how can he lower his temperature with sweat if his fluid volume is already low? Does this combination of stresses, heat, severe exercise, fatigue and lack of water volume, cause an imbalance in his electrolytes and cause irregular heart beat, etc.? An electrolyte imbalance can cause heart attacks!

I don't have any answers, but I do think Lasix must be used cautiously, and not too frequently. You must allow the horse time to recuperate from its effects. A Lasix horse needs help with electrolytes and time to recover.

The remarkable thing is that Lasix does improve some bleeders. Horses can run usefully with Lasix under certain conditions. If you race too frequently, your horse will start to show the effects and his performance will reflect this.

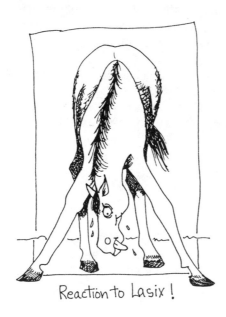

Reaction to Lasix!

My horses, trained with the progressive stacking of stress (over the time period recommended), don't seem to bleed. I don't think this is coincidental. There are many theories to consider. Is it the stress of the race, the red lining of the structure, that causes bleeding? Is it asking a horse, who has not been gradually brought up to the point of fitness necessary for the race, to run too hard, too soon? Horses are very honest, and capable of giving much more than is physically safe for them. Fillies are always in danger of giving too much. If you work them too hard, too soon you can ruin them for life. A horse should rise to the occasion and ease comfortably into to running his best for a sustained distance.

It is thought that bleeding does relate to speed work. We don't usually see it in horses doing long slow gallops.

Bleeding has been observed in Quarter Horses who were racing. Early studies indicated a higher percentage of bleeders than among Thoroughbreds. Quarter Horses are not given much racing foundation since they are asked to run only short distances. **The effort of going into pure speed without any long preparation could trigger a bleeding problem.** To me, it is like flooring the engine of your car without a good, gradual warm-up. Sudden, pure speed is hard on a cold engine. It's just as hard on an unfit horse's lungs and structure.

Epistaxis or bleeding, may have something to do with the fragility of capillaries and at times may be caused by respiratory illness. Since it is exercise induced in race horses, it probably has to do with asking too much, too soon, or red-lining the animal's system.

There are many concoctions on the market to help control bleeding. Some have a basis in diet, some are homeopathic, some naturally lower blood pressure, some like rutin, help coagulation and some are complete feed programs.

Bleeding is a very complex subject and if your horse has the problem, call the nearest university or speak with a good vet and try to determine what will help.

Be aware that there are also additives that can affect this problem. A situation that comes to mind is a filly that was sent to my farm to swim. She had undergone knee surgery. At that time MSM, a powder form of DMSO was being touted as a great thing to speed up the healing of joints. The theory was that DMSO opened the blood flow to the capillaries and the increased blood supply was good for quicker healing (more good blood in, more damaged material out). I was told to give specified amounts of MSM to this filly, twice a day. At the same time, a friend was suffering from chronically aching knees. The owner of the filly, suggested that my friend take a spoonful of the same stuff two or three times a day to get relief. Since at the time, everybody was talking about DMSO, I told my friend. He was in such chronic pain that he tried it. He did jokingly comment that aside from an inexplicable desire to snort, whinny and paw, he felt relief in his knees. Later, he started having uncontrollable nose bleeds. They were so bad he had to be taken to the hospital to have his nose packed. Back at home, he wondered if the nosebleeds were related to the DMSO. He stopped taking the powder and the nosebleeds stopped. He started taking the powder again and the nosebleeds started again. Obviously this was not a medically controlled experiment, but I kept the information in the back of my mind.

Finally, the mare was sent to the track. I was told that upon her arrival DMSO was administrated IV (intravenously) by a vet, because it would really help. Now she had had powdered DMSO, DMSO IV, and knowing the race track, they were probably painting her knees with DMSO too. The horse started to run and she bled. She was put on Lasix and when she ran again, she bled through the Lasix. They had to take her home.

I told the owner about my friend's observations and asked him if he thought there could be any connection. He asked his vet and reported back to me that the vet said,

"No. No relation whatsoever."

I personally believe these horses are given far too many things that try and "fool Mother Nature." You should keep your horse healthy, exercise him properly and give him time to rebuild from the extreme stress of a race.

As far as helping a bleeder goes, do your homework. There is new knowledge available everyday. Maybe someone out there has an answer.

Some vets have suggested that a horse might have a slight amount of bleeding, when trying his hardest. They go on to say, if the horse is given time to heal from the intense race or work, then there isn't a chronic problem. **They believe the problem starts when a horse has no real "re-build" time.** Racetrack routine encourages works and or races every five days or so. What happens if the lungs are healing and the horse is dosed with steroids and mood enhancers, and then worked or raced five days after his last bleeding episode? More damage occurs in the lungs, and the healing is retarded.

Then, because he's a bleeder, he's given Lasix and the plethora of other steroids on the day of the next race. Now he's running with medications that may enhance his performance while tearing apart his lungs. (Any emphysema sufferer will tell you how much Predisone (a steroid) helps their breathing and mental attitude - they'll tell you that their **symptoms** are relieved and they feel very aggressive.) Good qualities for a race horse but **no healing** has taken place. The symptoms of discomfort are removed, but the **damage** is still there!

The horse runs with these medications for various races until the damage being done catches up with him. It's not just using Lasix. It's Lasix plus all the steroids and pain-killers that cause such damage!

It is far easier not to have to deal with bleeding at all. The point is that most racetrack ailments are related to pushing a horse beyond his abilities. If you begin with a sound horse and follow my training program, your horse shouldn't bleed.

All of the rules mentioned apply to Florida Tracks, other states vary in their regulations.

Water is taken away from Lasix horses 4 hours before race!

BOWED TENDONS

There is no such thing as a "Little Bit Bowed." As many trainers are fond of saying, "It's like being a little bit pregnant"...you are or you aren't" The same holds true for a bowed tendon.

Bowed tendons are devastating for a race horse. Whatever his ability, it is forever impaired by bowed tendons. It is good money thrown after bad to try and bring back a horse with a bow. Unless he is exceptional and can run somewhere cheaper, and still win, the trial and tribulation involved aren't worth it. It is not cost effective and generally they'll give you hope, train well and then in the last work before the race (in traditional methods), or in the first race back they rebow.

Believe it or not, most of this anguish can be avoided,if you are tuned into your horse and follow my advice about monitoring his legs. This is also where the turnout and rest between works is so important. I have been training and\or breaking and prepping my own horses, since the late seventies. I recognize that a horse really can have a misstep or bad luck in a twist or fall and indeed bow a tendon. But that is the exception rather than the rule. There are many bowed tendons on the race track, due to the lack of good foundation in the training process, and because the horses were wrapped and medicated so much that you couldn't tell if a tendon was "cooking" or beginning to go. I can't stress enough the value of the solid progressive training and the extra time allowed in the process of development and how important foundation building is to the long term, overall structural integrity of the race horse.

Some horses, comformationally may be set up to have tendon problems. They may be very weak structurally with thin, weedy tendons, and/or with tied in tendons, or long cannon bones, or exceedingly long pasterns...all of which predispose such horses to breakdown when red lined. This kind of horse should never be trained for racing. He is not a good candidate for the rigors of the track.

Even wonderfully built strong tendons, short cannoned horses can break down. Look in the stallion catalogs...time and again you see bowed tendons. Almost 90% of the time they are bowed on the left leg. These are horses with great breeding and wonderful bone. How did it happen? The training process on the track. It's almost a text book case study on how to break down a horse. Start with a strong, good feeling animal with green unformed bone and tendon. Shoe him incorrectly, give him a long toe and no heel. Put him in a 12 x 12 ft. stall. Over feed him and give him too many vitamins. Don't let him out but once a day for 15 minutes to run like heck for a brief mile or so. Then walk him half and hour and put him back in the stall.

Ask anyone who knows anything about exercise physiology if any but super unusual horses can tolerate this kind of treatment. Of course, we have tendon break down...the animal is willing to give more than he has been properly prepared for and he is willing to run beyond his structure. Add in all of the chemical enhancements used in the name of good training and you'll see a complete program of breakdown. It is so predictable that I am appalled no one has truly tried to change this cycle of

destruction. Believe me, I love racing. I want it to succeed. We must act more responsibly on behalf of these magnificent animals.

It is simple to avoid bowed tendons. Monitor your horses legs. **When you perceive any heat or swelling in the tendon area** (you are monitoring every morning) back off, perhaps wrap for support for a day or two. **Never give medications that are going to fool you into thinking it has improved.** Give time and support. Read the warning signs. Studies have shown that stopping the insult before real damage is done may lead to full recovery. Make sure the tendon is completely back to normal before continuing training. It takes as long as it takes. **You must wait on this problem or ruin the horse!** Unfortunately the tendon is usually bowed before most people catch it, then it is too late. Retire the horse and learn.

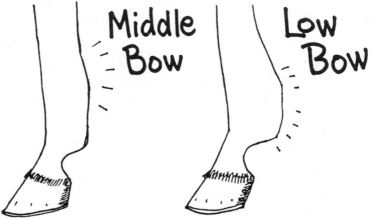

Middle Bow   Low Bow

Bowed Tendons turn thick and Firm later – The first sign of problems will be <u>heat</u> and <u>swelling</u>! <u>Don't Keep Training</u>!

Allow Rest! You have <u>no control</u> over a Bow caused by poor confirmation or by a bad move – You do have control over a tendon that is starting to Have slight heat or filling – If you <u>wait</u>!

185

To
MR. GREEN!

Rest, done
soon enough,
Heals most problems!

186

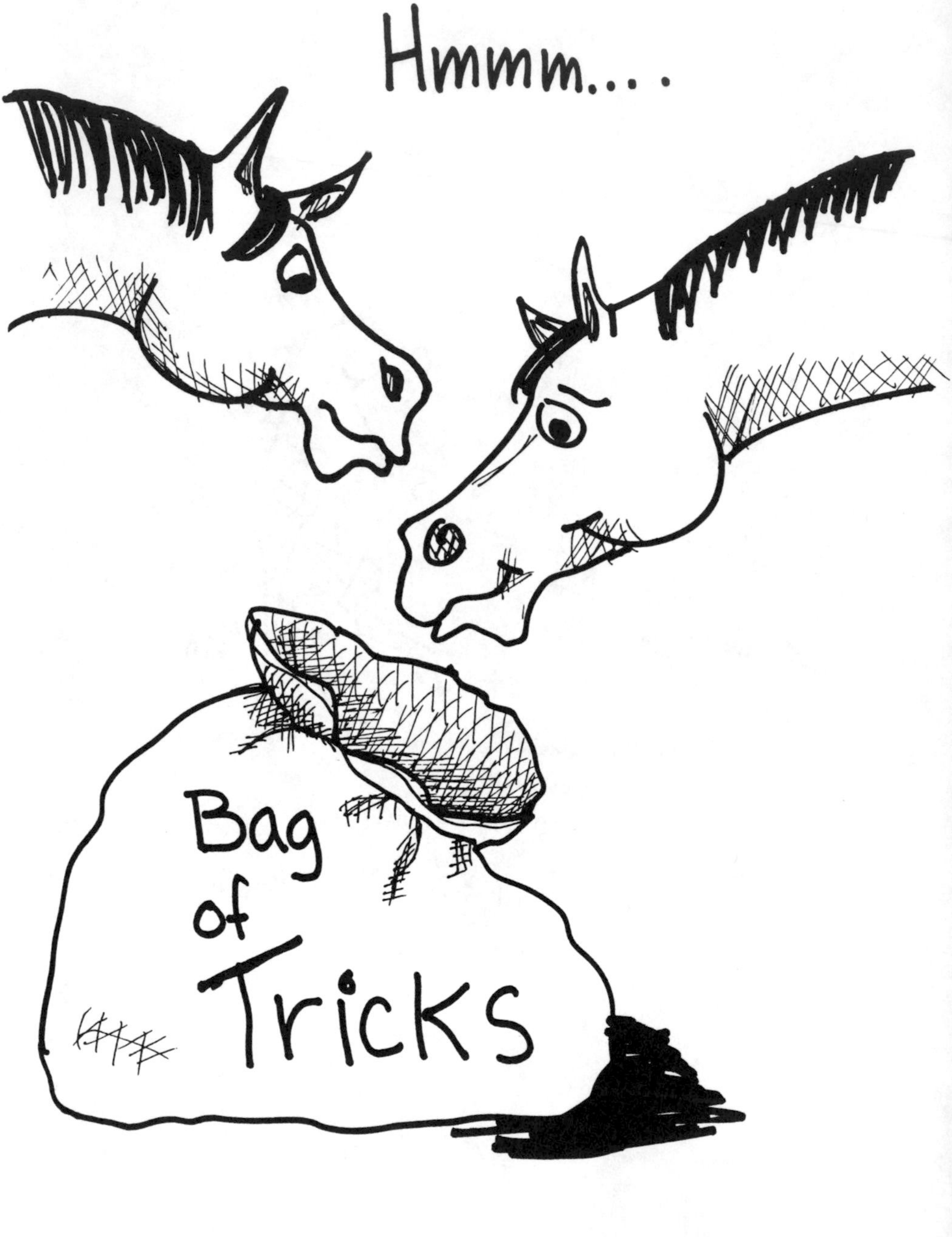
Hmmm....
Bag
of
Tricks

TRICKS

THE BAG OF TRICKS...SOLUTIONS TO VARIOUS AND SUNDRY PROBLEMS WITH HORSES AND TRAINING...

GIRTH GALL
When sores start to form where the girth is placed on the horse, plastic wrap or cellophane wrapped a few times around the girth may help. (Change girth covers if training various horses, to not pass on skin diseases and irritation!)

LOOSE PALATE PROBLEM
The horse makes a "funny noise" while running and between the vet, the rider, and the trainer, a loose palate is diagnosed. This means that the palate displaces itself while the horse is running. Sometimes wrapping Sealtex (a rubbery type bandage), around the bit will create a kind of mass that hold the horse's palate down. Usually a figure eight is then used to keep the horse's mouth closed. Surgery is not necessary when this little trick works. This will also eliminate the necessity of a tongue tie.

Bit with Sealtex wrapped on it to hold down a Loose or soft palate problem A figure eight is used To keep mouth closed!

VICK'S IN THE NOSE
Colts and fillies are very sensitive to odors...particularly of each other. To eliminate the danger of them thinking distracting thoughts, rub Vick's or any strong menthol based salve into the nostrils before racing and trailering your horses. It seems to kill the sense of smell for a while.

UNLOADING HORSES
Don't open the back trailer door or ramp until someone is at the horse's head with the shank...ready to back the horse out. Many times, the horse will see the door open behind him and start backing out while still tied up...then he has a fit when he finds he is still tied at his head. When loading, once the horse is in, then immediately close the back door or ramp so that he can't decide to back out while you are still fumbling with the butt bar. The butt bar and other things can be taken care of when the horse is well confined by the closed ramp or door.

HORSES THAT KICK OR STRIKE AT PEOPLE AND IN THE STALLS
Dog collars with small lengths of chains attached can be buckled on horses above knees or hocks to discourage persistent striking or kicking while in the stalls. When the horse kicks or strikes, the chains slap against his own legs and he learns not to do the negative behavior. (Idea from Donna Harper, DVM)

DRAWING UP ON RACE DAY

Many trainers take away the food and water from a horse on race day. Right away the horse knows he is in for it..he is going to race. I try to change as little as possible on race day. The horses have their usual feed at their usual time...(9 or 10 AM) and their normal hay. Maybe half and hour before I am going to get him ready, I'll take out the water but really, horses don't guzzle food or water before a race. There is a terrible old wives tale that says allowing the horse to have hay causes bleeding. It is completely unfounded. If you don't want them gorging on hay before the race, pull it out a few hours before post time. I have never had problems with horses who munch contentedly on race day.

PULLING FEED BUCKETS AN HOUR AFTER THEY ARE GIVEN

Horses are grazers who nibble all day in the wild. When I feed in the morning,the more aggressive horses gobble it all down fast. I prefer that they take their time and munch all day. They have been conditioned at the track to eat fast or it will be taken away. I don't think that is a good habit for the horses. It is much more desirable that they eat slowly and throughout the day. My horses usually finish up by noon. Since they have free choice hay, they continue snacking throughout the afternoon.

COOLING OFF HOT AND HIGH HORSES

Never try to make a hot or an excited horse stand still. It is much easier and better for him to keep him moving. It distracts him from his fear and works off the lactic acid buildup after a heavy work. It also works with the animal's natural instinct to move. Let's face it, we are not strong enough to hold them, if they really want to go. Let them think it was their idea.

COOLING HOT HORSES IN HOT WEATHER

In cooling my horses after a work or a race, in the terrible heat of the summer, I hose and hose them every turn around the barn to drop the temperature and cool the horse. It's so hot some days in Florida that the horses never dry off. They maintain a constant sweat. By hosing all over the body each time you walk them around the shedrow, you help them lower their overall body temperature. They cool out much more efficiently. You can feel the body heat reduce, as the cool water flows over the animal. We hose and put them in wet with a fan on them.

At home, after a summer hard gallop, their tack is pulled at the lakefront. The are taken into the lake to cool off. The lake water is so tepid, it does not shock them. It is important to keep them moving if they are still breathing hard. It took about 40 minutes to cool them, before I started using the "lake" method. Now it takes about ten minutes, plus ten minutes for floating and fool ing around. They come out feeling refreshed and relaxed. Since that is impossible at the track, we walk and hose, walk and hose.

NEW HORSES AT THE FARM

Allow any new horse time to adjust to the new home. Let him become secure in his environment. He must feel comfortable with his area. He learns quickly where to get his food and water and meets his friends over the fence. Don't try any training until you feel he is comfortable in his changed surroundings. (This usually takes three or four days.) When the animal becomes familiar with his area, he'll run back to his secure home...his stall or paddock, if he gets loose. That is why it is good to allow him to have his own particular stall or paddock. Don't change him to a different one every night.

NEW OR DIFFERENT EQUIPMENT

When trying new equipment, don't spring it on the horse the day of the race. Have him get used to it in the comfort of his stall. Blinkers, for example, are a very strange piece of equipment for the horse. When the horse wears them for the first time, (usually in his stall or paddock), he usually tries to back out of them. He seems to think that if he backs up, he'll be able to see. Eventually, he accepts that something mystical is not allowing him to see properly and settles down. Put them on for a few hours while the horse is in his paddock, where he is in his own territory and he won't try to run through a fence he can't see. Horses who have gotten loose with blinkers on have been known to crash into things in their confusion. An animal who is allowed to wear the equipment in his own space is able to learn his limitations with it on. When breaking two year olds, I have a head stall with a D bit that I put on them to wear for all day. They must eat with the bit on and endure it for hours. They learn how to keep it comfortable in their mouth and don't fret when I put on a complete bridle for the real training. Bandages, bell boots, vet wrap...all should be presented to the animal first in his own environment under non stressful conditions.

RING ON HOOF

When buying a horse, particularly a young one, always look at the wall of the hoof. It can give much recent history of the horse. If it is very firm and smooth sided that is good. Various ring like indentations are not. The rings can represent a very high fever, sickness, stress an extreme change in feed. (For example - in the yearling or two year old sales, you'll commonly see one ring about half an inch down from the coronet band. It probably occurred when the horse was pulled in off of the field to be "fattened" and "coddled" for the sale. An acute change in the horse's life-style took place. He was stalled and his feed was augmented without allow-

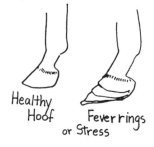

Healthy Hoof   Fever rings or Stress

ing the normal movement and exercise he previously enjoyed. When you go to sales, this type of hoof is a very common sight. Since the hoof grows about 1/4 to 1/2 inch a month, depending on the season, feed, environment and genetic background, you can estimate when the horse was confined. Since most sale horses need to be turned out for a month or two after you purchase them, don't eliminate a horse for a few rings. Just be aware of probable cause. A horse with many, many rings has probably foundered and should be avoided as a race prospect.

TONGUE TIES

Panty hose can be cut and made into very comfortable tongue ties. Jess Cloud

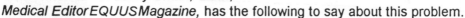

SORE STIFLES/LOCKED STIFLES

Fit horses, confined to a stall may have a temporary loss of control in the stifle. Matthew Mackay-Smith, DVM, *Medical Editor EQUUS Magazine,* has the following to say about this problem.

"Stall confinement of fit horses, particularly heavily muscled ones, and especially those tending to overstraigt hind legs, may lead to the temporary loss of control of the patella (knee cap) in the stifle so that it "locks up." Usually this is painless, but it looks alarming because the horse can't flex the affected leg(s), and hops about struggling to get a leg forward. Sometimes, the horse's reaction bruises the joint or strains it, causing lameness.

A recent review of stifle surgeries found that convalescence is often longer than anticipated, and the stifle(s) may become arthritic several years later. Thus, there is some reluctance among veterinarians to perform the surgery unless it is unavoidable.

If a horse starts locking his patella(s) after a rest, and was never known to do so before, then continuous turnout in a large paddock or pasture and progressive exercise to build muscle tone are usually sufficient to cure the problem. If there is recurrence in a horse who has done it before or who has had a lifelong tendency to "lock" one or both stifles, more strenuous calisthenics (working up hills, pulling a log) may be necessary to keep the stifles smoothly flexing."

GALLOPING YOUR HORSE

Try to have friends ride with you on occasion, so they can gallop along side, in front, and behind you. This accustoms your horse to other animals. Have them bump you and lean against you and your horse. Let your horse learn that this touching is no big deal. Always try to keep him relaxed.

BOLTING DOWN FOOD

Horses who have lived on the track sometimes bolt down their food. It is nice to see a hungry horse attack his food with gusto but eating too fast can be harmful and interfere with proper digestion. To slow him down, you can put LARGE smooth rocks in his feed bucket. He will have to work around them to get his feed. Be sure they are too large for him to bite into, we don't want broken teeth.

LITTLE FRIENDS

Some horses are very insecure. They may do well with a little goat or miniature

horse or some other animal. You'll see many such friends in the stalls with the animals at the track. In the receiving barn at one track, I saw two full grown horses both in one stall. One was obviously a Thoroughbred and the other a huge grade horse. The woman, (it would be a woman) explained to me that the mare was a bundle of nerves. She could run but was so nervous before the race that she would fret her energy away. When they tried having her pasture mate come along, she was much better. A good trainer does what he can to get the best performance from the horse. Sometimes you find yourself looking pretty silly. But that's okay. How did the horse run?

COMPANY

There is a saying that we use on the backside: Keep yourself in the best company and your horses in the worst company. It means put your horses in the easiest races you can find. . . the softer the competition the better the chances!

ROLLING

Even if you have no paddock or pen, a horse loves to roll - especially after his bath. If you can find a sandy area or a pile of sawdust somewhere around the backside it would be great to let him roll there before putting him back into the stall. Rolling helps him straighten out and stretch his back. It also allows him to scratch where he can't reach. It is very therapeutic and healthy for him!

Rolling helps Horses
stretch and scratch their
Backs !

Horses are Underpredictable!

EXPECT THE UNEXPECTED

In handling any young untrained horses, there is always an element of risk. As I have mentioned previously, I use Thoroughbreds as the example of the worst possible scenario. They can be the most volatile, high strung, over reactionary animals in the horse family.

One Easter Sunday stands out in my mind...I share it with you to **make you aware of the kind of risks you could encounter when working with horses. Realize that any undertaking with horses should be done with caution and care.**

The horses were loaded and I was ready to head for the track. I had left Alex, (my oldest son who was home for Easter with some Navy buddies), in charge of taking the saddles off the two year olds...they were in the "getting used to the saddle" phase of training. Each horse was strolling around his paddock with the equipment on.

One particularly flighty filly caught my eye, and I decided to supervise her unsaddling as she was hypersensitive to being handled. I stopped the truck, jumped out and called Alex over. Six foot four, two hundred and twenty pounds, Alex has always been very calm and kind around the horses...a steadying influence.

We both entered the small paddock, walking slowly toward the filly. I waited as Alex went quietly toward her head. She saw him coming and stood apprehensively. He spoke reassuringly to her in a cajoling manner. She seemed to be fine...then suddenly whirled around and nailed Alex right under the chest with both rear hooves, hitting him squarely.

Alex stopped...turned around, took three steps, dropped to his knees and keeled over backwards...laying still as death. I ran to him...his eyes were half open. Only the whites showed. He was not breathing...had no pulse. "Alex", I shouted. "Wake up!" Dropping to my knees, I grasped him around the waist and shook him. It was like shaking a lifeless rag doll...his arms flopped and his head lolled back. No response...none. "My God," I thought, "My son. He's dead. He stopped breathing. He can't die...not like this...not here in this dirty corral. It can't be happening." Such thoughts flashed through my mind as I tried pumping his chest and breathing life into him.

"Quick", I shouted to his friends who came running. "Call 9ll". I continued pumping and pounding with rhythm on his chest...sitting him up...jiggling him...anything to restore life to my son. He had no pulse, no respiration. "Please God, don't let him die! It can't be happening."

I vowed that I would never, ever have anything to do with horses, if my son died. Other thoughts flashed inexplicably through my mind, as I mentally pleaded with Alex to respond, while I was doing CPR (Cardio Pulmonary Resuscitation). Suddenly, he started trembling and shaking all over - a convulsion. Paramount in my mind was an ill mare that convulsed and then died. In a panic, I kept working on him. His eyes fluttered...he looked at me...he recognized me. "Gosh", he said,

"that was strange!" On my knees, I hugged and held Alex. He seem embarrassed...this huge hunk of a man being cradled in my arms like a baby. "Are you all right? Are you all right?", I kept asking. Silently praying that his mind and intellect would be intact. There had been no pulse or heartbeat for a sustained period of time. Though it seem like an eternity, it was probably only a few minutes.

He knew the day, the time, his name, and answered various questions coherently..albeit sheepishly. "How strange", he recounted, "I was there, somewhere, and I felt I had to do something. I couldn't remember what it was. Then it occurred to me...I had to breathe...that was it...I started, and there you were!"

I was just coming to the realization that my son was not dead...that he was okay...thank God. I looked up and remembered that the truck was still on and the horses in it were fretting and stomping. I was supposed to be in two races in Tampa Bay Downs that Easter Sunday. Alex assured me that he was fine. I insisted that he be checked out in the emergency room. He promised me that his friends would take him, but he didn't want me to miss the races because of him. CPR certainly saved his life. I encourage all of you to learn how to use it. You never know...you may save someone's life!

I headed down the road and marveled at how much we can appreciate life when we have the threat of death. The horses ran miserably but that was secondary to the fact that my first born was still alive and well!

....Just another day at the farm!

BEFORE WE SAY GOODBYE...

In the previous pages, I hope to have given to you, the ESSENCE of horse training. **You must adapt to your circumstances that which suits you. A trainer's role is to develop the PERSONAL BEST of each animal...without breaking him down in the process.** People think I'm naive when I say good training can be done without drugs and chemical enhancements. If I had not had the joy of a somewhat talented horse, I might have followed the advice of so many. Use the stuff or be at a disadvantage. But I had a decent horse...I kept her sound enough to run for more than four years and earn over $300,000. Though she was not brilliant, she was wonderfully game and useful. She ran over one hundred times and she only had problems when I couldn't get enough races to keep her fit. She was eligible for few races and needed to run every ten to fourteen days to be at her tightest. The joy of having a stakes class filly who never ran on medication, was never unsound, and who was turned out every day of her life to be a horse, has given me the courage to write this manual. I want others to have and achieve the same goals.

A few newspaper articles are included to give you an idea of what a game mare FIRST PREDICTION was.

Talented and truly gifted horses are few and far between. Most horses are lucky to win bottom of the barrel claiming races. But even this kind of racing can be fun...and your horse may last many years. If you run off the farm, the expenses are minimal and the horse can pay its way.

Enter the Racing Industry cautiously...one horse at a time...and invest your money carefully. Start out with a reasonably priced horse...the horse doesn't know what he cost. . . and follow these guidelines. You can be successful. Be patient and do your homework well. Learn everything you can about the Anatomy and Physiology of the horse. Read, study, and attend instructional seminars. Always follow your instincts about your animal. Use your common sense.

Beware of trainers and veterinarians who want to "give your horse a little something" to help him when he has an injury...and therefore keep him running when he shouldn't. Bute is fine, occasionally, and a lot of horses "warm out" of certain aches and pains. However, remember, injecting ankles and knees with cortisone, giving many steroids and continuing to race is setting your horse up for breakdown. Read the vet bills from your trainer at the track. Learn the names of drugs that are legitimately helping your animal and learn those which are painkillers given a day or two before a race. Banamaine, Ketofen, Steroids, etc., all may "help" a horse get through a race but are short term fixes with long term bad results.

Some of you will feel my suggestions are impractical in the "real life" atmosphere of horse racing. So be it. **I am in this for the long run...for the long term good of the horse and racing. WE MUST CLEAN UP OUR OWN ACT OR IT WILL BE DONE FOR US.** What better way than by example...by running sound, useful, horses year in and year out. Horses are not disposable items to be weeded through in search of the good horse. I must train each and every animal with the

proper foundation...that takes time...time that most owners are not willing to spend. Believe me, they spend time later, with chips in young joints and bowed horses. Spend it early or spend it later. My way allows you to raise and build up your animal easily, with no real pressure until the animal is mature and physically and mentally more able to withstand the rigors of racing.

Doesn't that make sense? A good foundation for children and horses is best done while they are young and growing. **What they become, once fit, healthy and sound, will depend on their inherent genetic ability...their own individual "gift" of speed. Understand--all the training and galloping and drugging in the world will not allow a horse to run faster than he is meant to run. Give him the time to develop the guts to withstand his own speed.**

I have enjoyed having this dialogue with you. If any of you have been inspired to pursue the great sport of horse racing with an attitude of fair play, I am thankful. **Each and everyone of you that starts racing sound, fit horses and wins, is a solid reinforcement that the little guy can win!** That's a great message for everyone. I hope our relationship doesn't end here. I am starting a newsletter and would like input from all of you out in the field. I plan to have names of trainers willing to work with our style of training. The newsletter will be a forum...a network of mutual advice...things are different in racing from one end of the country to the other. We can have a positive impact on racing and win races!

GOOD LUCK AND GOD BLESS YOU!

As we say
GoodBye...

BEFORE WE SAY GOODBYE...

In the previous pages, I hope to have given to you, the ESSENCE of horse training. **You must adapt to your circumstances that which suits you. A trainer's role is to develop the PERSONAL BEST of each animal...without breaking him down in the process.** People think I'm naive when I say good training can be done without drugs and chemical enhancements. If I had not had the joy of a somewhat talented horse, I might have followed the advice of so many. Use the stuff or be at a disadvantage. But I had a decent horse...I kept her sound enough to run for more than four years and earn over $300,000. Though she was not brilliant, she was wonderfully game and useful. She ran over one hundred times and she only had problems when I couldn't get enough races to keep her fit. She was eligible for few races and needed to run every ten to fourteen days to be at her tightest. The joy of having a stakes class filly who never ran on medication, was never unsound, and who was turned out every day of her life to be a horse, has given me the courage to write this manual. I want others to have and achieve the same goals.

A few newspaper articles are included to give you an idea of what a game mare FIRST PREDICTION was.

Talented and truly gifted horses are few and far between...Most horses are lucky to win bottom of the barrel claiming races. But even this kind of racing can be fun...and your horse may last many years. If you run off the farm, the expenses are minimal and the horse can pay its way.

Enter the Racing Industry cautiously...one horse at at time...and invest your money carefully. Start out with a reasonably priced horse...the horse doesn't know what he cost and follow these guidelines. You can be successful. Be patient and do your homework well. Learn everything you can about the Anatomy and Physiology of the horse. Read, study, and attend instructional seminars. Always follow your instincts about your animal. Use your common sense.

Beware of trainers and veterinarians who want to "give your horse a little something" to help him when he has an injury...and therefore keep him running when he shouldn't. Bute is fine, occassionally, and a lot of horses "warm out" of certain aches and pains.However, remember, injecting ankles and knees with cortisone, giving many steroids and continuing to race is setting your horse up for breakdown. Read the vet bills from your trainer at the track. Learn the names of drugs that are legitimately helping your animal and learn those which are painkillers given a day or two before a race. Banamaine, Ketofen, Steroids, etc., all may "help" a horse get through a race but are short term fixes with long term bad results.

Some of you will feel my suggestions are impractical in the "real life" atmosphere of horse racing. So be it. **I am in this for the long run...for the long term good of the horse and racing. WE MUST CLEAN UP OUR OWN ACT OR IT WILL BE DONE FOR US.** What better way than by example...by running sound, useful, horses year in and year out. Horses are not disposable items to be weeded through in search of the good horse. I must train each and every animal with the proper foundation...that takes time...time that most owners are not willing to spend. Believe me, they spend time later, with chips in young joints and bowed horses. Spend it early or spend it later. My way allows you to raise and build up your animal easily, with no real pressure until the animal is mature and physically and mentally more able to withstand the rigors of racing.

Doesn't that make sense? A good foundation for children and horses is best done while they are young and growing. **What they become, once fit, healthy, and sound, will depend on their inherent genetic ability...their own individual "gift" of speed. Understand—all the training and galloping and drugging in the world will not allow a horse to run faster than he is meant to run. Give him the time to develop the guts to withstand his own speed.**

I have enjoyed having this dialogue with you. If any of you have been inspired to pursue the great sport of horse racing with an attitude of fair play, I am thankful. **Each and everyone of you that starts racing sound, fit horses, and wins, is a solid reinforcement that the little guy can win!** That's a great message for everyone. I hope our relationship doesn't end here. I am starting a newsletter and would like input from all of you out in the field. I plan to have names of trainers willing to work with our style of training. The newsletter will be a forum...a network of mutual advice...things are different in racing from one end of the country to the other. We can have a positive impact on racing and win races!

GOOD LUCK AND GOD BLESS YOU!

ACKNOWLEDGMENTS

The following people have been a great source of information. I sincerely appreciate the time they have spent with me in person, on the telephone or through correspondence. Communication between all of us in the industry is of utmost importance if we hope to achieve our goal of being informed owners, trainers and veterinarians.

Tom Ainslie, Writer, *The Racing Form*; Thomas L. Aronson, Racing Resource Group, Inc.; Dr. W. Ashbury, University of Florida, Gainesville, FL; Ann Cain, Mullica Hill, NJ; Albert A. Cirelli, Jr., Professor, University of Nevada; Pat Clark, Circle Resources, Mansfield, TX; Michael Conder, Melbourne, FL; Sharon Creigier, Ph.D., Prince Edward Island, Canada; Trevor Denman, Track Announcer at Del Mar, Hollywood Park and Santa Anita; Michael Dickenson, Fair Hill Training Center, Elkton, MD; Donna Harper, D.V.M., Las Lunas, NM; Carol Holden, Sporting Life Farm, Middleburg, VA; Heather and George Humphries, *Horse Today Magazine,* Leesburg, VA; Dr. William E. Jones, D.V.M., Ph.D.; Mary Ann and David Kent, Kent Arabian Farm, Grand Rapids, MN; Lennart Krook, D.V.M., Ph.D., Cornell University; Mary Lebrato, Rio Linda, CA; C. Wayne McIlwraith, B.V.Sc., Ph.D., Colorado State University; Mary D. Midkiff, Equestrian Resources; Robert M. Miller, D.V.M., Thousand Oaks, CA; Dr. Ed Noble, D.V.M., Ocala, FL; Roy Poole, Jr., D.V.M., Ph.D., University of California at Davis; Dr. James Rooney, Professor, Veterinary Science, University of Kentucky; Alistair Webb, B.V.Sc., Ph.D., F.R.C.V.S., University of Florida, Gainesville, FL; Greg Wisner, Thoroughbred Pedigree Consultant, Dallas, TX:

Useful information and <u>Tra</u>ck <u>Te</u>rmino<u>log</u>y

insight into the
Front side
and
Back side !

Front side
Grandstand
ParaMutuel

Backside
Stable
Area
Racing Office

Information for Owners and Trainers

Before ever owning a racehorse, I had only been to the racetrack once in my life. I never bet, and my first day at the track was spent admiring the beautiful horses and the color and pageantry of the races. Initially, I knew nothing about races, bettors or the politics that go into race and nothing about the logistics on the backside. The BACKSIDE is the stable area of the race track. The FRONTSIDE includes the grandstand and clubhouse and is where patrons go to see the races and bet.

Depending on the layout of the track, certain offices are on the backside, within easy access of trainers. The RACING OFFICE is where trainers handle all the business of entering horses and filing ownership papers, turning in Coggins, etc.

Owning a race horse should be a pleasurable experience. Saturday afternoon television flashes ecstatic owners winning thousands of dollars for a minute and half or so of work on the part of their horses. Some of the winners cost millions in a sale...others as little twenty-five hundred. It looks easy. Go to a sale, buy a horse for what your pocketbook can spare, and win the Derby. Why not! These are not unreasonable goals. People on television do it all the time. Doesn't everything look easy? However, when you get involved, you will learn that there are centuries of effort and experience going into those aspirations.

Keep in mind that even with the BEST expert advice and millions of dollars, there is NO GUARANTEE that the horse will make it to the races...let alone win a race. Perhaps this is why we all feel we have a shot at it. Even the most obscure breeding may relate to great bloodlines and throw a winner.

Around forty thousand foals are registered with the Jockey club each year. Of those registered, only a small percentage ever win a race.

Rather than discourage you, I want to prepare you fairly for the reality of racing. An educated owner is a great asset to the racing industry.

In the following pages, I want to share with you the joys and anguishes of racehorse ownership. Whether you start out as a breeder, watching your own foals develop or, as an owner, buying a race horse prospect, you will find this one of the most challenging endeavors of your life. The business comes with no promises and plenty of pitfalls. If you believe that nothing of value comes easily, you are ready to be a racehorse owner.

Condition Book Page

SIXTY-SECOND DAY - Calder Race Course

SIXTH RACE   **ALLOWANCE**
Purse $14,000 (Plus $1,500 FOA). For Fillies Two Years Old which have
not won a race other than Maiden or Claiming. ....118 lbs.
Non-winners of a race other than claiming since June 15 allowed.. 3 lbs.
SIX FURLONGS

SEVENTH RACE   **ALLOWANCE**
Purse $15,000 (Plus $1,600 FOA). For Three-Year-Olds and Upward
which have not won a race other than Maiden, Claiming, or Starter.
Three year olds........................ 117 lbs.   Older.............................. 122 lbs.
Non-winners of a race other than claiming since June 15 allowed.. 3 lbs.
ONE MILE

EIGHTH RACE   **OVERNIGHT HANDICAP**

THE SOLO HAINA
$20,000
* (Plus $2,100 For Owners Award)
**A HANDICAP FOR FILLIES AND MARES THREE YEARS OLD AND
UPWARD.** WEIGHTS: SATURDAY, AUGUST 14.
Nominations Close Friday, August 13, 1993.
ONE MILE AND A SIXTEENTH (Turf)

NINTH RACE   **CLAIMING**
Purse $7,000. For Fillies and Mares Three Years Old and Upward
which have never won two races.
Three year olds.................. 114 lbs.   Older............................ 119 lbs.
Claiming Price $10,000; if for $9,000.................................. 2 lbs.
ONE MILE AND A SIXTEENTH

TENTH RACE   **CLAIMING**
Purse $12,000 (Plus $1,300 FOA). For Fillies Three Years Old
(Condition Eligibility). ....122 lbs.
Non-winners of two races at one mile or over
since June 15 allowed... 3 lbs.
One such race since then....................................... 5 lbs.
Claiming Price $25,000; if for $22,500.......................... 2 lbs.
(Maiden races, claiming and starter races for $20,000 or less not
considered.)
ABT. ONE MILE AND A FURLONG (Turf)

Closing Sunday, August 15
THE PRIVATE SECRETARY - $20,000
For Fillies & Mares 3 YO & Upward, SIX FURLONGS
To be run Friday, August 20
THE CATCHER LANE - $12,000
For 3 YO & Upward, ONE MILE & 1 FUR. (Turf)
To be run Friday, August 20

19

*This is really a difficult Race! A horse could have won **many** high claiming races and still be eligible here!*

*This race is limited to winners of **only** **one race** ... of **any** kind!*

hmm! which one for me!

Notice the difference in purses between Claiming and Allowance Races

THE CONDITION BOOK

Tracks conducting a live meet put out their *Condition Book* about every two weeks. This book lists all of the races the track hopes to fill for that time period. Usually eight to fourteen different races are offered each day. Those attracting most entries are used. Some tracks also write extras every day to accommodate fluctuations in the equine population at any given time. The goal of the Racing Secretary is to have competitive fields for the betting public.

Many trainers moan and groan when owners learn about the *Condition Book*. Owners over estimate the potential of their horse. They want him put in allowance races with big purses and tough competition. Trainers, on the other hand, want to put the horse with the easiest company. They want him to win and gain confidence, as he begins his career. Trainers want to work the horse up the ladder and make purses, as he rises to his level of competence. The saying on the backside is "keep yourself in the best company and your horses in the worst company". Owners, having paid forty thousand dollars or so to get the horse to his first race, have nightmares when the trainer wants to run him at twelve thousand. Much communication is necessary for both parties to be comfortable.

The maiden race and the non-winners of one and the non-winners of two races are going to be the easiest races the horse runs. Depending on whether the horse is running in claiming or in allowance races, soft spots may be found by reading the conditions of a race very carefully.

In the section on types of races, the differences between NW (non winners) of two races lifetime allowance vs NW (non winners) of two races other than claiming or maiden is discussed. If a horse is a NW of two races other than claiming or maiden, he probably has broken his maiden and may have won many claiming races. On the other hand, a NW of two races lifetime has only won one race. Big difference. Purses and competition may vary greatly even though they sound similar. Learning the subtleties of the *Condition Book* will help you greatly.

Trainers have a name for owners who decide they should choose the races for the horse: "owners from hell". One of my owners fit the category. He would call me and inform that he had entered his horse in thus and such a race. . .without even asking me about the horse's condition. Maybe the horse hadn't recovered from his last race. Maybe he wasn't quite right. Maybe he was off his head. When the owner was told that the horse wasn't ready or the race didn't suit him, he would say, "Well, if it really won't do you can scratch tomorrow." Scratching a horse frivolously is not good policy. As a trainer, you can get a reputation for entering and scratching. You can also be "stuck" in a race, when the field is short and your horse is needed for the race to go. If you are stuck, you must have a vet scratch (meaning a vet must state that your horse has a physical reason for not being able to run). Depending on the ground rules at the track, a vet scratch may put you on the vet's list for fourteen days. Then you might miss the race you really need. Be aware of all of the repercussions ahead of time. The racing office is trying to fill races in a competent manner. Don't waste their time with games. If owner and trainer are philosophically in tune, you

won't have these problems. You will work together.

Much of the following information has been taken from the *Appaloosa Club Racing Handbook.*

ROLE OF AUTHORIZED AGENT

If you sign and notarize an authorized agent form, the person named on the form may conduct your horse business for you. Often, the trainer is the authorized agent for the owner. He may buy, sell, or claim a horse for you. He may take money out of your account or put it in. Needless to say, trust is very important in this kind of relationship.

ROLE OF THE JOCKEY

The jockey is the other important member of the racing team. It is disturbing to hear disparaging remarks about them, or hear them referred to as pinheads, idiots, etc. Good jockeys do the job well. Great jockeys are gifted, instinctive riders. Not only do they have a knack for knowing where to be when, they can give the horse courage and desire to run. Great jockeys are artists. They take horses that are nervous, fractious and insecure, and mold them into willing partners of a racing team. Poor jockeys can lose the race with a fleeting instant of bad judgement.

Horses have completely changed their losing form, when coupled with a sensitive, gifted rider. To win, a horse must want to run. A good jockey knows how to channel the horse's energies into that goal.

Of course, the great jockeys are usually leading riders at major tracks. As small time players in the learning process of horseracing, you, as an owner and/or trainer must strive to find the best jockey available. Don't expect a leading jockey to choose your untried two year old maiden, first time out. Understand that the jockey's agent is hustling to get his rider the best mount in any given race. If the jockey hasn't been named on a better horse, he might try to pick up a ride on an unknown, on the theory that any horse can win.

However, if the form on your horse is miserable, don't be offended if the jockey declines your mount. A well known jockey wants to ride better horses and earn as much money as possible. The jockey won't want to risk his health and safety on a horse that looks green, unpredictable or unsound. Some of the jockeys at our local track are good friends. One year, I was running a bunch of "duds". I didn't even ask my regular jockeys to ride. They had much better chances on almost any other horse. I found a jockey, who was an excellent rider, eager for experience and willing to work with quirky horses. He was learning the trade and willing to ride anything.

This does not imply that you settle for less than the best jockey you can find. It means that you should not take it personally if the jockey refuses to accept your mount until the horse shows some talent and is controllable. Remember, all jockeys charge the same for the ride, plus 10% of the purse, if they win.

Be sure to discuss the idiosyncrasies of your horse with the jockey. Share with him all the information on whether the horse likes to run in front, on the inside, the

outside, etc. Then leave the running of the race to the jockey. Many trainers give very specific instructions as to where the horse should be every minute of the race. They become angry if the jockey doesn't follow these instructions to the letter. My feeling is that trainers should discuss their goals for the horse, but allow the jockey to use his judgement in attaining them. Be sure to listen to the jockey after the race.

You must assume jockeys are the competent experts in race riding. As an owner, you have the right to accompany the trainer, horse and jockey after the race. At the moment of dismounting your jockey makes the freshest and most informative comments about the horse and how he performed. The jockey will tell you about the horse. He knows whether the horse was frightened, intimidated, tired, fit, impressive, tried to bear out or in, if his teeth bothered him, if he was sore, lame, etc. You can learn so much listening to your rider. I am offended by enraged trainers screaming at jockeys, as they ride in to dismount, after the race. This is an embarrassment to the Great Sport of Racing.

Many trainers joke that when the jockeys bring the horses back to the finish line after the race, they are frantically trying to come up with some excuse as to why the horse didn't win. Be mature and realistic enough to understand the term "out run". The other horses in the race were faster than yours. Oh well, that's the way it goes.

Respect the jockey and assume they are trying their best to win. If your jockey is blatantly not following your orders or if you see a pattern of riding that you find suspect, change jockeys. Be aware that there are jockeys that don't play by the rules. One usually hears about such things on the backside. Be all ears, but take all comments with a grain of salt.

As you learn more about the business, both on the frontside and the backside, you will be able to choose your jockey wisely. Try to understand all of your obligations and the worst case scenario order to survive unscratched!

ROLE OF THE JOCKEY AGENT

This is usually the middle-man between the jockey and the trainer. A jockey agent must be a real hustler. He should be up early in the morning and help his jockey get to all the morning works. While the jock is on one horse, his agent should advise the next trainer to prepare the next mount. Since so much work must be done in so little time at the track, it is imperative that a popular jockey have coordination between his commitments. If a jockey "hangs up" a trainer and misses riding the horse, it can throw the trainer's schedule off terribly. A good agent keeps the trainer happy and the jock busy. If his jock is named on more than one horse in a race, he should follow-up and notify the trainer that he needs another rider. He must smooth feathers if he chooses one horse over another one. The agent wants his jock to ride the horse with the most chance of winning. But sometimes he is committed to a big stable and is obligated to ride all of the horses in it. Regardless of the chance to win in a particular race. **Top jocks can almost choose their mounts...the others take what they can get.**

Agents scout riders in much the same way baseball or football scouts find

players. They make trips to smaller tracks and try to find raw talent. Many riders come from Latin America. The agent may teach the rider how to shake hands, say, "Yes sir," and most importantly, "I understand"...even when he doesn't. They often share an apartment and the jock is molded and advised by his mentor agent. Certain agents are famous for developing talent. Many agents are retired from "real" jobs and have this as a second career. Since the agent's pay is a slice of what the jockey makes, he may need his pension to live on.

ROLE OF THE VALET

The valet is an employee who takes care of a jockey's equipment, sees to it that the correct silks are at his locker, that the rider has the proper weight in his lead pad, carries the saddle and equipment to the paddock and helps the trainer in saddling the horse, meets the rider after the race and carries the saddle and equipment back to the jockey's room.

PONY HORSES

Pony horses are really horses. They "pony" other race horses. To pony a horse means that the pony rider exercises the race horse, taking him on a led rope at the side of the pony. The race horse carries no weight. He is expected to move at the speed of the pony. Race horses can be so rambunctious that they want to run off with a rider. The trainer has such a horse ponied so that he won't burn up too much energy but will get exercise. Sometimes, when a race horse is young and insecure, a pony rider will accompany the race horse and rider to the track . The older horse steadies and comforts the young inexperienced animal. He may gallop at his side to get him going and then drop off as the race horse gains confidence.

The pony is also very useful on race day. Many race horses become very excited and ready to run when they see the track. The pony will accompany horse and rider and help control the race horse as he warms up before the race. Some jockeys worry about the horse "getting away" from them in the warm up. . . and will not allow the horse to gallop accompanied by a pony and lead shank. After a few races, as the horse becomes accustomed to the routine of racing, the pony is no longer necessary. Some trainers always have a pony . Others never have a pony.

If a horse gets away from a rider before the race and runs hard, the stewards may scratch him, on the grounds that the horse has already run his race and the betting public must be protected. That was frustrating for me. After hauling into the track to run, I wanted my horses to run. A mile gallop would be a warm-up for most of them.

Older horses can become very professional and workman-like. For the young and high strung animals, the pony and his experienced rider are a great asset.

THE FARRIER OR BLACKSMITH

As a new owner, do you know that your horse's shoes might cost more than yours, and that he needs a new set every six weeks? This is generally an extra

expense on your monthly training bill and may run from forty to eighty dollars or more, depending on the area of the country and the complexity of the job.

Trainers at some tracks change the shoes if the track turns sloppy, or use one kind of shoes for turf and another for dirt. Changing shoes too frequently is not good for the wall of the hoof. **At some race tracks, if you change the style of the shoe, you must get permission from the stewards.** This is because the shoe style can impair or improve the performance of the horse. One trainer I knew used heavy, thick steel shoes on his horse for all training and working. When race time came, he changed the shoes to light weight aluminum and the horse felt much more agile. His performance improved with the change. At today's major tracks, he probably couldn't get away with it.

I have wanted to start some of my young horses racing barefoot. When asking permission, the stewards tend to be somewhat inflexible. They say a horse that starts barefoot will have to race the meet barefoot. With those options, it was better to put shoes on than risk putting my animals at a disadvantage.

If the horse is crooked legged, shoeing can help his performance dramatically. If he hits himself when he runs . . . his front foot cutting his ankle, etc. . . . various shoes must be tried until the right combination is found.,

Horses with hoof problems may need more frequent sessions with special treatments. There are many new products and innovative styles for the hoof. It is important that your trainer be experienced enough to separate a gimmick or fad style of shoeing from a therapeutic, innovative device. Usually there will be university studies on new styles and rational testing to show the usefulness. Ask the trainer what he is doing and see if it makes sense to you...if it sounds like witchcraft...draw your own conclusions.

OWNERS, TRAINERS AND DEALS

Always clarify the monetary arrangement with your trainer. It is imperative that costs be set on the training of your horse and that you understand the best and worst possible scenarios.

A common tradition is that the trainers receive 10% of the win purse. Some ask and get 10% of all earnings . . . second, third and fourth place. Nothing is automatic unless defined as such. Understand what your trainer expects to get from the earnings of the horse. It is best to write down the details and sign the document.

A common practice is for the owner to pay day money. For example, a base price of $30 a day. This should cover feed, usual supplements, shavings, and daily maintenance of the horse. Vet bills, shoeing and special feeds or equipment will cost extra. One of my first trainers charged me for safety pins and cotton used to wrap the horses legs. He also charged extra for electrolytes and salt. Since I had been paying $35 a day in the early '80s, this kind of bookkeeping was abusive.

At most tracks, the trainer doesn't pay for the stalls or the upkeep of track. If he is at a training center or at his own farm, he will have that extra overhead. Depending on the agreement, he may or may not charge for hauling from farm to track or from

track to track. I knew one trainer that had no trailer and no place to train his horses where he had them stabled. Four or five days a week he charged his owner thirty dollars to haul the horse to gallop at the track. Needless to say, this doubled the training bill and that owner, quite upset, moved his horse upon receipt of the first bill.

A trainer should have the tools of his trade. He should have saddles, a variety of bridles and other necessary equipment to conduct his business. If your trainer wants you to pay for buckets, stall guards, and other items that should be general expense items, be cautious. Owners should pay for special equipment pertinent to their horse . . .for example, a set of blinkers with a particular cut to them or an unusual bit.

Extra costs above the day rate may be for other services. Pony horses, used a couple of times a week to take your horse to the track, might be listed as an added charge. Having your horses' hair clipped when coming from a cold climate to a hot climate could cost twenty or thirty dollars. If a trainer has his own pony and his own set of clippers, he may provide those and other services, at no extra charge.

Above the initial day rate, your bill will include the vet charges. Some trainers go overboard with vets. They pull blood continually, have ultrasound treatments, laser treatments, Jugs (fluids put in IV), and a plethora of medications administered. X-rays are done frequently (remember . . . if it shows on the X-ray, the damage has already been done). Some owners love this technology and are willing to pay for it. Make your philosophy clear. Be sure your trainer understands how you want your horse treated. Communication and mutual trust is important for both parties. Vet charges have been known to cost as much as or more than training fees. A horse needing that degree of medical support perhaps should not be at the track. (See Drugs and Medications Section.)

It is not unusual to have extra costs on race day. Disposable leg wraps, such as Vetwrap, cost around $10. There are all kinds of "natural" herbs, sold in one dose tubes, that your trainer might use, if he believes they will help. An oral paste composed of natural ingredients is preferable to an injection if it is used to help the horse. It depends on whether or not the trainer gets the results he wants. In any case, these little tubes cost from $4 to $10 each. There may also be a hauling fee on race day, from one track to another or from the farm to the track.

Most trainers are trying to do a competent job and are aware of the costs. If you have good rapport with your trainer, he will keep you up to date, and you should have no major surprises.

DEALS

In an ideal world, all owners have plenty of money and trainers don't have to make deals. Not so in the real world. The economic situation is such that we have all had to become creative in our endeavors. Trainers may make a 60-40 or 50-50 split or whatever you both agree on. Half the horse may be given to the trainer or percentages of earnings, etc. It is important to define what expenses are paid by whom before splitting the earnings. A friend just called with a perfect example of this problem. The deal was 40-60. My friend retained ownership of the horse and

40% of his earnings. She was paying 100% of all extra expenses such as pony, vet and shoeing. She was surprised to find the trainer deducted his 10% earnings fee off the top before factoring the 40-60 figure. She also found that he had given highly questionable and unauthorized treatments and medications to the horse. He told the track bookkeeper that he had access to her account and received the earnings checks. Much after the fact, my friend found that from the $47,000 her horse earned, she was given a total of $7,000. It was a hard lesson to learn.

In doing DEALS, define the following: Who pays for shoes, ponies, treatments, feed, hauling, and vet bills. Percentage of ownership may be written right on the horses' papers. All the contingencies should be spelled out.

I have lost money on the majority of my deals. This is usually because I get untried horses and must spend time in developing them, only to find they don't have talent. Chances of having a winner are slim. We are all pursuing the dream of the one who can bail us out.

If you own a useful, performing animal, trainers will be more willing to make a deal. A formed, talented horse is a joy to train.

A trainer came to our area looking for horses. He called the owners of solid allowance horses and offered to train them free of charge. The current trainer of one of these horses, heard about the call and gleefully told me how he had "punched the daylights out" of the pushy newcomer.

THE AGONY AND THE ECSTASY

Some friends formed a syndicate, went to the sales, bought a fairly expensive horse and started the process of racing their GREAT HOPE. First I got weekly reports about how the filly was doing everything right. How she loved to gallop and was doing very impressive works. Then she had some predictable setbacks. After sore shins, coughs, inconsistent works, and problems in the gate, the trainer picked a date and said the horse would start. How exciting! What anticipation! The friends called me. They had already planned the next race, a little stake, that she could go in after her first out and, of course, first win. They told me they had the leading rider and he was very high on the filly. She went off favorite, the owners convinced she would smoke the field. She did run a very viable race but finished second. This is not bad for a first race. The jockey, however, was now a bum that did not pressure on the filly in the stretch. . . "If he had, she would have won....he fell asleep in the stretch!" I suggested they buy the tape and watch the reruns. They did and saw the jockey really rode as well as could be expected. The horse simply tired. She would probably be fine and tighter for the next race. When a horse loses, owners seek excuses...some reason why he didn't win. The main reason most of the time is that the horse was outrun. Good horses will win in spite of difficulties, bad breaks, boxed in, too wide, etc. They win in adversity. Cheap horses barely win, when everything goes just right. They are the claimers that fill the bottom races. As an owner, be judicious. See what really happens in the race and learn about your horse.

As a trainer, I get the horse to the first race to see what he does and how he comes out of it. Then I eliminate the excuses that might have caused him to lose. If he broke poorly, more gate work. If he hits himself, farrier work and leg wraps. If he shied or seemed to hang, blinkers. If he was uncontrollable, different equipment. Each new piece of information gleaned from the rider in the race and observed by me must be interpreted in terms of the performance of the horse. When we finally get a fair race from a fit horse with no interference or problems, we know what we have. If he was running high, you can always drop him. If he was at the bottom, maybe he can win through his conditions.

The Trainer tries to find the right spot for his HORSE

SYNDICATES, PARTNERSHIPS AND VARIATIONS!

One of the most positive trends in horse racing in recent years has been the increase in the number of racing partnerships. For a number of reasons, these partnerships (and they can be extremely varied in their makeup) lend themselves to enjoyment of the sport at its very best.

Most notably, from a business standpoint, it is far better to own part of a good horse than it is to own all of a mediocre one. Basically, good horses cost about the same to maintain as "cheap" horses. The differences are that they (a) usually cost a good deal more to acquire and (b) they have the potential of earning substantial income. Many owners who in the past attempted to operate on a middle-class budget while searching for a rags-to-riches horse have come to see that there are usually more rags than riches created by that approach. However, armed with their hard-earned lessons, and hopefully having experienced at least a taste of the thrills of winning, they are now taking a more intelligent approach to the sport by joining forces with friends.

That leads to another of the benefits of group ownership: fun with friends. I have trained for some very diverse groups who, though they may have had little in common otherwise, did share one trait. They had a terrific time racing their horses. Some were high-dollar players who wanted to be participants in every major decision. Other partnerships were compromised mainly of fun-loving race fans who chipped in, bought a couple of horses, and merely wanted to know in advance when the horses would race. Most groups fall somewhere between those two extremes. But with proper preparation and proper guidance, along with the patience and perseverance which is obligatory, nearly any group can eventually experience joyous, unforgettable days (or nights) at the races.

The best thing about racing partnerships, though, is that the participants, through their combining of resources, are able to purchase a better racing prospect initially. Recent racing lore is replete with stories of successful partnerships whose relatively modest investments have brought them ownership of stakes winning horses. Almost without exception, these successful partnerships are typified by: 1) a capable, honest, highly-communicative trainer and 2) a written agreement which names one partner as the main liaison between the trainer and the group.

by Scott Wells, Hollywood Park

While in the past, many owners approached racing with the attitude that racing is the Sport of Kings and they intended to be kingly, these days, many are realizing that the phrases "strength in numbers" and "the more the merrier" have their place in today's racing climate.

HORSE IDENTIFICATION

Every horse entered in a race is positively identified to be the horse that it is stated to be on its registration certificate. Every horse which is racing at approved tracks must be tattooed on the inside of the upper lip with an official identification number, which is placed on the horse's registration certificate and becomes part of its identifying features along with the natural markings and characteristics.

Each horse is definitely identified prior to his race by the official **track identifier** and thoroughly examined by the track veterinarian to assure that he is in fit physical racing condition. If there is any discrepancy in identification or a sign of any physical disability, the horse will be withdrawn, or scratched, from the race.

The Tatoo man (horse identifier) checks to see that the horse matches his papers!

TRACK AND COMMISSION VETERINARIANS

The track veterinarian is responsible for the examination of each horse to ensure that all entries are in a "racing sound" condition. This includes pre-race morning examinations, close observation during the parade to the post, at the starting gate and during and after the race. He is responsible for the inspection of all horses registered with the racing secretary and for maintaining the veterinary list of all horses officially scratched from a race. He is also responsible for control of all communicable diseases of animals, insect control and inhumane acts against horses including neglect in feeding, watering and care.

The commission veterinarian is in charge of all sample collections and must be available for stewards at scratch time and any time they desire identification of drugs or examination of a horse for tampering. He may not practice medicine on the racehorse; he may not wager nor may he sell drug supplies. It is his responsibility to study new medications of the unethical patent medicine variety, any formula changes in old medications and newly available medications, and to disseminate this information to the practicing veterinarians and trainers.

STATE RACING COMMISSIONS

The various state racing commissions, by law, supervise the implementation of their rules and regulations regarding the operation of all racing within the state. The commission which governs each state is authorized by law to prescribe the rules of racing, grant the franchise for racetrack operations, determine how many tracks may operate within the state, limit the number of days of racing, approve purse schedules, pass the appointment of officials for meetings and supervise the strict licensing of all racetrack personnel. Licenses are issued only after thorough investigation. You must be licensed in each state you are going to race. State rules and regulation supersede breed registry or association rules.

State racing commissions are also responsible for the testing of each race winner to see that no drugs were present which may have affected the condition of the horse. After every race, the winner and any other horse designated by the stewards are taken to the state racing commission's testing enclosure where urine, saliva and/or blood samples are taken. (The first three horses in stakes races are normally tested.) The state veterinarian seals, tags and delivers the specimens to the laboratory, in most cases a member of the Association of Official Racing Chemists, where an extensive series of chemical tests are run on each sample to ensure that no drugs or prohibited medications were present which may have affected the racing condition and performance of the horse.

Although the problems and ways of dealing with them vary greatly from state to state, the commissions, through the Association of Racing Commissioners International, are able to act as one body on important issues and establish precedents concerning racing matters.

RACING SECRETARY

The racing secretary has perhaps the hardest job in racing.

His duties are many-fold and important for he is directly responsible for the end result - the horses competing on the track in races which he first created on paper and brought into being.

Although the racing secretary is employed by the racing association or management, he has an unrelenting responsibility to:

The Public - Under the rules of racing, the racing secretary must provide the public with the best and most entertaining card of races he can provide with the horses available.

The Management - It is his duty to create a stakes program and write a condition book that will attract the best quality of horses that are available to the track.

The Owners and Trainers - When the racing secretary approves stalls for a stable of horses, he obligates himself to the owner and trainer of the horses because in accepting them, he is saying they will fit into his scheduled program at the race meeting. He must be fair to them without compromising his responsibility to the public or management.

No single racing official can contribute more to the success or failure of a race meeting than the racing secretary. He must bear all of his obligations in mind at all times and uphold them, being dignified and impartial but firm in his attitude.

STEWARDS

The stewards are like the umpires or judges at the track. Problems between individuals . . . owners, trainers, grooms may be aired in front of them. Infractions of ground rules at the track , smoking under the shedrow, fighting, horses arriving late in the paddock for the race . . . are aired out in front of the stewards. The stewards may fine you, or suspend you, or do both, depending on the severity of the problem. They may take the purse money back, after the fact, if the medication tests show signs of overdoses.

The Stewards' most visual job, in relation to the public, is settling disputes in the actual races. If a jockey claims a foul or interference during the race, the stewards review the films and judge the incident. There are cameras all around the racing strip. If there is an objection or inquiry, the stewards review the films. If they can't see the infraction on the film, they will not recognize it happened. Film replays have improved their judgement tremendously.

All suspensions and fines are reported by them to the state racing commission and in turn to the Association of Racing Commissioners International so that offenders may be barred from taking part in other race meetings in that state or any other during the period of suspension. The stewards have complete jurisdiction over a race meeting.

PADDOCK JUDGE

Approximately 25 minutes before the race, the horses are taken to the paddock where they are saddled under the supervision of the paddock judge. The saddling is done by the trainer with assistance from the jockey's valet.

The paddock judge is in charge of the building or enclosure where the horses are saddled for a race. He has control over the individuals who may be admitted into that area. He verifies the racing equipment of each horse and checks to ensure that special equipment, such as blinkers, is added. He gives the orders necessary to take the horses to their stalls, saddle the horses, order the jockeys by means of an electrical bell or similar device to report to the paddock and to parade around the walking ring in the paddock. This allows the public a chance to view the horse from all sides and gives the state veterinarian a chance to inspect the horse. If the horse is deemed unsound, the horse is scratched from the field and put on the veterinary list. The stewards are notified immediately as is the mutuel department. The

paddock judge starts the parade to the post and, if serving as a patrol judge at the same time, leaves the paddock with the horses and proceeds to the specific tower or stand to which he is assigned.

CLERK OF SCALES

The clerk of scales at many tracks has complete control of the jockey's room and all who work there, as well as all equipment. At the larger racetracks, he normally has in his crew an assistant clerk of scales, a supervisor of the jockey room, a color man who cares for and stores the racing colors, a number cloth and equipment custodian, security men and numerous valets.

It is his responsibility to ensure that the weight carried by the jockey is the weight assigned and that each jockey has the proper equipment. He weighs all jockeys with their tack before and after the race. A jockey's weight includes his riding clothing, saddle and pad. Before the result of a race is declared official by the stewards, all jockeys must weigh in, full view of the stewards and the public. If underweight after the race by more than two pounds, the mount may be disqualified.

The clerk of scales posts all over-weights and will not allow any jockey to ride with an overweight of more than two pounds until the overweight is accepted by the trainer. He calls changes to the announcer, calculating room, mutuels, racing form, stewards, officials and the receiving barn. He does not allow a jockey to pass the scale at more than seven pounds overweight except under conditions where the trainer may waive allowance previously claimed. The sex or age allowance generally cannot be waived. In most areas, twoyearold fillies are allowed three to five pounds. The clerk of scales is also responsible for providing the paymaster an accounting of riding fees due each jockey.

THE STARTER

The starter takes charge of the horses once they leave the paddock and summons them to the starting gate. The horses and jockeys parade past the stands for everyone to see and make their final selection for wagering. Ponies may be used to lead a horse to the start according to the wishes of the owner and trainer who must pay the pony boy for his services.

Post time is the specified time horses are to enter the starting gate. It also notifies patrons of the time available for wagering. Following the parade, the starter may excuse the horses as he may deem proper because of injury or incorrigibility. He gives all orders and takes all necessary measures to ensure a fair start. Most starters start the field from in front of the gate and are stationed on a raised platform with a view of all horses.

The job of loading the horses into the gate can be dangerous. However, the

dangers of the job can be greatly reduced by thorough training and practice. The gate is towed to the various starting positions by a tractor-type truck and is moved off the track after the start of the race. As a safeguard system, the gate truck can be backed up by a regular tractor which can tow the vehicle.

Along with actual loading of the horses, the crew is responsible for maintenance of the gate. The individual gates are operated by electromagnets and must be checked periodically as a precautionary measure. All moving parts must be lubricated on a weekly basis.

PATROL JUDGES

Patrol judges supervise every race and assist the stewards in enforcing the rules and regulations. The patrol judges observe the races from elevated platforms situated at the clubhouse turn, finish line and the 1/2 and 1/4 poles at a typical mile track. Along the straightaway, generally two patrol judges are used, with one being stationed approximately at the half-way mark of the race and the other at the finish line. Their primary responsibility is to closely watch the running of the race from their particular vantage points. With the aid of binoculars, they look for rule violations such as reckless riding, interferences, lack of jockey effort and other practices which could be of detrimental effect to the outcome of the race.

Viewing the race from their assigned stand, the patrol judges report findings to the stewards via intercom and prepare a written report of each race. They are responsible for reviewing the film of the race and conduct showings for jockeys and horsemen when instructed by the stewards and/or at stated times.

With the use of the video-tape system combined with the patrol judges, the stewards have a readily available reference system at their disposal.

VIDEO TAPE PATROL

Video tapes are generally made of each race for use by the stewards, patrol judges and placing judges and are usually taken from two positions - head-on and from the side. This enables the stewards to view the race from every aspect and in the case of an inquiry, to review the race immediately. By using the tapes, any conflict of opinion as to what may have happened is eliminated, and careful analysis of any reported incident by any official in any part of the race is available.

These tapes are replayed for the spectators over monitors at many tracks and are also available for reviewing by trainers and jockeys for training purposes, or by horse owners who may have missed seeing the actual running of the race.

The tapes of all races are reviewed by the board of stewards the following day. At this time, they look for any infractions and assess any fines or suspensions they deem necessary.

PLACING JUDGES

Three placing judges assist the stewards in determining the order of finish of each race. It is advisable to have three judges and as the horse crosses the finish line, they write down the complete order of finish. They have a small board with

numbers on it so they can post the order during the race and race fans can check the board if they lose track of their horses. The placing judges and stewards are aided in their decisions by photo-finish pictures if the finish is close (within a half a length).

Although the order of finish may be hardly perceptible by the spectators or even the stewards, the photo-finish pictures are accurate and the placing judges and stewards can distinguish in fractions of inches the order of finish. Photo finish pictures are always posted in various places around the grandstand area in order for spectators to satisfy themselves about the finish of any race. The placing judges post the official finish after the race according to the photo finish camera.

When the finish of a race is close and a photo is called for, the word "photo" will flash on the tote board. One of the most unique systems ever conceived to provide the placing judges with absolute proof of the results of horse racing is the photo-finish camera. The camera system was developed in 1937 through the efforts of three key people: Bing Crosby, Buddy Fogelson and Bogart Rogers. With the photo-finish camera, the placing judges, in making close decisions, have as their ultimate reference a permanent photographic record of the finish of every race accurate to within 1/100th of a second.

It should be kept in mind that in any instance where the pictures furnished are not adequate or usable, the decision of the stewards will be final.

THE DAILY RACING PROGRAM

Each day after the entries are drawn for the next racing day, all of the information is sent to the printer, and daily programs are printed.

Some tracks carry the past performances on each horse along with post position, distance and other pertinent information in their daily programs, while other tracks print only the essential information (horse's name and breeding, post position, distance, jockey, weight, owner, trainer, etc.). At tracks where past performance lines are not printed in the program, the spectator can find the information on each horse in the *Daily Racing Form*. Performance lines in the track's program and those in the Daily Racing Form are identical, since all the information comes from the permanent records which are maintained on a computer and are supplied to the Racing Form and individual racing associations.

The examples show the type of program with an explanation and an explanation of the past performance lines which appear in the programs and the Daily Racing Form.

LICENSES

All persons actively involved in racing must be licensed.

This includes racing officials, all track employees, jockeys, owners and trainers and their employees.

Licenses are obtained from the racing commission office at the track. Anyone wishing to obtain a license must fill out an application supplied by the state racing commission and return it to the racing commission office at the track. A photograph and fingerprints are recorded for identification and, with the application, are given to the stewards to review. In most cases, the stewards speak with the applicant or in the care of a trainer, give a test.

Licenses must be held in each state in which the licensee races. The application procedure is repeated each year. In most states, photographs are taken once every three years and finger prints are taken only once.

OWNERS

As the owner of a race horse, you have many responsibilities and should be aware of the following:

Horses must be registered in your correct name. Beware of partnerships, nicknames, ranch or stable names, assumed names, etc.

Fees must be paid or arrangements made with the trainer to pay all fees, such as entry fees, jockey mounts, tattooing, etc.

In most cases the owner must provide jockey silks. Colors are registered when the owner applies for a license in each and every state in which he will race.

If an owner changes trainers, he must notify the racing secretary and cause the new trainer to sign his name on said owner's registration.

The personnel of every stable must be registered.

After horses have been registered and owners listed with the racing secretary, no horse will be transferred, unless claimed at the meeting, without permission of the stewards. The stewards will require a notarized bill of sale from the registered owner.

The purchase or transfer of any horse on the grounds at any track, whether by private sale, claiming or public auction, does not guarantee the new owner a stall for such horse unless approved by the racing secretary and/or the stewards. The management has the right to allocate stalls to those horses which fit the racing program as well as those horses which are sound.

Horses sold to any person or stable not registered for racing must be removed from the grounds within 24 hours unless approved by the racing secretary and/or the stewards.

Before a horse may be entered, its owner must secure an owner's license from the racing commission. The stewards may grant a reasonable delay in the case of absentee owners.

TRAINERS

As the trainer of a race horse, you have many responsibilities and should be aware of the following:

No horse shall be qualified to start in any race unless he is in the hands of a licensed trainer.

No trainer shall practice his profession except under his own name.

A trainer shall attend his horse in the paddock and shall be present to supervise

his saddling unless he has obtained the permission of a steward to send another licensed trainer as a substitute.

Each trainer shall register with the racing secretary every person in his employ.

A trainer is responsible for the condition of each horse trained by him.

A trainer shall not have in charge or under his supervision any horse owned, in whole or in part, by a disqualified person.

No trainer shall move or permit to be moved any horse or horses in his care from the grounds of an association without written permission from the association.

When a trainer is to be absent for a period of more than two racing days from his stable or the grounds when his horses are racing, and his horses are entered or are to be entered, he must provide a licensed trainer to assume the complete responsibility of the horses he is entering or running. Such licensed trainer shall sign in the presence of the stewards a form furnished by the State Racing Commission accepting
complete responsibility of the horses entered or running.

Only the trainer is authorized to withdraw the registration certificate from the racing secretary's office.

Trainer, Owner, and Veterinarian —
The Relationship !

GOOD COMMUNICATION !
A MUST !

GLOSSARY

Firing?

Blister?

Maiden?

CRiBBiNG?

Sesamoiditis?

Bog Spavin?

DAM?

SiRE?

GLOSSARY

ACTH - This is a hormone that stimulates the adrenal glands to produce cortisol, a steroid. If used over a long period of time in conjunction with corticosteroids, it will suppress the horse's own adrenal glands. It is very harmful long term. Make sure you know what is being given to your horse. The accumulation of all of these medications definitely affect the overall structure and health of your horse.

AEROBIC - Means with air. The phase of training where your horse gallops within himself, comfortably and for miles.

ALLOWANCE RACE - A better quality race where horses run without a claiming price. Every track has a limit on the price of claiming races. Allowance races are a step above the highest claiming races. In allowance races certain conditions (non winners of two races in a lifetime, for example) are met. A good allowance horse is a very valuable commodity.

ANABOLIC STEROIDS - These are the steroids you hear so much about in human sports. They create more muscle mass on the animal and make fillies and geldings aggressive. Not a surprise since the steroid is an artificial testosterone. Long term use of this on fillies can impair their ability to reproduce. Muscle can be hyper developed and tear itself from the bone.

ANAEROBIC - This means without air. When the horse is galloping hard and is going into oxygen debt he is in an anaerobic state. He will be huffing and puffing after the run to repay the oxygen debt to his muscle. The further he can go before running out of air, the better the race horse he will be.

BLEEDER - A term used for horses suffering from Exercise Induced Pulmonary Hemorrhaging. In certain states these animals are put on Lasix, a diuretic.

BLISTER - A chemical ointment or liquid which, when applied to a limb, causes an acute inflammation. It is used to treat chronic conditions such as an osselet, ring bone, bowed tendon, etc. When a trainer says he is going to "blister" the ankle, the tendon, the hocks, the knees, etc., it means he is going to apply a caustic chemical that will cause severe inflammation to the area. The theory is that the inflammatory reaction will bring blood supply to the area and hasten healing. Aggressive massages might do the same without as much trauma to the animal. Ask trusted vets what they think.

BOG SPAVIN - A chronic distention of the joint capsule of the hock that causes a swelling of the front-inside aspect of the hock joint.

BOOKKEEPER - The person who manages track disbursements.

Make sure you disburse your Earnings!

224

BOWED TENDON - A debilitating injury that keeps a horse from ever running to his best ability.

BREEZE - To encourage a horse to gallop out to his full speed but usually done without whipping. That's saved for the "work".

BUCKED SHIN - A painful swelling on the front surface of the cannon bone.

CAPPED HOCK - A swelling found at the point of the hock and caused by a bruise. It usually stems from kicking in horse vans or stalls.

CHEAP SPEED - A horse that can run the first two furlongs in 22 seconds, but then peters out and finishes the race poorly has "cheap speed". He has the mechanical ability to run 11 second furlongs - but lungs, structure, or something doesn't allow him to carry his speed the distance.

CLAIMING RACES - These are races that have evolved so that horses of equal ability may have a chance to win. A horse that is more talented than the rest of the field will stand a risk of being claimed if put in a race he can win easily. If he is put where he belongs, any horse in that particular race could be the winner. These races came about to give the public a fair chance at betting and to give less than great horses a place to run. Even if it is at the "bottom" they still have an opportunity to be useful for their owners and trainers. I have always hated claiming races, because if I put my horse where he can be useful, and he is, he may be claimed, and all my work is lost. Our dream is allowance horses that don't risk being claimed in every race. Unfortunately, good allowance horses are few and far between.

CLOCKER - The official timer hired by the race track to record timed workouts.

COLIC - A term used to describe any abdominal pain in the horse.

COLORS - The jockey's silk or nylon jacket and cap provided by the owner.

COLT - A male horse under the age of five.

The CLOCKER times the workouts of Horse

CONTRACTED FEET - Abnormal contractions of the heel.

CORTICOSTEROIDS - Any of a number of hormonal steroid substances obtained from the cortex of the adrenal gland. They may be used to inject joints to decrease inflammation. Rest is a must when used therapeutically. If used systemically, many trainers believe they enhance the horse's overall performance and make him more aggressively. Be aware of the ramifications of long term use.

225

COUPLED ENTRY - Two or more horses belonging to the same owner or trained by the same person. They run as an entry comprising a single betting unit. Their program number regardless of position would be 1 and 1A. A bet on one horse of an entry is a bet on both.

COW HOCKS - A conformation fault where the hocks are very close together while the rest of the rear legs are widely separated and toed out.

CRACKED HEELS (GREASED HEELS/SCRATCHES) - A weeping, moist dermatitis found on the back of the pastern just above the quarters.

CRIBBING (STUMPSUCKING) - An incurable vice or habit largely learned by imitation. The cribbber closes his teeth on any convenient surface (manger, gate, part of the stall partition, etc.), extends his neck and swallows a deep draft of air with a grunting sound.

DMSO - Dimethylsulfoxide This solution is often mixed with other concoctions, such as steroids. It opens the pores and allows the medications to be absorbed into the bloodstream. Typically, it is an anti-inflammatory.

DAM - A female parent (mother).

DEAD HEAT - A tie occurring when photo-finish cameras shows two or more horses crossing the finish line simultaneously

ELECTROLYTES - Salts that maintain blood balance. These are usually found in a well balanced feed program. However, if a horse is over stressed, he may need them short term after hard races.

EDEMA - An abnormal collection of fluids in body tissue.

ENDOSCOPE - A flexible tube with an optical attachment on the end, enabling the vet to inspect the horse internally. The instrument used by the vet when he scopes the horse.

EQUINE INFECTIOUS ANEMIA (EIA swamp fever) - An infectious disease of horses. It occurs in acute, chronic or inapparent forms, characterized in the acute or chronic stage by intermittent fever, depression, progressive weakness, weight loss, edema and anemia.

FIRING - The terrible custom of burning the front of the cannon bone, generally because of bucked shins. See Setback Section.

FURLONG: Eight of these make a mile. One is 220 yards.

226

GELDING - An altered, or castrated, male horse of any age.

HAND - A unit of measurement (four inches) by which a horse's height is measured from the ground to the withers. A horse that stands 15 hands is five feet tall at the withers.

HANDLE - The amount of money wagered on each race by the betting public.

HORSE - A stallion five years of age or older.

JOINT CAPSULE - A sac-like membrane that encloses a joint space and secretes joint (synovial) fluid.

JUG - A mixture of IV fluids with vitamins and electrolytes (and who knows what). It is given to horses by vets at the racetrack.

LASIX - A brand name drug for furosemide, a diuretic.

MAIDEN - A horse that has never won a race. "To break the maiden" means to win his first race.

NEURECTOMY - An operation in which the sensory nerve is severed with the idea of permanently eliminating pain that arises from that area.

OSSELETS - A swelling of the front part of the fetlock joint. The swelling may be due to arthritis of the fetlock join or to a bony growth.

OSTEOCHONDROSIS - A bone disease probably caused by severe over feeding and or too much calcium supplementation. May also be caused by overuse of drugs, mainly steroids.

OVER-REACHING - When the rear toe strikes the quarter of the front foot on the same side while the horse is in motion. Another name for grabbing his quarters, this usually happens when a horse stumbles upon breaking away from the starting gate.

OVERNIGHT - A race for which entries close 72 hours or less before post time for the first race on the day the race is to be run. Also, the mimeographed sheet available to horsemen at the racing secretary's office showing the entries for the following day.

PADDOCK - The area where the horses are saddled and viewed prior to a race. The paddock is always adjacent to the jockey's quarters.

PONY - The good old faithful horse, usually an Appaloosa, Paint or Quarter Horse that helps the young, inexperienced horse!

QUARTER CRACK - This is a crack found in the wall of the hoof in the area of the quarter. It often runs from the bottom of the wall up to the coronet.

227

QUITTOR - An infection involving the cartilage of the coffin bone that drains through tracts at the level of the coronet band.

RACING SECRETARY - This is the person who puts together the Condition Book at the track. He writes the races he thinks can be filled by the horses at his track. If you need a particular race, speaking to him will help. Many times he will write the race. If it doesn't fill, don't blame him. Many times trainers complain that the secretary is not sensitive to their needs. Usually, the secretary is happy to write whatever will fill the card.

RECEIVING BARN - The horse hotel, so to speak, at the racetrack.

REDLINE - This is a term used frequently in this manual. It means that the horse is doing his ultimate best, trying his hardest, giving you all he's got, stressing every fiber of his body to his own personal best. This should really only be done under race circumstances. The horse will need time to rebuild from such a work out.

RING BONE - A bony enlargement seen in front and on both sides of the pastern. If it is under the top of the hoof, it is called a low ring bone. If it is found halfway up the pastern, it is call a high ring bone.

ROARER - A horse with paralyzed vocal chords. The condition causes fluttering noise when the horse makes a quick move. It interferes with the horse's ability to race, especially in distance races.

SCALPING - The toe of the front hoof hits the pastern of the rear foot on the same side, when the horse is in motion.

SESAMOIDITIS - The sesamoids are two pyramid-shaped bones found at the rear of the fetlock joint and act as a pulley for the flexor tendons. When they become arthritic and coated with mineral deposits, the condition is know as sesamoiditis.

SPEEDY CUT - Occurring when the front foot hits the inside of the hock or the rear foot hits the outside of the front cannon bone. It is caused by poor conformation and/or poor shoeing.

SPIT BOX - The State Barn where the horses go to be tested for drugs.

SPRINTER - A horse than can run fast at 6 furlongs or less is called a sprinter.

STAKES - These are races that have paid entry fees. A horse that runs in Stakes is a better than average allowance horse and his winnings will pay his entry into the Stakes. If he can't earn enough to pay his own way in, then probably he shouldn't be competing at that level. Remember, the horse tells you how good he is by what he wins.

STARTER - This is the official who is head of the gate crew. He gives the okay for the horse to get his gate card. No horse may start racing without an official gate card.

THOROUGHPIN - Puffy swelling which appears on upper part of hock and in front of the large tendon.

THRUSH - A degenerative condition of the frog.

TIE-UP - Spasm of rump muscles - In a fit horse possibly caused by high energy grain and lack of exercise. In an unfit horse it may be caused by over-exercise .

WINDSUCKING - This occurs when a filly, while running hard, sucks wind in through her vagina. Even when cooling out, you may hear the intake and expelling of the air under her tail. It sounds like she is passing gas. This can be painful . It is usually caused by conformation where the tail is set high and the opening to the vagina is at a particular angle. It is easily remedied by having the vet take a few stitches at the top of the entrance to the vagina.

WOLF TEETH - Extra teeth found just forward of the first upper molar. They must be extracted, as they are tender and interfere with the bit of the bridle.

WORK - One step up from a breeze and a tad below a real race, this is the timed tryout on the racetrack that gives you an idea of your horse's true ability. When a horse is "worked" he is generally pushed to the limit, against another horse or alone. The rider will hit him and ride him hard.

Note: Many of these terms are taken from *Equus Magazine.* My thanks to them.

Faster!
Faster!

STANDARD DISTANCES
(one mile track)

220 to 440 yards
4 furlongs
4½ furlongs
5 furlongs
5½ furlongs
6 furlongs

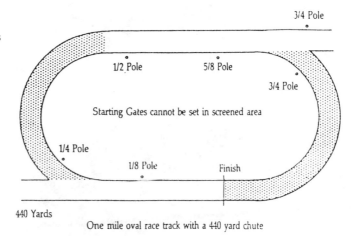

One mile oval race track with a 440 yard chute

STANDARD DISTANCES
(1/2 mile track with 440 yard chute)

220 to 440 yards
2½ furlongs
3 furlongs
½ Mile plus 70 yards
4½ furlongs
5 furlongs
5½ furlongs
6 furlongs

One half mile oval race track with a 440 yard chute

TRACK CONDITIONS

FAST (F) — Footing at its best, dry and even.
GOOD (GD) — Rated between fast and slow.
SLOW (SL) — Damp and clinging, between heavy and good.
HEAVY (HY) — A drying track, between muddy and slow.
MUDDY (M) — Soft and wet.
SLOPPY (SY) — Condition immediately after a rain, usually has firm footing beneath its surface.

RECOMMENDED READING !

RECOMMENDED READING

My philosophy is to read everything possible about horses and racing.
me books stand out in my mind. Their authors show a great sensitivity
the horse. This is a list of a few that should help you.

ADAMS' LAMENESS IN HORSES
By Ted S. Stashak

AINSLIE'S COMPLETE GUIDE TO THOROUGHBRED RACING
By Tom Ainslie

THE BODY LANGUAGE OF HORSES
By Tom Ainslie and Bonnie Ledbetter

DRUGS AND THE PERFORMANCE HORSE
By Thomas Tobin

EQUINE SPORTS MEDICINE
By William Jones

THE FIT RACEHORSE and THE RACEHORSE OWNER'S MANUAL
By Tom Ivers

IMPRINT TRAINING OF THE NEWBORN FOAL
By Robert M. Miller

THE LAME HORSE
By Dr. James R. Rooney

LYONS ON HORSES
By John Lyons

PRINCIPLES OF HORSESHOEING II
By Dr. Doub Butler

RACEHORSES AT RISK
By Lennert Krook and George Maylin

Read, Read, Read !

Your recommended reading should include some magazines. They will keep you abreast of new developments in the industry.

EQUUS MAGAZINE has excellent and well written articles. Many of them explain complex subjects in layman's terms. There are always good articles on equine sports physiology and training.

THE BACKSTRETCH is the magazine for the United Thoroughbred Trainers Association. You don't have to belong to subscribe. It has good articles that will keep you abreast of the racing situation. . . generally from the trainers viewpoint.

THE HORSEMAN'S JOURNAL is the trade magazine for the Horsemen's Protective and Benevolent Association. It deals with racing and the racing industry.

THE BLOODHORSE is the magazine of the Thoroughbred Owners and Breeders Association. It comes out weekly and really keeps you up to date and informed about what is going on where in the Thoroughbred racing world.

THE DAILY RACING FORM is the state of the art, best newspaper around to get a history and form on the horses running. The articles are current and there is an edition at every major track for every racing day. It is the best money you can spend to get racing information.

Arabian, Appaloosa, Paint and Quarter Horses are raced throughout the country. Contact the Racing Division of the Breed Registry to receive more information about their programs.

By the way · · ·

I will be starting a <u>newsletter</u> and compiling a <u>list</u> of <u>Trainers</u> who will be willing to work with you Readers —

If you are a Trainer and would like to be on the list, call or write !

If you are interested in the <u>newsletter</u> or the <u>Trainers list</u>, send a <u>self</u> <u>addressed</u> and <u>stamped</u> <u>envelop</u> to:

Janet Del Castillo
3708 Crystal Beach Road
Winter Haven, Fla
33880

If you would like a farm Consultation call 813-2998448

If you would like to share your experience with the newsletter readers — send me an article !

Thought Provoking Letters to Editor!

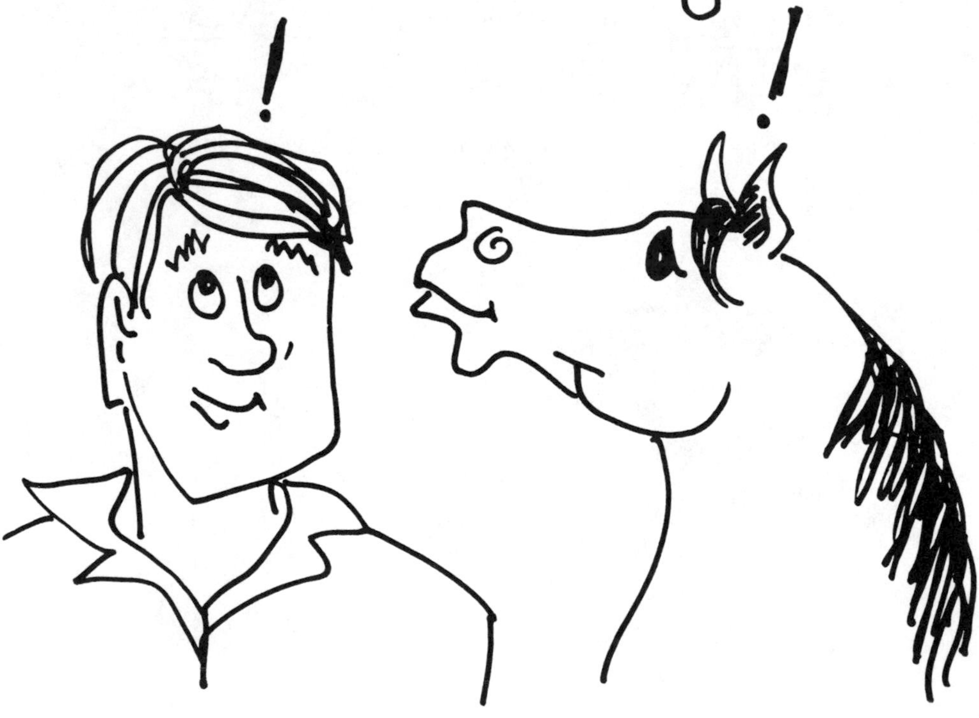

Masking drugs need investigating now

I have more than a 50-year association with horseracing. I have heard most all of the criticisms of the Triple Crown format that have been raised since the latest disaster. The only possible exception is the Chrysler Triple Crown bonus. As Mark Simon noted (Daily Racing Form, June 20), this bonus is an obscenity which should be eliminated.

My view is that if you take immature horses and run them three times in five weeks at distances that most have never tackled and are not likely to try again, while putting 126 pounds (121 pounds for fillies) on them in dangerously large fields, you are going to have serious trouble for the horse.

This is not anything new – the criticism is obvious and has been around as long as I have. So I doubt anything will be done to correct it.

However, in all the verbiage, why has the possibility of masking drugs being a contributing factor not been mentioned? If, for example, a joint is injected with cortisone at the optimal time prior to a race, it may become impossible for the jockey, the track vet, the stewards or Ross Perot to determine that the horse is unfit to run.

I am not pointing the finger at anyone, nor do I imply that cortisone is the only such drug available. There may be others of choice. All I am saying is that I believe that a masking drug, injected into the joint, is not discoverable by a blood test. Truesdail Lab and all their science be damned, because the drug is not likely to enter the bloodstream. The most thorough exam – pre-race – is not apt to discover the fitness problem being masked because of the effectiveness of the drug being used.

Why has this possible contributing factor to the problem not been discussed?

Charles E. Samuel
Stockton, Calif.

THE OLDER, THE BETTER

Editor:

As the industry prepares for the coming technology of DirectTv (*The Blood-Horse* of April 17, page 1865), be forewarned that we may find horse racing going the way of fur coats. The all-too-common occurrence of horses breaking down simply will not withstand the public scrutiny.

Perhaps it's time for a new vision—racing horses older, sounder, and therefore longer. Could Arazi have been our much-needed superstar had he not needed surgery at the tender age of two? Or A.P. Indy, had he been able to run longer than just enough to prove himself? I see little use in 2-year-old racing and wouldn't mind if the Triple Crown was for 4-year-olds.

From a business point of view, isn't it sensible to run your investment sounder and stronger? From a humane point of view, don't we owe it to these beautiful creatures that have served us so well?

Tori Keith
Knightdale, N.C.

Editor:

Racing isn't fun anymore. It used to be, and it could be again, but not without a complete overhaul. Every horse I ever owned got injured. After my best and favorite horse fractured a cannon bone, resulting in an 18-month lay-up, it became a test of nerves just to watch him run.

And now the best horses are going down. Despite undoubted expert care and love, it happened to Go for Wand, Union City, and Prairie Bayou. It is happening too much, and the hard part is that it often happens unexpectedly to horses who have never had a problem before.

But that is not entirely true. Very often, catastrophic breakdowns are not a sudden event. Just like a paper-clip that is bent back and forth over and over, a series of micro-fractures accumulate until suddenly the whole thing gives way. That is what happens to overworked bone. The bottom line is that we race horses too young and too much.

It is time for some big changes. Every racing event in a horse's life should be pushed back one full year. The lightest training should start no earlier than age two. Maiden races should start no earlier than age three. Yes, all the great races such as the Champagne Stakes (gr. I) and the Hopeful Stakes (gr. I) should be for 3-year olds. Horses should run in the classics at age four. The extra time will be good not only for the horses, it will help horse racing too. Tragedies will occur less frequently. Horses will have longer healthier careers, allowing horse lovers to follow their favorite horse. That develops the kind of good will that the sport desperately needs.

Next, horses should not race year round. Every horse needs some time off. We humans, with the bills to pay, will not do that unless it is mandated. We keep running horses until they are injured or worse. If we don't change our ways, animal rights groups will do it for us, and rightfully so.

Donald A. Cocquyt
Simi Valley, Calif.

A sample of letters to the Racing Form and Bloodhorse Magazine

These are caring people - looking for Solutions

WHAT do YOU THINK?

236

In defense of jockey Luis Collazo

To the Editor:

It was interesting to read that the stewards at Philadelphia Park slapped a $250 fine on jockey Luis Collazo for not doing a very good job of riding a horse named North Branch Kid. Now, if we could only fine the stewards, the owner and trainer of the horse and, yes, let us not forget the track veterinarians. All of these people are far more guilty of wrongdoing that is jockey Collazo.

What we have here is official racing's traditional response to one of its most basic problems: the sport is being surreptitiously conducted under one set of rules, while the public has been deceived into betting it under another set.

An uninformed racing public — and that unfortunately includes most of the people who bet their money every day — probably assumes Collazo is some kind of a three-headed villain — a little "pinhead muck sack" who, on purpose, did them in and robbed them of their right to win. Nothing could be further from the truth.

The truth needs to be told, probably for the first time, that those in horse racing really do play by one set of rules — many of them unwritten and unspoken, but quite understood — while the public bets horses under "official rules," which are that in name and perception only.

The scenario that got Collazo in trouble plays itself out over and over almost every day at every race track in the country. Dozens of injured, sore and bad legged horses are permitted to run. Racetracks desperately need them to fill those nine or 10 races each day, and they need them to insure full fields in all those gimmick races, where higher payoffs are the desired attraction.

The problem with letting horses such as North Branch Kid be entered in races is not that jockeys won't let them run, but that trainers are permitted to keep entering them and track veterinarians become conveniently distracted as the horses limp through their race-day health inspections.

Every day, trainers are coerced into running such horses, with that being demanded by racing secretaries who are under tremendous pressure to fill a card. Even when trainers tell the racing office the horse is not fit to run and might not "get by the vet," nobody cares to listen. The horse is needed, "so put 'em in."

When these horses are entered, a jockey, out of loyalty to the trainer, will accept the mount and then make some effort to get him around the course. The trainer knows the public is getting robbed; the jockey knows the public is getting robbed; the track vets know the public is getting robbed; the general manager of the racetrack knows the public is getting robbed. And nobody cares as the racing fan is robbed.

The real responsibility of stopping sore and lame horses from running rests with the track veterinarians, who examine each of the horses on race day, as is required by the "official" rules. But these vets know early in their employment they will not be on the payroll for long if they scratch too many of them.

Joe Abbey, the chief steward at Philadelphia Park, sounded somewhat the fool when he explained to Daily Racing Form the Collazo fine.

"This horse was obviously in distress," said Abbey. "The rider said the horse was making all kinds of noises during the race and when questioned, the outrider confirmed this. We also found out this horse had been on the vet's list in New Jersey last year. The trainer stated he did not want to run the horse, that he was going to turn him out, but the owner wanted to run him one more time."

And Collazo was fined?

And then Abbey said the most ridiculous thing of all: "We have told these riders repeatedly, if they think a horse is in distress and he can't be ridden in a fitting manner, then the horse should be pulled up."

Wait a big minute here. Why pull the horse up during the race? Since 99 percent of all these horses show these very negative signs during their pre-race warmup, why not simply scratch them before they run? And, herein lies the big catch, and it is something those of us who have been in racing for many years are not supposed to discuss.

Those official rules of racing say that once the gates open, the horse is a starter. This means that the race track gets its big commission on all the money bet. If the horse was scratched before the race, there would be a refund and the track would not get anything but aggravation.

Needless to say, this certainly puts stewards such as Abbey in a real ethical dilemma themselves. Unfortunately, money usually wins out over ethics, and the public keeps getting robbed.

It is my fantasy wish that one day, when the field is made up of sore horses — as is quite often the case — that the jockeys at Philadelphia Park will do just what Abbey suggests, and ease them all. Will Abbey and his fellow stewards declare the race "no contest," or will they declare them all starters and let the track keep the money?

It is absolutely shameful to fine Collazo, who is an innocent victim, while horseracing hides behind those unwritten and unspoken rules. He is the innocent party in all of this and we would suggest the stewards take another look at the situation, fine themselves $250 each and then go after the owner and trainer.

Kelso Sturgeon
Bel Air, Md.

August 12, 1993

Daily Racing Form
10 Lake Drive
Highstown, New Jersey 08520

Dear Editor:

Please spare us any further articles about the difficulties of champion
race mares in producing foals. I think if I read one more time about
the heartache of Genuine Risk or Lady's Secret (etc., ad nauseam), and
her latest failure to get in, stay in, or to give live birth to, a foal,
I will do something drastic (like join PETA).

Is anyone, like me, stupid enough to think that the rampant use of
synthetic male hormones (read: steroids) has anything to do with the
problem? I do not know if the two mares mentioned above were so
treated, but both sexes are routinely given a myriad of hormones
commencing before their second birthdays, when they probably approximate
the development of 8 to 12 year-old children. Ask any gynecologist what
the effect on a girl's future fertility would be if she were given male
hormones before she started her menstrual cycle.

I have a friend who is a Ph.D. in physiology and an expert on the
effects of steroids. He had been contacted by a prominent trainer about
designing a steroid therapy regimen for horses to obtain the maximum
effect. Knowing nothing about the races, he called me (an inveterate
horseplayer) to find out if steroids were legally prohibited, to which
I responded that, not only were they not illegal, their use was as
standard as daily feeding. He was shocked to learn that essentially
pre-pubescent females were receiving treatment, adding that fertility
problems would be the expected result. And females are not the only
ones suffering from this abuse. He made it clear that it would be
possible for the muscle mass of males to become so powerful that the
muscles could actually produce more torque than the bones could
withstand, resulting in snapped weight-bearing bones in the middle of a
race.

All this makes me wonder if some of the horrible injuries we have seen
on televised races in the last few years have actually had a reverse
cause-effect relationship from that which is obvious: does a horse take
a bad step because he snapped his cannon bone, rather than the other way
around?

Like a bunch of unrepentant tax cheats, trainers are quick to say
"everyone's doing it" in defense of this abuse. Yet that is precisely
the point - everyone is doing it and horses are being injured in the
process. Since they are standard procedure for virtually all horses,
steroids provide no competitive advantage; their prohibition would
likewise create no competitive disadvantage. And maybe, just maybe, we
would be spared the spectacle of horrific equine injury.

Very truly yours,

Mark H. Boykin

Racing Organizations and Information

THE
JOCKEY
CLUB

821 Corporate Drive
Lexington, KY 40503-2794
Telephone (606) 224-2700
Fax (606) 224-2710
Telex 856599

Every Thoroughbred which races in the United States, Canada and Puerto Rico must be registered in The American Stud Book.

This Thoroughbred Registry is maintained by The Jockey Club, an organization established in 1894, which issues all Certificates of Registration.

Registration in the Stud Book ensures the correct identification of every Thoroughbred and, as such, is essential to the integrity of Thoroughbred racing.

A new owner should always compare the markings on their horse with its description on the Certificate of Foal Registration at the time of purchase and when the horse reaches its final destination. If the horse and its description do not match, the sooner this is discovered, the better.

For racing and breeding purposes, any transfer of ownership must be endorsed by the seller or their agent on the back of the Certificate of Foal Registration. But the Certificate is not a deed of ownership and should never be relied upon as such.

The Jockey Club's Registration Department is based in Lexington, Kentucky, where a group of dedicated staff which understands the Thoroughbred business is ready to help with any problems.

Dedicated to the improvement of Thoroughbred breeding and racing, The Jockey Club is also involved in numerous subsidiary and associate organizations.

These include The Jockey Club Information Systems, Inc., a computerized on-line information and sales catalogue production service; Equibase, racing's central performance database; the news and sports media service, Thoroughbred Racing Communications. Inc.; the Grayson-Jockey Club Research Foundation, which raises funds for equine veterinary research; and The Jockey Club Foundation, providing relief of poverty and distress among indigent members of the Thoroughbred industry and their families.

240

POST OFFICE BOX 4367, LEXINGTON, KY 40544
TELEPHONE (606) 276-2291 FAX (606) 276-2462

THOROUGHBRED OWNERS AND BREEDERS ASSOC.

The TOBA is a national non-profit association founded in 1961. Its 3,116 individual members, essentially owners and breeders, include association memberships of 35 state breeders associations, whose constituency of licensed owners encompass another 28,000 persons.

The TOBA has a 35-person Board of Trustees and an additional eight(8) State Trustees, which governs the activities of the association.

The TOBA works primarily on national projects that will benefit the interests of owners and breeders in all regions.

TOBA has members in all 50 states and 19 different countries. 11% of its membership live in Kentucky, where the TOBA home office is located. 9% are from New York, 8% from California, with Texas, Illinois, Maryland, New Jersey and Florida also having a significant core of members.

TOBA members individual dues are $220 annually, which includes a subscription to The Blood-Horse magazine, its key supplements and a host of other money-saving membership benefits.

The current president of the TOBA is Miss Helen C. Alexander. Vice-Presidents are Ronald K. Kirk(Kentucky), John Ed Anthony(Arkansas) and Rollin W. Baugh(California).

Among its activities, the TOBA: (1) is the custodian of the vital North American Graded Stakes Committee, (2) publishes The Blood-Horse magazine weekly for the industry, (3) actively recruits and trains new owners, (4) is the leading catalyst for a national image-building marketing campaign for horse racing, (5) has an active task force looking into possible improvements in the workers compensation insurance arrangements for horsemen, (6) maintains a network regional watch for significant outbreaks of equine diseases, (7) offers a multi-state licensing service for its members, (8) answers dozens of questions made by phone to the TOBA offices, providing a vital information service to the industry.

For more information about membership, write: TOBA, P.O. Box 4367, Lexington, Ky. 40544, or call (606) 276-2291.

241

We're headed for the finish line and we need your help! A couple of weeks ago we sent you the background information on what NATO will try to do for the sport of Thoroughbred racing in general and for owners in particular. In case you mislaid the membership card, here's another copy! Please join the hundreds of your fellow owners who have already joined.

For further information please call 1-800-545-7777.

National Association of Thoroughbred Owners, Inc. (NATO)

MEMBERSHIP APPLICATION FORM FOR LICENSED THOROUGHBRED OWNERS

Enclosed is my dues payment of (circle one): One year – $75   Two Years –$135   Three years – $195

LAST NAME _____ FIRST NAME _____ SIGNATURE _____

STABLE NAME _____ NUMBER OF THOROUGHBREDS OWNED _____

ADDRESS _____ CITY _____ STATE _____ ZIP _____

(___) _____ STATES LICENSED TO RACE IN _____
PHONE   FAX

Knowing we need additional funds to get NATO out of the starting gate, I have enclosed an additional contribution of $ _____

Make checks payable to National Association of Thoroughbred Owners Inc. and send to: **P. O. Box 878, Unionville, PA 19375.** NATO is a not-for-profit corporation.

MAKE COPIES OF THIS FORM AND GIVE THEM TO YOUR FRIENDS. WE THANK YOU FOR YOUR SUPPORT!

THOROUGHBRED RACING COMMUNICATIONS, INC.

Thoroughbred Racing Communications, Inc. (TRC) is a national media relations office that was formed in July, 1987, to expand awareness of Thoroughbred racing. It is funded by founding organizations The Jockey Club, Breeders' Cup Ltd., and the Thoroughbred Racing Associations (TRA).

Among the media services provided by TRC are: **TRC News**, a weekly newsletter to media representatives and industry officials; video and audio feeds from major races and events to television and radio networks; and the **TRC Notebook**, a compilation of notes from the Thoroughbred world and a preview of weekend racing, which is distributed weekly on the Associated Press wire.

TRC also produces a weekly, nationally syndicated radio show "*The Thoroughbred Connection*," hosted by sportscaster Jim McKay as well as **TRC Video News Features**, brief, ready-to-air profiles of intriguing personalities in Thoroughbred racing, which are sent to -- and distributed by -- network newsfeed organizations as well as entertainment programs.

In July, 1993, TRC, in association with PHoenix Communications, launched a nationally syndicated racing magazine television show called "*Thoroughbred World.*" Hosted by announcer/racing commentator Tom Durkin, the monthly show airs on Prime Network and is comprised primarily of features on personalities and events in Thoroughbred racing.

From February to November each year, TRC also conducts a weekly **National Thoroughbred Poll**, as well as a **Triple Crown Poll** from March through June, which appear in newspapers throughout the country.

In 1988, TRC produced "Wire to Wire: Enjoying a Day at the Races," an educational brochure designed to aid racetracks in their efforts to attract new fans.

TRC also serves as the licensing agent for the manufacture and distribution of products bearing the Secretariat identification. Proceeds from TRC-licensed or TRC-produced merchandise benefit equine medical research funded by the Grayson-Jockey Club Research Foundation.

The executive director of TRC is Tom Merritt. The TRC staff consists of Bob Curran Jr., Director of Media Relations & Development; Howard Bass, Manager of Media Services; Peggy Hendershot, Manager of Information Services; Jenifer Van Deinse, Coordinator of Program Services; and Joan Lawrence, Coordinator of Media Services.

Executive Director
M.A. Sullivan
P.O. Box 19232
Portland, OR 97280, USA
Phone   (503) 644-9224
Fax   (503) 626-7039

Association of
Official Racing
Chemists

The AORC (Association of Official Racing Chemists) was formed in 1947. The Association is composed of individual chemists engaged by official racing regulatory bodies. These chemists analyze racing samples submitted from these official sources. Samples are tested from flat racing, harness racing, show events, and greyhound racing from both North American and international origins.

Advantages of AORC membership include the exchange of technical information resulting in procedure improvements. These procedural advances in detection and identification of drugs in biological samples result in improved coverage in the laboratories.

Emphasis is placed on proficiency testing through various programs of quality control for the members in racing laboratories. At present there are members in 21 countries some of whom analyze samples for other national racing jurisdictions, also. 59 laboratories have professional chemists holding AORC membership.

Submitted by M. A. Sullivan, AORC executive director
7-22-93

244

AMERICAN QUARTER HORSE ASSOCIATION

P. O. Box 200 ▪ Amarillo, Texas ▪ 79168
2701 I-40 East ▪ Amarillo, Texas ▪ 79104
(806) 376-4811

AQHA Racing Department:
The AQHA Racing Department is the official recordkeeper for American Quarter Horse racing, compiling the results of recognized races from the United States, Canada and Mexico. The Department maintains all official statistics, oversees the racing tattoo program and handles awards. Department members also represent the sport at racing industrywide events and coordinate AQHA's national advertising campaign, the only one of its kind in the entire horse racing industry.

Assistance for potential racehorse owners:
The AQHA Racing Department maintains a listing of state racing associations that a potential racehorse owner can contact for assistance in purchasing a racing American Quarter Horse. The Department has sales schedules, racing deates and information about major violations by jockeys, trainers and owners as reported by racetracks, state racing commissions and the Association of Racing Commissioners International. The following resources also are available:

* *The Quarter Racing Journal.* AQHA's award-winning monthly racing magazine includes industry news, features, race coverage, statistics about the leading horses and horsemen and an annual review. For United States residents, a one-year subscription of 12 issues is $17. To subscribe, call the *Journal* Circulation Department at (806) 372-1192.

* "America's Horse." AQHA's monthly program on ESPN features the American Quarter Horse in all the breed's activities and includes coverage of major racing events. Check cable television listings.

* "How to Wager on America's Fastest Athlete." This 48-page guidebook explains handicapping American Quarter Horse racing, with statistics on leading jockeys and trainers, and explanations of handicapping methods. Free.

* "Winning at American Quarter Horse Racing: With Special Application to the Thoroughbred Player." Narrated by Rick Baedeker of Hollywood Park, this 40-minute video explains the similarities and differences between wagering on American Quarter Horse and Thoroughbred racing. $19.95

* "Owning America's Fastest Athlete." This 12-minute video explains acquiring a racing American Quarter Horse, choosing a trainer and the opportunities available in the industry. The video ends with the award-winning music video "Running Blood" by Michael Martin Murphey. $9.95

To order the handicapping guide and videos, call the AQHA Racing Department at (806) 376-4811.

245

Pacific Coast
Quarter Horse Racing Association

Helping California's Quarter Horse Horsemen

- Administration of 7 major California Futurities & Derbies:

  (1) Ed Burke Memorial Futurity [Gr 1]   (5) California Sires Cup Futurity [R3]
  (2) Governor's Cup Derby [R1]   (6) California Sires Cup Derby [R3]
  (3) PCQHRA Breeders Futurity [R2]   (7) PCQHRA Breeders Derby [R3]
  (4) Governor's Cup Futurity [R2]

- Full-time legislative advocacy in Sacramento
- Administration of Cal-Bred Awards Program for breeders, race horse owners & stallion owners
- Administration of PCQHRA Annual Yearling & Mixed Stock Sale
- Contract representation for horsemen at all California race meets with Quarter Horse participation
- Providing the only recognized representation of Quarter Horse interests before the California Horse Racing Board
- Promotion of California racing opportunities for Quarter Horsemen across the United States
- Publication of the only regular California Quarter Horse newsletter to keep horsemen informed on racing issues
- Publication of the most complete directory of Quarter Horse racing interests in California
- Membership and participation in national organizations working to develop & improve the economic future of the Quarter horse industry

Representing California's Quarter Horse Horsemen Since 1951
PACIFIC COAST QUARTER HORSE RACING ASSOCIATION

P.C.Q.H.R.A.

For More Information On Quarter Horse Breeding
& Racing Opportunities In California
Call: (310) 493-4273

P.O. Box 8403
5070 Highway 8 West
Moscow, Idaho 83843
(208) 882-5578 · FAX 1 (208) 882-8150

Appaloosa
Horse
Club

Roger L. Klamfoth, Executive Secretary
Daniel J. Marsh, Treasurer
Lynn Theissen, Administrative Assistant
Lex Smurthwaite, Registrar

APPALOOSA RACING

"The Appaloosa Horse Club is dedicated to preserving, improving, promoting and enhancing the breed known as the Appaloosa. The Appaloosa is a breed with a color preference."

This mission statement was adopted by the ApHC's Board of Directors in 1989 and amended in 1992, and serves as our reference point in everything we do as an association.

An Executive Race Committee which is a part of and operates within the scope of the Appaloosa Horse Club provides a committee through which the racing members of the Appaloosa industry may have direct input into the ApHC's racing program. The purpose of this committee is to enhance Appaloosa racing by promoting interest and education through various articles, newsletters, press releases, workshops, seminars and representation of the breed at various industry functions. The committee assists in developing policies, helps with Appaloosa Racing Association programs and reports activities, desires and actions of the racing industry to the Board of Directors of the Appaloosa Horse Club. It promotes parimutuel races in accordance with the applicable State Horse Racing Commission rules and regulations for Appaloosa horses registered with the ApHC and works with track management, owners, trainers, racing associations, etc., when requested. At it's annual meeting all stakes races are reviewed and grades are issued for those meeting the criteria set forth by the committee. The committee is responsible for selecting the Champion running horses each year and for the individuals inducted into the Appaloosa Racing Hall of Fame.

The Racing Department is the official record keeper for Appaloosa racing and is responsible for compiling the results of all recognized races in the United States and Canada, maintaining all the official statistics, overseeing the racing tattoo program and handling all awards. It maintains a listing of all state racing associations and racing dates and provides past performance lines upon request by the Daily Racing Form and other race reporting agencies, race tracks, or individuals. The department is responsible for the annual racing review as reported in the Appaloosa Yearbook and for the bimonthly Appaloosa Racing Newsletter which includes industry news, features, statistics on leading horses and horsemen and current race coverage.

The monthly breed publication, APPALOOSA JOURNAL, in addition to its regular industry coverage, reports racing briefs with limited articles featuring major stakes races.

Appaloosa racing continues to grow in popularity attracting many new people to the breed. For more information about our breed which excels at middle distance races contact the Racing Department, P.O. Box 8403, Moscow, Idaho 83843. Telephone (208) 882-5578, Extension 276.

247

NATIONAL ORGANIZATIONS

U.S. Dept. of Agriculture-Animal & Plant Health Inspection Services:

Administrator	Washington, D.C.	(202) 447-3668
Veterinary Services	Washington, D.C.	(202) 447-5193
Animal Care (Horse Protection Act)	Hyattsville, MD	(301) 436-7586
Equine & Miscellaneous Diseases	Hyattsville, MD	(301) 436-5913

Food & Drug Administration - Center for Veterinary Medicine:

Veterinary Equine Specialist	Rockville, MD	(301) 443-3420

Industry:

The Jockey Club Executive Office	New York, NY	(212) 371-5970
The Jockey Club Registry Office	Lexington, KY	(606) 224-2700

Horse Council:

American Horse Council	Washington, D.C.	(202) 296-4031

Racing Organizations:

American Horse Racing Federation	Washington, D.C.	(202) 296-4031
Association of Official Racing Chemists	Portland, OR	(503) 644-9224
Association of Racing Commissioners International	Lexington, KY	(606) 254-4060
Breeders' Cup Limited	Lexington, KY	(606) 223-5444
Equibase Company	Lexington, KY	(800) 333-2211
Horsemen's Benevolent & Protective Association	New Orleans, LA	(504) 945-4500
International Racing Bureau	Lexington, KY	(606) 276-5228
Jockey Agents' Benevolent Association	Elmont, NY	(516) 561-0120
Jockey's Guild	Lexington, KY	(606) 259-3211
National Museum of Racing	Saratoga Springs, NY	(518) 584-0400
National Steeplechase & Hunt Association	Elkton, MD	(301) 392-0700
National Turf Writers Association	Louisville, KY	(502) 452-6965
Race Track Industry Program	Tucson, AZ	(602) 621-5660
Society of North American Racing Officials	Oak Park, IL	(312) 848-1891
Thoroughbred Racing Associations of North America	Lake Success, NY	(516) 328-2660
Thoroughbred Racing Protective Bureau	New Hyde Park, NY	(516) 328-2010
Turf Benevolent Association	Jamaica, NY	(212) 297-8831
Turf Publicists of America	East Rutherford, NJ	(201) 935-8500
United Thoroughbred Trainers of America	Detroit, MI	(313) 342-6144

Breeders Associations:

American Thoroughbred Breeders Alliance	Timonium, MD	(301) 252-2100
Thoroughbred Owners & Breeders Association	Lexington, KY	(606) 276-2291

Equine Health & Research:

American Association of Equine Practioners	Lexington, KY	(606) 233-0147
American Farrier's Association	Lexington, KY	(606) 233-7411
American Veterinary Medical Association	Schaumburg, IL	(708) 605-8070
Grayson-Jockey Club Research Foundation	Lexington, KY	(606) 224-2850
Maxwell H. Gluck Equine Research Center	Lexington, KY	(606) 257-4757
Morris Animal Foundation	Englewood, CO	(303) 790-2345

Publications:

The Blood-Horse	Lexington, KY	(606) 278-2361
The Daily Racing Form	Hightstown, NJ	(609) 448-9100
Horsemen's Journal	Lexington, KY	(606) 223-9800
Racing Times	New York, NY	(212) 336-7600
Thoroughbred Racing Communications	New York, NY	(212) 371-5910
Thoroughbred Times	Lexington, KY	(606) 223-9800

ALABAMA

Birmingham Racing Commission	Birmingham	(205) 328-7223
Birmingham Race Course	Birmingham	(205) 838-7500
Alabama Thoroughbred Owners & Breeders Association	Birmingham	(205) 838-7404

ALASKA

Alaska State Horsemen's Association	Anchorage	(907) 696-6408

ARIZONA

Arizona Department of Racing	Phoenix	(602) 542-5151
Arizona Racing Commission	Phoenix	(602) 542-5151
Horsemen's Benevolent & Protective Association	Phoenix	(602) 942-3336
Apache County Fair	St. Johns	(602) 337-4364
Cochise County Fair	Douglas	(602) 364-3819
Coconino Fair	Flagstaff	(602) 774-5139
Graham County Fair	Safford	(602) 428-6240
Prescott Downs	Prescott	(602) 445-0220
Rillito Park	Tucson	(602) 293-5011
Santa Cruz County Fair	Sonoita	(602) 455-5553
Turf Paradise	Phoenix	(602) 942-1101
Yuma County Fair	Yuma	(602) 726-4420
Arizoniá Thoroughbred Breeders Association	Phoenix	(602) 942-1310
Arizona State Horsemen's Association	Phoenix	(602) 258-2708

ARKANSAS

Arkansas State Racing Commission	Little Rock	(501) 682-1467
Horsemen's Benevolent & Protective Association	Hot Springs	(501) 623-7641
Oaklawn Park	Hot Springs	(501) 623-4411
Arkansas Thoroughbred Breeders' Association	Hot Springs	(501) 624-6328
Arkansas Breeders' Sales Co.	Hot Springs	(501) 624-6336
Arkansas Horse Council	Little Rock	(501) 851-3366

CALIFORNIA

California Horse Racing Board	Sacramento	(916) 920-7178
Federation of California Racing Associations	Arcadia	(818) 574-7223
Horsemen's Benevolent & Protective Association	Arcadia	(818) 447-2145
Bay Meadows	San Mateo	(415) 574-7223
Del Mar	Del Mar	(619) 755-1141
Fairplex Park	Pomona	(714) 623-3111
Ferndale	Ferndale	(707) 786-9511
Fresno	Fresno	(209) 453-3247
Golden Gate Fields	Albany	(415) 526-3020
Hollywood Park	Inglewood	(213) 419-1500
Los Alamitos	Los Alamitos	(714) 751-3247
Pleasanton	Pleasanton	(415) 846-2881
Sacramento	Sacramento	(916) 924-2088
Santa Anita Park	Arcadia	(818) 574-7223
Santa Rosa/Sonoma	Santa Rosa	(707) 545-4200
Solano/Vallejo	Vallejo	(707) 644-4401
Stockton/San Joaquin	Stockton	(209) 466-5041

249

California Thoroughbred Breeders Association	Arcadia	(818) 445-7800
Barretts Equine Sales	Pomona	(714) 629-3099
California Thoroughbred Sales	Del Mar	(619) 755-6807
California State Horsemen's Association	Santa Rosa	(707) 544-2250

COLORADO
Colorado Racing Commission	Denver	(303) 894-2990
Horsemen's Benevolent & Protective Association	Lafayette	(303) 665-6764
Gateway Downs	Holly	(303) 537-6866
Colorado Thoroughbred Breeders Association	Denver	(303) 293-8212
Colorado Horsemen's Council	Arvada	(303) 469-5863

CONNECTICUT
| Connecticut Division of Special Revenue | Newington | (203) 566-2756 |
| Connecticut Horse Council | Bethany | (203) 525-8037 |

DELAWARE
| Delaware Thoroughbred Racing Commission | Wilmington | (302) 577-3288 |
| Delaware Park | Stanton | (302) 994-2521 |

FLORIDA
Florida Division of Pari-Mutuel Wagering	Tallahassee	(904) 488-9130
Florida Pari-Mutuel Commission	Miami	(305) 470-5675
Horsemen's Benevolent & Protective Association	Opa Locka	(305) 625-4591
Calder Race Course - Tropical Park	Opa Locka	(305) 625-1311
Gulfstream Park Racing Association	Hallandale	(305) 454-7000
Hialeah Park	Hialeah	(305) 885-8000
Tampa Bay Downs	Oldsmar	(813) 855-4401
Florida Thoroughbred Breeders' Association	Ocala	(904) 629-2160
Fasig-Tipton Florida	Lexington, KY	(606) 255-1555
Ocala Breeders' Sales Co.	Ocala	(904) 237-2154

GEORGIA
| Georgia Thoroughbred Owners & Breeders Association | Atlanta | (404) 451-0409 |
| Georgia Horse Foundation | Atlanta | (404) 261-0612 |

IDAHO
Horsemen's Benevolent & Protective Association	Meridian	(208) 888-4519
Idaho State Horse Racing Commission	Boise	(208) 327-7105
Cassia County Fair	Burley	(208) 678-7985
Eastern Idaho Fair	Blackfoot	(208) 785-2480
Gem County	Emmett	(208) 365-6144
Jerome County Fair	Jerome	(208) 324-7209
Le Bois Park	Boise	(208) 376-7223
Oneida County Fair	Malad	(208) 766-2247
Pocatello Downs	Pocatello	(208) 234-0181
Rupert Fairgrounds	Rupert	(208) 436-4793
Sandy Downs - Teton Racing	Idaho Falls	(208) 529-8722
Idaho Thoroughbred Breeders Association	Boise	(208) 375-5930
Idaho Horse Council	Castleford	(208) 537-6664

ILLINOIS

Horsemen's Benevolent & Protective Assn. (Chicago)	Cicero	(708) 652-2201
Horsemen's Benevolent & Protective Assn. (Illinois)	Caseyville	(618) 345-7724
Illinois Department of Agriculture - Horse Racing Programs	Springfield	(217) 782-4231
Illinois Racing Board	Chicago	(312) 814-2600
Arlington International Racecourse Ltd.	Arlington Heights	(708) 255-4300
Balmoral	Crete	(708) 672-7544
Fairmount Park	Collinsville	(618) 345-4300
Hawthorne Race Course	Cicero	(312) 780-3700
Sportman's Park	Cicero	(312) 242-1121
Illinois Thoroughbred Breeders & Owners Foundation	Fairview Heights	(618) 344-3427
Illinois Thoroughbred Breeders & Owners Foundation Sales	Fairview Heights	(618) 344-3427
Midwest Equine Sales	Arlington Heights	(312) 392-2227
Horsemen's Council of Illinois	Urbana	(217) 333-1784

INDIANA

Horsemen's Benevolent & Protective Association	Guilford	(513) 782-2800
Indiana Horse Racing Commission	Indianapolis	(317) 233-3119
Thoroughbred Association of Indiana	Lafayette	(317) 589-3838
Indiana Horse Council	Indianapolis	(317) 786-6646

IOWA

Horsemen's Benevolent & Protective Association	Altoona	(515) 967-6528
Iowa Racing & Gaming Commission	Des Moines	(515) 281-7352
Prairie Meadows	Altoona	(515) 967-1000
Iowa Thoroughbred Breeders & Owners	Perry	(515) 465-3809
Iowa Horse Industry Council	Cedar Rapids	(319) 396-9366

KANSAS

Horsemen's Benevolent & Protective Association	Edmond, OK	(405) 359-0625
Kansas Racing Commission	Topeka	(913) 296-5800
Eureka Downs	Eureka	(316) 583-5528
The Woodlands	Kansas City	(913) 299-9797
Kansas Thoroughbred Association	Medicine Lodge	(316) 886-9824
Kansas Thoroughbred Association/Sales	Beloit	(913) 738-3749

KENTUCKY

Horsemen's Benevolent & Protective Association	Louisville	(502) 363-1077
Kentucky State Racing Commission	Lexington	(606) 254-7021
Churchill Downs	Louisville	(502) 636-4400
Ellis Park	Henderson	(812) 425-1456
Keeneland Association	Lexington	(606) 254-3412
Turfway Park Race Course	Florence	(606) 371-0200
Kentucky Thoroughbred Association	Lexington	(606) 278-6004
Kentucky Thoroughbred Owners & Breeders	Lexington	(606) 277-1122
Fasig-Tipton Co.	Lexington	(606) 255-1555
Lexington Breeders' Sales	Lexington	(606) 252-0540
Keeneland Association	Lexington	(606) 254-3412
Matchmaker Breeders Exchange	Lexington	(606) 259-0451
Stallion Access/Fasig-Tipton	Lexington	(606) 255-1555

LOUISIANA

Horsemen's Benevolent & Protective Association	New Orleans	(504) 945-1555
Louisiana State Racing Commission	New Orleans	(504) 483-4001
Delta Downs	Vinton	(318) 589-7441
Evangeline Downs	Lafayette	(318) 896-7223
Fair Grounds	New Orleans	(504) 944-5515
Jefferson Downs	Kenner	(504) 466-8521
Louisiana Downs	Bossier City	(318) 742-5555
Louisiana Thoroughbred Breeders Association	New Orleans	(504) 947-4676
Breeders Sales Co. of Louisiana	New Orleans	(504) 947-4676
Fasig-Tipton Louisiana	Lexington, KY	(606) 255-1555
Louisiana Thoroughbred Breeders Sales Co.	Carencro	(318) 896-6152
Southwest Equine Sales	Carencro	(318) 234-2382

MARYLAND

Maryland Million, Ltd.	Timonium	(301) 252-2100
Maryland Racing Commission	Baltimore	(301) 333-6267
Laurel Race Course	Laurel	(301) 725-0400
Marlboro	Upper Marlboro	(301) 952-4740
Pimlico Race Course	Baltimore	(301) 542-9400
Timonium	Timonium	(301) 252-0200
Maryland Horse Breeder's Association	Timonium	(301) 252-2100
Maryland Horse Breeder's Foundation	Timonium	(301) 252-2100
Maryland Thoroughbred Horsemen's Association	Baltimore	(301) 265-6842
Equivest Breeders Sales Co.	Timonium	(800) 666-4677
Maryland Horse Council	Timonium	(301) 252-2100

MASSACHUSETTS

Horsemen's Benevolent & Protective Assn. (New England)	Revere	(603) 893-9806
Massachusetts State Racing Commission	Boston	(617) 727-2581
Marshfield Fair	Marshfield	(617) 834-6629
Northampton	Northamption	(413) 584-2237
Massachusetts Thoroughbred Breeders Association	North Andover	(508) 683-4565

MICHIGAN

Horsemen's Benevolent & Protective Association	Livonia	(313) 261-5700
Michigan - Office of the Racing Commissioner	Livonia	(313) 462-2400
Ladbroke - Detroit Racing Corporation	Livonia	(313) 525-7300
Mount Pleasant Meadows	Mt. Pleasant	(517) 773-0012
Michigan United Thoroughbred Breeders & Owners Assn.	Livonia	(313) 422-2044
Midwest Thoroughbred Sales	Livonia	(313) 522-1675
Michigan Horse Council	Lansing	(517) 655-4880

MINNESOTA

Horsemen's Benevolent & Protective Association	Shakopee	(612) 496-7772
Minnesota Racing Commission	Eden Prairie	(612) 341-7555
Canterbury Downs	Shakopee	(612) 445-7223
Minnesota Thoroughbred Association	Burnsville	(612) 892-6200
Minnesota Thoroughbred Association/Sales	Hamel	(612) 478-6068
Minnesota Horse Council	St. Paul	(612) 457-5948

MISSISSIPPI

Mississippi Thoroughbred Breeders Association	Madison	(601) 856-8293
Mississippi Horse Council	Tupelo	(601) 844-4988

MISSOURI

Missouri Horse Racing Commission	Jefferson City	(314) 751-3565
Missouri Thoroughbred Owners & Breeders Association	Willard	(417) 742-2624
Missouri Equine Council	Sullivan	(314) 457-8423

MONTANA

Horsemen's Benevolent & Protective Association	Billings	(406) 256-8364
State of Montana Board of Horse Racing	Helena	(406) 444-4287
Cow Capital Turf Club	Miles City	(406) 232-3758
Flathead Fairgrounds	Kalispell	(406) 756-5628
Great Falls	Great Falls	(406) 727-8900
Helena	Helena	(406) 443-7210
Marias Fair	Shelby	(406) 434-2692
MetraPark Race Track	Billings	(406) 256-2400
Ravalli County Fairgrounds	Hamilton	(406) 363-3411
Western Montana Fair	Missoula	(406) 721-3247
Montana Thoroughbred Breeders Association	Black Eagle	(406) 965-3420
All West Sales & Racing	Billings	(406) 259-8455

NEBRASKA

Horsemen's Benevolent & Protective Association	Grand Island	(402) 473-4121
Nebraska State Racing Commission	Lincoln	(402) 471-2577
Ak-Sar-Ben	Omaha	(402) 556-2305
Atokad Park	South Sioux City	(402) 494-4502
Columbus	Columbus	(402) 564-0133
Fonner Park	Grand Island	(308) 382-4515
Lincoln	Lincoln	(402) 474-5371
Nebraska Thoroughbred Breeders' Association	Grand Island	(308) 384-4683

NEVADA

Nevada Racing Commission	Las Vegas	(702) 486-7616

NEW HAMPSHIRE

New Hampshire Pari-Mutuel Commission	Concord	(603) 271-2158
Rockingham Park	Salem	(603) 898-2311
New Hampshire Horse Council	Durham	(603) 862-2131

NEW JERSEY

Horsemen's Benevolent & Protective Association	Robbinsville	(609) 448-0192
New Jersey Racing Commission	Trenton	(609) 292-0613
Atlantic City Racing Association	Atlantic City	(609) 641-2190
Garden State Park	Cherry Hill	(609) 488-8400
The Meadowlands	East Rutherford	(201) 935-8500
Monmouth Park	Oceanport	(201) 222-5100
Thoroughbred Breeders' Association of New Jersey	Bordentown	(609) 298-6401
Equivest Breeders Sales Co.	Northfield	(800) 666-4677
New Jersey Horse Council	Quakertown	(201) 735-2682

NEW MEXICO

New Mexico State Racing Commission	Albuquerque	(505) 841-4644
The Downs at Albuquerque	Albuquerque	(505) 265-0943
The Downs at Santa Fe	Santa Fe	(505) 471-3311
La Mesa Park	Raton	(505) 455-2301
Ruidoso Downs	Ruidoso	(505) 378-4431
San Juan Downs	Farmington	(505) 326-4551
Sunland Park	Sunland Park	(505) 589-1131
New Mexico Horse Breeders' Association	Albuquerque	(505) 262-0224
Ruidoso Horse Sales Co.	Glencoe	(505) 653-4242
New Mexico Horse Council	Albuquerque	(505) 344-8548

NEW YORK

Horsemen's Benevolent & Protective Assn. (Finger Lakes)	Canandaigua	(716) 924-3004
Horsemen's Benevolent & Protective Assn. (New York)	Jamaica	(718) 641-4700
New York City Off-Track Betting Corp.	New York	(212) 704-5000
New York State Racing Commission	New York	(212) 219-4230
New York State Racing & Wagering Board	New York	(212) 219-4230
New York State Regional OTB Corporations:		
Catskill Regional OTB	Pomona	(914) 362-0400
Capital Regional OTB	Schenectady	(518) 370-5151
Nassau County Regional OTB	Hempstead	(516) 292-8300
Suffolk Regional OTB	Hauppauge	(516) 434-4500
Western Regional OTB	Batavia	(716) 343-1423
Aqueduct	Queens	(718) 641-4700
Belmont	Elmont	(516) 488-6000
Finger Lakes	Farmington	(716) 924-3232
Saratoga	Saratoga	(518) 584-6200
New York State Thoroughbred Breeding & Dev. Fund Corp.	New York	(212) 832-3700
New York Thoroughbred Breeders	Elmont	(516) 354-7600
Fasig-Tipton New York	Elmont	(516) 328-1800
New York State Horse Council	Churchville	(716) 293-2561

NORTH CAROLINA

North Carolina Thoroughbred Breeders Association	Hillsborough	(919) 967-8592
North Carolina Horse Council	Raleigh	(919) 552-3536

NORTH DAKOTA

North Dakota Racing Commission	Bismarck	(701) 224-4290

OHIO

Horsemen's Benevolent & Protective Association	Grove City	(614) 875-1269
Ohio State Racing Commission	Columbus	(614) 466-2757
Beulah Park	Grove City	(614) 871-9600
River Downs	Cincinnati	(513) 232-8000
Thistledown	North Randall	(216) 662-8600
Ohio Thoroughbred Breeders & Owners	Cincinnati	(513) 241-4589
Beulah Park Sales Co.	Grove City	(614) 871-9600
National Equine Sales	Springfield	(513) 324-5558
Ohio Horseman's Council	Miamitown	(614) 833-1211

OKLAHOMA

Horsemen's Benevolent and Protective Association	Oklahoma City	(405) 427-8753
Oklahoma Horse Racing Commission	Oklahoma City	(405) 848-0404
Blue Ribbon Downs	Sallisaw	(918) 775-7771
Fair Meadows at Tulsa	Tulsa	(918) 743-7223
Remington Park	Oklahoma City	(405) 424-1000
Will Rogers Downs	Claremore	(918) 341-4720
Oklahoma Horsemen's Association	Oklahoma City	(405) 843-8333
Oklahoma Thoroughbred Association	Oklahoma City	(405) 840-3712
Heritage Place Sales Company	Oklahoma City	(405) 682-4551

OREGON

Horsemen's Benevolent & Protective Association	Portland	(503) 285-4941
Oregon Racing Commission	Portland	(503) 229-5820
Crook County Fairgrounds (Crooked River Roundup)	Prineville	(503) 447-6575
Eastern Oregon Livestock Show	Union	(503) 562-5828
Grants Pass	Grants Pass	(503) 476-3992
Harney County Fairgrounds	Burns	(503) 573-6447
Klamath County Fairgrounds	Klamath Falls	(503) 883-3796
Lone Oak Park/Salem	Salem	(503) 378-3247
Portland Meadows	Portland	(503) 285-9144
Oregon Horsemen's Association	Springfield	(503) 746-6564
Oregon Thoroughbred Breeders' Association	Portland	(503) 285-0658

PENNSYLVANIA

Horsemen's Benevolent & Protective Association	Grantville	(717) 469-2970
Horsemen's Benevolent & Protective Assn (Philadelphia Pk)	Bensalem	(215) 638-2012
Pennsylvania State Horse Racing Commission	Harrisburg	(717) 787-1942
Penn National	Grantville	(717) 469-2211
Philadelphia Park	Bensalem	(215) 639-9000
Pennsylvania Horse Breeders' Association	Kennett Square	(215) 444-1050
Fasig-Tipton Midlantic	Kennett Square	(215) 444-9000
Pennsylvania Equine Council	Kennett Square	(215) 444-5800

RHODE ISLAND

R.I. Dept. of Business Reg., Div. of Racing & Athletics	Providence	(401) 277-6541

SOUTH CAROLINA

South Carolina Department of Agriculture	Columbia	(803) 734-2210
Thoroughbred Association of South Carolina	Camden	(803) 432-6513
South Carolina Horse Council	Orangeburg	(803) 534-7312

SOUTH DAKOTA

South Dakota Racing Commission	Pierre	(605) 773-3179
South Dakota Horse Council	Brookings	(605) 693-3820

TENNESSEE

Tennessee State Racing Commission	Nashville	(615) 741-1952
Tennessee Department of Agriculture, Marketing Division	Nashville	(615) 360-0160
Tennessee Thoroughbred Owners & Breeders Association	Nashville	(615) 292-0245
Tennessee Breeders Sales Co.	Nashville	(615) 292-0245
Tennessee Horse Council	Nashville	(615) 297-3200

TEXAS

Horsemen's Benevolent & Protective Association	Aubrey	(817) 365-2441
Texas Horse Racing Association	Austin	(512) 480-8288
Texas Racing Commission	Austin	(512) 974-8461
Bandera Downs	Bandera	(512) 796-3081
Texas Thoroughbred Breeders' Association	Austin	(512) 458-6133
Texas Thoroughbred Breeders Sales Co.	Austin	(512) 458-6133
Thoroughbred Horsemen's Association of Texas	Bryan	(409) 822-1970

VERMONT

Vermont Racing Commission	Montpelier	(802) 828-3429

VIRGINIA

Virginia Racing Commission	Richmond	(804) 371-7363
Virginia Thoroughbred Association	Warrenton	(703) 347-4313
Virginia Horse Council	Riner	(703) 977-5707

WASHINGTON

Horsemen's Benevolent & Protective Association	Renton	(206) 228-3340
Washington Horse Racing Commission	Olympia	(206) 459-6462
Harbor Park	Elma	(206) 482-2651
Longacres	Renton	(206) 226-3131
Playfair Race Course	Spokane	(509) 534-0505
Sun Downs	Kennewick	(509) 582-5434
Walla Walla	Walla Walla	(509) 527-3247
Yakima Meadows	Yakima	(509) 248-3920
Washington Thoroughbred Breeders Association	Seattle	(206) 226-2620
Rainier Bloodstock	Enumclaw	(206) 825-3717
Washington Thoroughbred Breeders Sales Cooperative	Seattle	(206) 226-2620
Washington State Horse Council	Seattle	(206) 255-5892

WEST VIRGINIA

Horsemen's Benevolent & Protective Assn. (Charles Town)	Charles Town	(304) 725-7001
Horsemen's Benevolent & Protective Assn. (Mountaineer Pk)	New Cumberland	(304) 387-9772
West Virginia Racing Commission	Charleston	(304) 348-2150
Charles Town	Charles Town	(304) 725-7001
Mountaineer Park	Chester	(304) 387-2400
West Virginia Thoroughbred Breeders Association	Charles Town	(304) 725-3203

WISCONSIN

Wisconsin Racing Board	Madison	(608) 267-3291
Wisconsin State Horse Council	Madison	(414) 263-4303

WYOMING

Wyoming State Pari-Mutuel Commission	Cheyenne	(307) 777-5887
Central Wyoming	Casper	(307) 235-5775
Energy Downs	Gillette	(307) 682-0552
Sweetwater Downs	Rock Springs	(307) 382-7846
Wyoming Downs	Evanston	(307) 789-8873
Wyoming Horse Council	Douglas	(307) 358-2417

CANADA

The Jockey Club of Canada	Rexdale, Ont.	(416) 675-7756
Racetracks of Canada	Mississauga, Ont.	(416) 826-2520

ALBERTA

Alberta Racing Commission	Calgary	(403) 297-6551
Northlands	Edmonton	(403) 471-7379
Stampede Park	Calgary	(403) 261-0214
Canadian Thoroughbred Horse Society	Calgary	(403) 287-0960

BRITISH COLUMBIA

British Columbia Racing Commission	Burnaby	(604) 660-7400
Horsemen's Benevolent & Protective Association	Vancouver	(604) 984-4311
Exhibition Park	Vancouver	(604) 254-1631
Sandown Park	Sidney	(604) 386-2261
Canadian Thoroughbred Horse Society	Surrey	(604) 574-0145

MANITOBA

Horsemen's Benevolent & Protective Association	Winnipeg	(204) 832-4949
Manitoba Horse Racing Commission	Winnipeg	(204) 885-7770
Assiniboia Downs	Winnipeg	(204) 885-3330
Canadian Thoroughbred Horse Society	Winnipeg	(204) 832-1702

ONTARIO

Horsemen's Benevolent & Protective Association	Inglewood	(416) 675-3805
Horsemen's Benevolent & Protective Association (Eastern)	Rexdale	(416) 675-3805
Ontario Jockey Club	Rexdale	(416) 675-6110
Ontario Racing Commission	Toronto	(416) 963-0520
Fort Erie	Fort Erie	(416) 871-3200
Greenwood	Toronto	(416) 698-3131
Woodbine	Toronto	(416) 675-6110
Canadian Thoroughbred Horse Society	Rexdale	(416) 675-1370
Woodbine Sales	Rexdale	(416) 674-1460

QUEBEC

Quebec Racing Commission	Montreal	(514) 873-5000
Canadian Thoroughbred Horse Society	Montreal	(514) 333-6067

SASKATCHEWAN

Saskatchewan Horse Racing Commission	Saskatoon	(306) 343-9566
Marquis Downs	Saskatoon	(306) 242-6100
Canadian Thoroughbred Horse Society	Saskatoon	(306) 374-7777

PUERTO RICO

Puerto Rico Racing Sport Administration	San Juan	(809) 762-5210
El Comandante	Canovanas	(809) 724-6060
Puerto Rico Thoroughbred Breeders Association	Hato Rey	(809) 759-9991

Ft Lauderdale Times
Pompano - Sun
July 21, 1985   7/21

Dave Joseph

HORSE RACING

'Prediction' making fond memories for trainer and charity

There are fond memories, Janet DelCastillo says, but not many of victory.

Between bushtrack racing and bad breeding, DelCastillo, 40, has had little luck and fewer winners with the thoroughbreds she has trained.

After eight years, she can't recall any of her horses as "noteworthy. It seems they've always been bottom-of-the-line claimers."

In Winter Haven, where DelCastillo lives with her three children, the locals don't care a lot about horse racing. In February they turn their attention to the Boston Red Sox, headquartered there for spring training. The rest of the year Winter Haven is known as the home of Cypress Gardens.

But DelCastillo may yet change the way they think. In the middle of Winter Haven, on 12 acres, DelCastillo has what seems to be a legitimate stakes horse in First Prediction.

The horse has been in the money six of her 10 races, and in her last start finished second in a division of Calder's Gloxinia Stakes.

DelCastillo isn't the only one profiting from First Prediction's success. The Florida Horsemen's Children's Home in Ocala for "problem" boys and girls shares.

When Ed MacClellan of the children's home offered to sell DelCastillo the filly and another horse in March for a bargain-basement $5,000, DelCastillo didn't have the money.

"I was helping them with artwork at the school, and Ed asked if I wanted the two," DelCastillo said.

The horses had been donated to the school, and "he said that I could pay him when I had the money."

When First Prediction began earning some purse money, DelCastillo didn't forget. Now, every time First Prediction earns a check, the children's home gets a donation.

DelCastillo's odyssey began 10 years ago. Born and reared in San Francisco, she trained polo ponies until she joined the Peace Corps and went to Colombia, where she met her husband.

After living in Buffalo and Staten Island, the DelCastillos moved to Winter Haven and started racing horses.

"One day my husband said that we should get some race horses, so we got a few mares and we bred them," DelCastillo said.

"We raced [quarter horses] at Pompano, then we got thoroughbreds. But after putting around $16,000 into the horses we were lucky if they were running in $2,500 races at Tampa [Bay Downs]."

Finally, along came First Prediction, a 3-year-old by On To Glory-Around The Bend.

First Prediction is not a large filly, but she has showed enough to be considered a runner.

After breaking her maiden at Tampa Bay Downs in March, the filly has continued to improve.

After running respectably in two allowance races at Hialeah, the filly moved to Calder and finished second to C'Mon Liz in the Gloxinia two weeks ago.

Appearing to weaken after C'Mon Liz passed her entering the stretch over Calder's turf coure, First Prediction made a run at the victor in the closing yards to place.

In lieu of a track, DelCastillo has used her back yard. She builds her horses up with slow five-mile gallops through orange groves.

"It's really more like a trail," mostly heavy sand, which DelCastillo says builds up stamina.

"I think it's like a child," she said. "If you expose a horse to a lot of things, then it's only a question of speed. I think my training builds up a horse and makes it a stronger piece of equipment."

After building up the endurance and then testing her horses with intervals of speed workouts, she swims them in a mile lake behind her house, "sometimes two times a day if it's hot."

The rest of the time, DelCastillo quarters her horses in her eight-stall barn as little as possible.

"I think a horse needs sun and vitamin D," she said.

"Sure, mine have a few problems with some cuts and nicks they get on our fences, and their coats always look bleached, but their bodies are much more solid, and I've never had any tendon problems because of the long, slow foundation."

The foundation has been laid for Saturday's $50,000 Office Queen Stakes for 3-year-old fillies over Calder's 1 1/16-mile turf course.

"I really think we've got a chance," DelCastillo said. "All I've ever really wanted all these years was a horse I could throw in the van to race that I wasn't afraid was going to get claimed.

"I've waited a lifetime for this, and I may not get another chance."

So Friday Janet DelCastillo will van First Prediction the 4½ hours from Winter Haven to Miami in hope of winning the Office Queen.

There will be a lot of people pulling for DelCastillo, but none more than the boys and girls at the Florida Horsemen's Children's Home.

We didn't win the Office Queen Stakes — But we had fun trying!

260

Can nice girls finish first?
Calder race tells the story

By LUTHER EVANS
Herald Turf Writer

First Prediction held only a head advantage over charging Truly when they reached the eighth pole in Saturday's $47,650 Black Velvet Handicap before 9,884 fans at Calder.

On which filly would you have bet your money at that point?

Truly was the 2.20-1 favorite. She is is a daughter of the great stallion In Reality, bred by the eminently successful Frances A. Genter. She is trained by Frank Gomez, Calder's all-time-leading winner of stakes with 58. She was being ridden by Jose Velez Jr., Calder's 1985 riding champion with 109 winners.

First Prediction went off as a 15.30-1 long shot. She is a daughter of On to Glory and was bred by Paul Marriott, who culled her from his yearlings as being too small and gave her to the Florida Horsemen Childrens' Home in Citra, Fla. Later, Janet Del Castillo bought her on credit as part of a two-filly package for $5,000.

The primary training of First Prediction consists of Del Castillo, admittedly "a large woman," galloping her through a Winter Haven orange grove and also swimming the filly in a nearby lake. Saturday, First Prediction was being ridden as usual by Benny Green, a nice guy who has to scuffle to make a living ... unfortunate for a jockey with his ability.

At the sixteenth pole, First Prediction and Truly had swept past front-runner Merry Cathy and C'mon Liz and still were at each other's throats. Now, by all logic, you would have bet on Truly. Right?

Wrong.

First Prediction, under a super ride by Green, refused to yield more than a few inches in the drive and outgamed Truly by a nose to earn her first stakes victory.

"I knew she had the guts to do it," said Del Castillo.

But the first female owner-trainer to win a Calder stakes this season didn't come down to earth to analyze 4-year-old First Prediction's unexpected added-money triumph until 10 minutes after it had been accomplished. She had rushed onto the track, leaping high with every other stride, to hug Green and his mount before they got to the winner's circle. And all the time, she was whooping in sheer ecstacy.

Del Castillo was entitled. When Ed McCellan, the children's home director, decided that the home couldn't care for the fillies and offered to sell them to her, she tried to say no. "I was in the middle of a divorce, had four kids, and no money," she said. "But I couldn't resist buying them, if on credit."

The other filly never panned out, but before Saturday, First Prediction had earned $94,241 in 35 starts with a 6-8-7 record. And that had alowed Del Castillo to pay off the $5,000 debt last year. But she didn't stop there. Since then, every time First Prediction earns a check, the home gets a donation from her. The next contribution will be the biggest — First Prediction collected $29,790 in the Black Velvet.

First Prediction carried 114 pounds over the mile and 70 yards in 1:45 3/5 and paid $32.60, $10.20 and $5.20. Truly returned $3.60 and $2.60 and Hall The Lady $3.60.

End of an improbable — but heartwarming — report on a horse race.

23 in Desert Vixen

The six-furlong Desert Vixen, the opening test in the fifth annual Florida Stallion Stakes series, headlines the card at Calder today. It has been split into two divisions because of 23 entries.

Twelve 2-year-old fillies will compete in the first division and 11 in the second.

Ocali Gal, Rapturous and My Nicole are expected to be among contenders in the first division.

Allaise, a winner at Belmont Park, and Calder victors Blues Court and Jill Of All Trades head the second division.

Words Cannot describe The joy of this Win!

At Calder, 'Prediction' turns dream to reality

*Ft. Lauderdale Times
Pompano Sun
August 24 '86*

By DAVE JOSEPH
Racing Writer

MIAMI — Against all odds, dreams can still come true. Just ask Janet Del-Castillo.

Two years ago while visiting the Florida Horsemen's Children's Home in Citra, DelCastillo bought two horses on loan from the home's administrator Ed MacClellan for $5,000. One, an On To Glory filly named First Prediction, had been donated by breeder Paul Marriott so the home's neglected children could ride her for recreational purposes and later breed her, not to become a stakes-winning filly at Calder Race Course.

"I remember having no money at the time," DelCastillo recalled. "I didn't even know if I would be able to keep my farm (in Winter Haven) at that point. But a voice from heaven said, 'Take a shot.' I figured once she started winning I could pay the $5,000 off."

That's how sure DelCastillo was that First Prediction would not only become a winner, but a stakes winner. Some called her a dreamer, but DelCastillo wouldn't give in.

On her Winter Haven farm, she trained First Prediction through sandy trails of orange groves and took her for swims every day in a lake behind her farm

Despite everyone telling her that she had wasted her money — that you couldn't expect to win when you ship in overnight from a tiny farm to a major racetrack — DelCastillo dreamed on. And Saturday at Calder, her dream came true.

Racing third down the backstretch, First Prediction and jockey Benjamin Green came driving down the middle of the stretch to nose out Frances A. Genter's Truly to win the $47,650 Black Velvet Handicap.

A 15-1 longshot, 4-year-old First Prediction took the lead just past the eighth pole and held game while favorite Truly and jockey Jose Velez Jr., battled with her neck-and-neck to the wire. First Prediction covered the mile and 70 yards in 1:45 3/5.

First Prediction was second in an allowance race Aug. 15 at Calder. Instead of preparing her for the Black Velvet by galloping her as she usually does through the groves, DelCastillo prepped the filly with daily swims on the farm. During the day, DelCastillo turns First Prediction out in a pasture.

"It's a dream come true," said Del-Castillo, who danced for joy in the winner's circle after the race. "Today she

SEE **CALDER** / 14C

CALDER

FROM **PAGE 1C**

First Prediction turns dream to reality at Calder

just wouldn't give up.

"Everyone always told me you couldn't ship a horse in like this and win. But in this particular case, it's all worked."

DelCastillo's good fortune has also helped the children's home. After First Prediction's prior victories — she has won seven races and placed in 22 of 36 — DelCastillo has donated $1,000 to the home. "And you can bet they'll be getting another check tonight," she said.

Breaking fifth in the nine-horse field, Green moved First Prediction up along the rail around the first turn and settled into third going down the backstretch behind C'Mon Liz and Merry Cathy. It was an unusual move, because First Prediction's best running style is usually to close from well off the pace.

"I was closer than I expected to be today," Green said. "But she was running strong so I let her run."

While C'Mon Liz was setting fractions of 24, :48 2/5. First Prediction continued inching closer to the front. By the time Green hit the 3/8th pole, First Prediction was full of run, as was Truly, closing from sixth.

DelCastillo

"As we came around the 3/8th pole she was picking up horses and they weren't really moving away from her too much," Green said. "She just kept on going."

Two-wide entering the stretch, First Prediction took the lead from Merry Cathy at the eighth pole. A neck behind on the outside Truly was closing. But First Prediction would not give in. The filly continued on strongly in the last sixteenth and to the wire.

"I am so glad she is a legitimate horse," DelCastillo said. "I am so glad."

So is the Florida horsemen's Children's Home.

First Prediction paid $32.60, $10.20 and $5.20. Truly paid $3.60 and $2.60 and Hail The Lady, who closed from eighth, returned $3.60 to show.

262

Commoner almost dethrones royalty

By LUTHER EVANS
Herald Turf Writer

First Prediction, a racing commoner who works out in a Winter Haven orange grove, almost put the squeeze on aristocratic Fragrant Princess in Calder's $52,030 New Year Handicap before 12,267 fans Thursday.

First Prediction, purchased in a two-horse package for a mere $5,000 from the Florida Horsemen Children's School near Ocala two years ago, charged between horses in the final furlong but just missed catching winner Fragrant Princess by a head. But her rally from last place in the early going did enable her to finish one length ahead of Greentree Stable's Perfect Point, who had been expected by many to deprive Harper Stables' Fragrant Princess of her third consecutive victory.

Trainer Luis Olivares sprinted down from the fourth floor just in time to make the winner's circle. "I told you to expect me here because I was here after Powder Break won the La Prevoyante last Jan. 1," he said. "I like to start every year in a big way. And I think my Flying Pidgeon will win the W.L. McKnight Handicap at 1½ miles on Wednesday, closing day."

Olivares has gone on from such January success to earn the title as South Florida's outstanding trainer of the past two winter seasons. "I believe that three is an even better number," he said.

Fragrant Princess carried 116 pounds over the nine furlongs in 1:55 and paid $8.60, $5 and $4.60. First Prediction (113 pounds) returned $6 and $3.60. Regal Prin-

cess, whom trainer Jose "Pepe" Mendez had sharp enough to lead most of the way under Walter Guerra, paid $3.80.

Fragrant Princess disposed of Regal Princess and Donna's Dolly inside the eighth pole and seemed to have matters in hand when First Prediction began her powerful bid that made the finish exciting.

There is financial parity today between Fragrant Princess, a 4-year-old Diplomat Way filly, and First Prediction, a 5-year-old On To Glory mare. Fragrant Princess' $34,150 purse increased her earnings to $163,531. First Prediction's $9,050 second-place money increased her winnings to $152,464.

And who, you may ask, is nervy enough to get aboard First Prediction and gallop her through an orange grove? Owner-trainer Janet Del Castillo, that's who.

The Jan. 1 crowd wagered $1,722,256.

third-place Regal Princess.

Julio Pezua, who rode First Prediction for the first time for trainer Janet Del Castillo, thought that jockey Heriberto Valdivieso had allowed Fragrant Princess to drift in and shut off his gray mount late in the drive. Stewards studied race films and decided that the winner had been clear when she lugged in and did not force Pezua to check the runner-up.

It was a good horse race. And it probably would have been even better except for heavy early-morning rain bringing five scratches after the 1⅛-mile test had been taken off the turf course. Included among the defectors was

This was amusing!

The story covered the horse that lost more than the horse that won!

263

Tale of Gift Horse
And Home for Kids

Lew Zagnit / TAMPA BAY

OLDSMAR, Fla.—You take a horse with a broken leg, add a trainer, a divorcee trying to make it on her own, and tie in a home for dependent children, and what have you got? No, not a remake of "Annie Meets National Velvet." You have the Gold Coup—Janet del Castillo—Florida Horsemen's Children Home story, which is being played out at this meeting. You can catch the latest installment of this real life melodrama on Saturday, when del Castillo runs Gold Coup in a $5,000 claiming race here.

Now a little background on the cast. "The Florida Horsemen's Children's Home offers long-term residential care for neglected and dependent children; children from families with problems or whose parents are divorced," explained director Ed MacClellan, when contacted by phone at the Florida facility.

MacClellan had for 12 years served as the director of the Rodeheaver Home, a boys ranch in Putnam. Thus he was an obvious selection when people within the horse industry here, particularly Joe Durkin of the Florida Horse Magazine, decided there was a need for a similar facility in Marion County.

"We started raising money four years ago, and George Steinbrenner, through his New York Yankee Foundation, gave us a grant for one half of the land purchase. We raised the other half by donations. We do not receive any government funds. We are supported entirely by donations.

"We turned 1-year-old in November," said MacClellan. "We have one cottage for 12 kids, 60 acres of land, and 15 head of horses. Our staff consists of one set of cottage parents and a relief set of cottage parents, one of whom doubles as a secretary. We also have a thrift store in Ocala.

"We have paddocks for the horses, but no barns, but we are trying to raise funds to build barns."

Part of the support the horsemen contribute comes in the form of horses who are donated for the children to take care of or, if possible, are sold to race, which is how del Castillo became involved.

A couple of years ago, she paid $5,000 for two thoroughbreds who had been donated to the home. One of them just recently broke his maiden, but the other one turned out to be a pretty good runner. He name is First Prediction, and the 5-year-old On to Glory mare just went over the $170,000 mark in earnings with a second in an allowance race at Hialeah last Saturday.

First Prediction, who was donated by breeder Paul Marriott, has been a steady and useful campaigner partly by design, and possibly partly due to a mistake by del Castillo, who took out her trainer's license three years ago after she and her husband were divorced.

"I think part of the reason she's so strong," said del Castillo, the mother of three teenaged children, "is that I never start my horses until they're 3-years-old. And, when I was galloping First Prediction around the orange grove I thought I was going three miles a day, but I was actually going closer to five and a half.

"She was the first one I got from the children's home. They've gotten wonderful support from the horse community, certainly from Clayton O'Quinn, and Helmuth Schmidt. I've worked with them the most at picking up the horses that were donated, trying them out and either getting rid of them, or trying to run them. And Gold Coup, who was donated by Evelyn Poole, was the first one good enough to run in the childrens home's name.

"I got him sometime in the middle of last summer "continued del Castillo, who spent time serving in the peace corps." He had a fractured cannon bone, and was very body sore. The first thing I did was bring him home, geld him, and turn him out. Then I started long slow gallops. I tried him a few times in Miami, but I think he was just tuning up, and he's gotten better since. He's been on the board or won every race he's been in since."

Gold Coup is owned in partnership with the children's home, (even through the children, who are of course minors, are not allowed at the track due to state law) and del Castillo's mother and stepfather. Thus half the money the 5-year-old Gold Stage gelding makes, which totals about $4,000 so far, goes to support the home.

And the best thing about this story is there's no happy ending, just a happy continuation.

C. V. B. Cushman Dead; Rode in '30 Carolina Cup

RANCHO PALOS VERDES, Cal.— Charles V. B. Cushman, who rode in the inaugural running of the Carolina Cup Steeplechase in 1930, died here on January 13 at the age of 84, it was learned Thursday. He was one of four generations of the Cushman family to participate as amateur and professional riders.

Mr. Cushman, whose grandson, John, won the Carolina Cup in 1982 aboard Quiet Bay, operated Eastland Farm Stable and campaigned stakes winners. In 1928 he paid a then record yearling price of $75,000 for New Broom, a Whisk Broom II colt. He is survived by his widow, Elizabeth; two sons, two daughters, 14 grandchildren and eight great-grandchildren.

Leading Filly
and Mare Earners

(Includes horses who have started at least once in North America. Lifetime earnings of horses who have raced in foreign countries are included through the date of last start in North America.)

(Includes Racing of January 18)

This was another horse I got from the Childrens' Home

He went to Canada and I lost track of him !

Daily Racing Form Jan 31, 1987

264

Art Grace

Horse racing

Gulfstream announcer and his memorable goof

I have listened to a lot of track announcers (Hialeah's Tom Durkin, a notable exception) mangle a lot of pronunciations, but my favorite is the most recent, by Gulfstream's Ross Morton.

As far as I know, there is only one way to pronounce "benign." It has to rhyme with fine. Unless it is Morton's interpretation of the 4-year-old filly Benign Begum.

When she ran at Gulfstream the first time on March 20, I thought I must have been fantasizing when I heard Morton refer to her, throughout the seven-furlong race, as, so help me, "Bennigan Begum." (He also mispronounced "Begum," but that's understandable.)

Nah, it couldn't be. I decided to wait until Benign Begum ran back in order to make sure I had not been hallucinating. She finally showed up again in the first race last Sunday. And sure enough,

Grace

Morton called her "Bennigan Begum" with every rundown as the field plodded its way through the mile and a sixteenth.

I think I'll go out for dinner tonight ... for a hamburger and fries at that popular restaurant on 163rd street. You know the one I'm referring to: Benign's.

* * *

Apparently, I am not the only race track person to have been smitten by Patty Smyth's new solo album, especially the title song, "Never Enough."

Janet Del Castillo, a very nice lady who owns and trains First Prediction, has decided that "never enough" is the way to handle her horse. A more appropriate theme would be "enough is enough."

First Prediction, a 5-year old mare, has been one of my favorites for a long time. She is, or rather was, a stone closer who made a big run virtually every time.

I liked her a lot when Bennie Green was riding her at Calder last year and positively loved her when Julio Pezua got the mount beginning Jan. 1 this year. It was a perfect marriage, a closer with a

great finishing rider.

She just missed in the New Year's Handicap at Calder, at 7-1, and won at 8-1 at Hialeah nine days later. She then finished second in the Bal Harbour and third, beaten a neck and a nose to Anka Germania and Chaldea, in the Columbiana. Next time out she closed big again to finish second in the Key Largo.

At that point she had to be considered an iron horse, the Margaret Thatcher of Florida racing. She already had run five times in six weeks in 1987 after a very rigorous campaign in 1986.

She was back in one week later at Tampa Bay and finally the regimen caught up with her. She finished fifth, beaten 14½ lengths.

Undiscouraged, DelCastillo vanned her back to Hialeah for the Black Helen two weeks later. First Prediction never got out of a gallop, finishing 11th.

I got the message loud and clear two weeks later at Gulfstream when First Prediction turned back to seven furlongs and finished a weak fifth. When she failed to fire going short I knew the romance was over between us.

When she showed up still again, just eight days later in the Suwanee River Handicap, I wasn't about to bet on her. She finished fifth.

Surely Del Castillo would give her a rest now? Yeah, three whole days. Four days later First Prediction was in the Rampart Handicap, in body but not in spirit. She was last all the way, finishing 16 lengths behind the next to last horse.

First Prediction is nominated for Saturday's mile-and-a-half Orchid Handicap and next Wednesday's seven-furlong Old Hat Handicap. She will warm up for those stakes today in the ninth race, an allowance feature at a mile and a sixteenth on the grass. Unless 20 races in 29 weeks prove a mite debilitating, I'm sure she will be able to make the Orchid and Old Hat.

I went through the same depressing experience with another personal favorite, Command Attention, owned and trained by Nathan Kelly. Command Attention hasn't been around much lately but his last start, at Gulfstream March 26, was the 140th of his career.

The 9-year-old gelding was running in

stakes races two years ago. I will never forget the afternoon in October, 1985, when he won an allowance race on grass at Calder by a nose and paid $59.80.

How sad it was to see him running for a $5,000 claiming price at Tampa last December, finishing seventh, 15 lengths behind Spindle City.

He raced only 16 times last year because he had to laid up from July to December. But if he could make it to the paddock he didn't miss any dances in previous four years. He ran only nine times as a 2 year old and only 13 times at 3. But from 1982 through 1985, he maintained a twice-a-month schedule without buckling.

If he was a cat I'd take him home and let him enjoy the good life.

First Prediction already has matched Command Attention's busiest year — 27 starts in 1983. She equalled that total last year and is well on her to surpassing it this year.

More's the pity. Horses are not machines, but sometimes they are treated as though they were.

[handwritten:] This article was a complete surprise to me — I had arrived at the track the night before and I was never interviewed.

[handwritten:] Read on → the next days article tells "The Rest of the Story!"

265

Racing Green

Art Grace

Horse racing

April 17, 1987

Del Castillo has a right to feel wonderful

Grace

In this column yesterday, I excoriated owner-trainer Janet Del Castillo for what I considered poor, and possibly abusive, management of her horse First Prediction. After running extremely well against top competition all winter, the 5-year-old mare appeared to have been ground down by an exhausting schedule — 20 races in 28 weeks.

I was moved to voice my displeasure when First Prediction ran three times in 12 days at Gulfstream, twice in major stakes, and had run five very poor races in a row. Immediately before going off form, First Prediction had finished third, beaten a neck and a nose, to top fillies Anka Germania and Chaldea in the Columbiana at Hialeah Feb. 1 and two weeks later came from last to finish second to Singular Bequest in the Key Largo.

Then came five terrible races, the most recent in the Rampart Handicap April 5. But there are two sides to most stories and Miss Del Castillo surely was entitled to present a defense. She came to see me yesterday and did so, an hour before First Prediction ran still again in the ninth race which, to Janet's discomfiture, had been switched from grass to dirt.

"I know it looks terrible on paper," she said. "All people see is that she ran on March 24 and April 1 and April 5. What they don't realize is that I can't ever work this mare like a normal horse.

"Every time I try to work her, she ties up (suffer severe cramping). If I let that happen, it takes two months to get her ready to run again. So I never work her. She has to run at least every 10 to 14 days. If she's off longer than that I have to start from scratch again.

"If I ever felt she had a physical problem, if she ever went off her feed, I'd stop on her immediately. She's like a part of my family . . . she's in our yard (Del Castillo lives in Winter Haven) when she's not running. I could never abuse her. She's absolutely sound.

"She's been running poorly, but I've been trying to get her back into her rhythm. I know it looks bad when she runs in a tough race like the Rampart with only three days rest. What they'd never understand is that I needed that race to get her back to her optimum form. Not many people use a $125,000 stakes as a work, but I did. I never was able to be very subtle.

"She's been acting just fine; I expect she'll run well today. If it hadn't been taken off the grass I'd really like her . . . she doesn't seem to like dirt. But I still expect her to run a whole lot better.

"After what you wrote in the paper today, I hope the people don't throw rocks at me when I go to the paddock. If she runs bad again, I'd consider resting her until Calder opens (in six weeks)...which would mean it would take me four races to get her ready again. That's something I can't really afford to do.

"If I had to choose yesterday to lambaste Miss Del Castillo, at least my timing was exquisite. First Prediction was so utterly worn out that she came from next to last on the backstretch and wore down front-running Bereavement in the last 50 yards to win the mile and a sixteenth allowance feature by a length, Julio Pezua, of course, rode her flawlessly.

After the race, Miss Del Castillo could not resist rushing to the press box and tell me, "I told you so."

Well, indeed she had. Practically everyone except Janet had agreed with my criticism, but I'm the only one who went public with it. She had a right to rub it in. It was the least she could do.

"I feel wonderful, it's such a relief to know I wasn't wrong," she said. "For a while I was starting to doubt myself."

Before the race Janet had felt First Prediction could not run well on dirt 'except for Calder (which has a unique racing strip). She was running super on grass down here, then I made the mistake of running her at Tampa (seven days after the Key Largo at Hialeah).

"She didn't like the track and didn't fire (finishing a bad fifth). When she ran back in the Black Helen it was against killers and she was widest of all in a 15-horse field into the first turn. She didn't have a chance.

"At that point, I had to try and get her back into her rhythm. I ran her seven furlongs and she did close ground. But she couldn't handle those fractions, :22, :44 and change, 1:10. And she didn't like the dirt. The only place to run her next was the grass stake at Gulfstream (Suwanee River) and the fractions were so slow she couldn't make up ground.

"With a horse like her, who comes from way out of it, things have to break right (a realistic early pace by the speed horses) for her to run well. But I felt she needed that race, and one more, to reach her level of competence.

"The reason I ran her back four days later (in the $125,000 Rampart Handicap) is that I got suckered into it. Just before the entries closed, they called me and said only four horses were entered. It turned out to be seven.

"I told Pezua not to abuse her if she didn't have a shot. The pace was slow again and he realized there was no point beating on her.

"It's no fun to have to train her in front of everybody in the afternoons. She has to get her works in her races. She doesn't do well in a stall.

"I have her in a normal environment at Winter Haven, in cycle with nature. She's out in the pasture every day, in the sunshine, not locked in a stall. She swims every day. That's it.

"A horse can't talk to you; you have to go by your perceptions. I can tell you she hasn't gotten sour in two years; she's never refused to eat up. She's like a working man who puts on his hard hat and goes to work every day. 'Another day, another dollar.'

"If the race sets up right (with early speed) she'll be there. If it doesn't, she won't. If I can run her with no more than 10 to 14 days between races, I don't have to be concerned about not working her. If it's 20 days I fall two races behind with her.

"It's tough when I have to keep running her in stakes but it's the only way to keep her in her rhythm.

"Most people have no idea how tough this game can be. They've never had to load a hysterical 2-year-old filly on a van at 5 in the morning and take her to Tampa to work."

First Prediction ran 19 times in 1985, 24 times last year, and already has run 11 times this year. She has finished in the money in 32 of those 54 starts, winning nine. She went over the $200,000 mark in earnings with a $13,200 winner's purse yesterday.

While I still have reservations with Miss Del Castillo's handling of First Prediction, she aced me in straight sets yesterday and the overall results have been good.

Last year at Hialeah First Prediction ran twice in five days and finished second both times. She ran at Calder Aug. 2, 15 and 23 and won twice and finished second once.

Before the slump hit late in February this year the mare ran eight times in 2½ months and every race was a corker. After her performance yesterday, I doubt she ever will break down. Her career will end when the iron starts to rust.

266

Racing Daily Form

Copyright © 1987 by Daily Racing Form, Inc. All rights reserved.

VOL. 17. No. 130   HIGHTSTOWN, N.J., SUNDAY, MAY 10, 1987   PRICE $2.00

Fieldy Heads Gulf's Very One

HEADLINES and Front Page on Racing FORM! Guess WHO WON? "...Not Fieldy!"

By WILLIAM C. PHILLIPS

GULFSTREAM PARK, Hallandale, Fla.—Arriola and Seltzter's Fieldy, an Irish-bred 4-year-old who dead-heated for win with Fama in a division of the Grade III Suwannee River Handicap on turf April 1 and then was unplaced in the Grade II Orchid 'Cap on grass April 18, heads a field of 11 fillies and mares entered for the inaugural running of the $62,700 The Very One Handicap, which features a Mother's Day card here Sunday.

The race will be decided at a mile on the turf for a winner's prize of $37,620.

Craig Perret will return from the North to ride Fieldy at topweight of 115 pounds.

Janet del Castillo's First Prediction, a winner of her last two starts, is next in the weights at 114, with leading jockey Julio Pezua back in the saddle.

The field is completed by J. Robert Harris Jr.'s Thirty Zip, 113, Earlie Fires; J. C. Dudley's Tri Argo, 112, Robert Lester; Barbara Hunter's Duckweed, 111, Jose Velez Jr.; Mike J. Doyle and Sherry Farm's Miss Enchanted, 111, Steve Gaffalione; Southlake Stable's Lady of the North, 110, Pezua on another call; Dana S. Bray Jr.'s Evening Bid, 110, Santiago Soto; Buckram Oak Farm's Royal Infatuation, 110, Constantino Hernandez; Joanne and R. Thornton's Tuscadoon, 108, Mike Lee, and Mrs. Henry D. Paxson's Lustrous Reason, 108, James Reed.

Fieldy showed her class in France as a 2-year-old by winning the Group I Marcel Boussac at Longchamp. She was off form for three other races in France as a 3-year-old, but trainer Steve W. Young reports that whatever her problem was, it no longer exists. His statement is supported by her two winning races and a close second in her United States race this year. Fieldy was not a factor in the Orchid, but that race was at a mile and a ha'f, and Young described the race as "an experiment" to see whether she could handle the distance.

"She couldn't," he said, "but the mile will suit her fine."

First Prediction has gained a large following on the story how she was a yearling purchase from an orphanage home near Ocala and is trained by her owner in an orange grove next to a lake in Winter Haven. The attractive 5-year-old gray mare by Or to Glory has come from off the pace for a number of top efforts on the turf, including a third in a three-way photo finish at

Hialeah this past winter with Anka Germania and Chaldea in the Grade III Columbiana Handicap, and a rousing two and one-half length tally on the grass her last start, beating Truly.

larry Geiger has found Thirty Zip performs best when her races are spaced a month apart and this event fits the schedule perfectly. She was fourth behind the crack filly Life at the Top in the Grade III Rampart Handicap that was run on the main track on April 5. Three weeks before that, she finished strongly at a mile on the turf and just missed catching Small Virtue in a division of the Joe Namath Handicap.

The 4-year-old Tri Jet filly also ran well on the grass at Calder last fall when third behind Anka Germania and Slew's Exceller in the Calder Breeders' Cup Handicap.

Prominent

First Prediction seeks third straight Florida win Sunday.

267

HORSE RACING

Photo/JIM RAFTERY

Thirty Zip (2) doesn't have enough zip to catch Julio Pezua and First Prediction Sunday.

First Prediction has enough gas to capture third straight victory

By FRAN LaBELLE
Staff Writer

HALLANDALE — The photos had been taken, horse and jockey dutifully kissed and Janet Del Castillo was about to answer any questions about First Prediction's 2½-length victory in Sunday's $62,700 Very One Handicap at Gulfstream.

"Do you think we can tell her how we ran out of gas on the turnpike now?," said her son, Alex.

"Don't tell me any more," Del Castillo said.

As it turns out, Alex and his brother, Hernando, ran out of gas near the Pompano Beach exit of the turnpike Friday while shipping in First Prediction for Sunday's 1-mile turf test for older fillies and mares. After a 20-minute wait, the van was back on the road.

Fortunately, Del Castillo left the driving to Julio Pezua Sunday. This time, no one ran out of gas.

Pezua, whose victory was his second of the day and increased his record season's total to 75, got something extra from First Prediction in the stretch to get by J.R. Harris Jr.'s Thirty Zip. It was First Prediction's third straight victory, and it came before a Mother's Day crowd of 10,752.

"I had to lay up closer to the pace than usual because the race was only a flat mile," said Pezua, who stayed fourth behind Tri Argo, favored Fieldy and Tuscadoon until the stretch. "I saved all the ground I could and was able to get through inside. My horse made the lead in the stretch, but then the [Thirty Zip] went by here. When my horse saw that, she dug in and went ahead to win the race."

Del Castillo said her main worry was that the early fractions of :23 4/5, :41 1/5 and 1:11 1/5 would mean Pezua would have to use his mount earlier than he would like.

"It was a wild race," said Del Castillo, whose charge turned in a winning time of 1:35 1/5 for her second stakes victory. "But First Prediction's been knocking at the door. She's a game little thing, and God bless Pezua. He knew enough to keep her close."

First Prediction, a 5-year-old daughter of On To Glory-Around The Bend by Hagley, returned $7.80, $4.20 and $3.00.

It is also thought that Del Castillo will use part of the winner's purse of $37,620 to gas all of her vehicles.

NOTES: Pezua has been named on another stakes contender. He will ride Easter Mary for trainer **Sonny Hine** in Wednesday's $41,195 Honey Fox Stakes for 3-year-old fillies at a mile and a sixteenth... Gulfstream will offer simulcasting of the Preakness next Saturday.

268

Breeding Business: Romance and Glory

Racing Form

5/19/87

Bill Giauque / FLORIDA

OCALA, Fla.—Imagine, just to test your business sense, a smallish, late, gray 2-year-old filly. Consider also the parentage of this filly. She came into this world as the daughter of a modest but successful Florida sire and a more or less undistinguished dam.

Further imagine that the breeder, a man of means, donated the filly to a home for children, who, for one reason or another, need supervision from other than their parents.

The supervisor of this home, unable to get an offer of more than $500 for the filly and another home of similar origin and condition, finally sells the horses to a woman trainer for $5,000, to be paid whenever.

The new owner runs her horse operation with her three children. She is in the middle of a divorce, trains her horses in an orange grove and ships from the farm to the track to race, a four-and-a-half-hour trip, if the traffic is light.

Based on this scenario, would you predict success for the principals involved? If you said yes, you have the business sense of the man who bought a share in John Henry, the heart of a Hollywood movie producer and your address is the Magic Kingdom ... but you are right.

The stakes-winning filly, First Prediction, has earned owner-trainer Janet Del Castillo more than $200,000. She paid the Florida Horsemen's Children's Home for the two horses long ago, and according to Children's Home president Ed Mac Clellan, Del Castillo sends a check for $1,000 every time First Prediction wins a race. Not only that but breeder Paul Marriot got his tax writeoff for the donation, and he continues to receive Florida breeders' awards every time the filly wins.

"The most anybody offered was $500 apiece," MacClellan recalled. "I knew they were worth more than that, so I sold the package (to Del Castillo) for $5,000, but she didn't have to pay anything up front."

On the buying end of the transaction, Del Castillo remembered, "Ed McClellan called me, said he had two horses for sale. One was a May filly 14-months old. The Florida Horsemen's Children's Home didn't even have fences up yet. In the middle of trying to say, 'No,' this voice from above said. 'Shut up and take the horses'."

Because Del Castillo trains her horses long and slowly in the deep sand of the nearby orange grove, First Prediction was not rushed to the track at 2. Still, her training performance did not give rise to any burst of confidence in the trainer.

"She absolutely trained like a very, very ordinary horse," said the Winter Haven trainer. "I would never have said this one is going to be great. In fact, I offered another trainer a half-interest in her for $2,500. He didn't have any money, either."

Two years ago in February after First Prediction rolled up a couple of seconds and a third, an agent offered $25,000 for the filly. "When you get a horse for $2,500, and someone offers you $25,000, that is a lot of money," the owner said. "I went to the kids and everyone said, 'Oh, Mom, don't sell the filly'."

After the daughter of On to Glory broke her maiden at Tampa Bay Downs, Del Castillo shipped to South Florida for a crack at the big time.

"I was so stupid I didn't know you couldn't ship in and win," the unorthodox trainer said. "But she was fit and had a tremendous stretch run to win a $25,000 claiming race.

"I was going to put her back in a $35,000 claimer, but Roger McElhiney told me not to run for $35,000 or she'd get claimed. First Prediction ran third in an allowance race, and afterward someone offered me $50,000 so she probably would have been claimed away at the lower price. Every time I was going to lose her someone always helped me."

In all First Prediction has started 59 times with 11 wins and 14 seconds and earnings of more than $250,000.

In the latest chapter of this movie-like story, the gray filly defeated Thirty Zip in a thrilling stretch run in The Very One Handicap. "She was passed by Thirty Zip in deep stretch, and she came again to win," said Del Castillo with excitement still in her voice.

The owner's three helpers and children are Alex, 19; Hernando, 18; and Victoria, 15. The Very One Handicap was the first time the boys had been allowed to transport a horse five hours down the Florida Turnpike for a race. They made the trip the night before the race.

"In the winner's circle, my son turned to me and said he ran out of gas on the turnpike," Del Castillo revealed. "The gas gauge was not working right. Here the poor little filly is coming down to run in one of the biggest races of her life, and she is stuck on the side of the Turnpike."

First Prediction has given the woman from Winter Haven credibility and a belief in dreams.

"You must not ever forget," she explained, "there is serendipity in life. Getting this wonderful horse is the greatest thing that ever happened to me. She has made so much that it would be awful not to remember."

And the checks continue to arrive at the Florida Horsemen's Children's Home.

This is my favorite story!

269

'Prediction' Risks Skein In Gulf 'Cap

By WILLIAM C. PHILLIPS

URF AUTHORITY

Daily For

WEDNESDAY, MAY 20, 1987

GULFSTREAM PARK, Hallandale, Fla.—Janet del Castillo's First Prediction, who has become a favorite of Florida racing fans, seeks her fourth straight triumph in the second running of the $39,620 Candy Eclair Handicap here Wednesday. Six fillies and mares are entered to compete at a mile and a sixteenth for a winner's purse of $23,772.

The public has become enraptured with First Prediction's background: a yearling purchase from a home for orphans and wayward children near Ocala, trained in her owner's orange grove next to a lake in Winter Haven, and brought to the racetrack for her afternoon engagements in a van driven by Castillo.

The fans have been impressed, too, by Del Castillo's display of joyful emotions after she has saddled her mare for a winning race, and the apparent comaradarie she shares with Julio Pezua, the mare's regular rider this season.

First Prediction began her skein by beating Bereavement by a length in a mile and a sixteenth allowance race on April 16. She defeated Truly by two and a half lengths in a mile race on the grass May 1, and outgamed Thirty Zip by a nose in a dramatic stretch duel to capture The Very One Handicap at a mile on the turf nine days later.

A winner of 11 races in a career of 59 races, accruing $255,520 in purses, the 5-year-old gray daughter of On to Glory will carry 115 pounds.

Mr. and Mrs. Cleo Hall's 4-year-old Judy's Red Shoes, a multiple stakes winner, whose earnings total $269,349, is topweighted at 116 pounds. Santiago Soto will ride.

Ross Heritage Farm & Baird's Lady Vernalee, a winner of three straight, including the Sweetest Chant and Lady in Waiting handicaps, will carry 114 and Robert Lester will ride.

The field is completed by Frances A. Genter's Truly, 114, Jose Velez Jr.; R. & J. Thornton's Tuscadoon, 108, Mike Lee, and C. & E. R. Dixon's Warm and Soft, 107, Norberto J. Palavencino.

This will be the first race for Judy's Red Shoes since she was third in a division of the Joe Namath Handicap here at a mile on the grass March 15. She was the winner of a mile and a furlong overnight race on dirt in three starts at Hialeah this winter and won seven of 19 outings last season.

Lady Vernalee has been raced as a sprinter but the 4-year-old Hold Your Peace filly's recent performances have been so strong the stable decided to give her a shot at the longer distance. Tuscadoon is the only rival in this race with the speed to challenge her early, and if Lady Vernalee steals off to a long lead she could be hard to catch.

Santiago Soto
Has Mount in Gulf 'Cap

This is the day my filly came down with a virus, foundered and almost died!

It was a full year before she returned to race!

270

Mixing oranges and horses

Dick Evans

On the Money

The dew glistens atop the oranges as the sun rises. Suddenly, the birds stop chirping and the ground starts to shake. From around the bend come three thundering thoroughbreds in a race down the narrow lanes between the rows of heavenly laden trees.

For three miles, the horses maneuver the tight curves and straightaways through the groves around Winter Haven, Fla. Then, it's everyone in the lake for a cool dip.

Is this anyway to train thoroughbreds?

According to Janet Del Castillo, it's the best way.

"I raise them like I raised my three children,

Del Castillo

by using good old fashioned common sense," said Del Castillo, 43, a former Peace Corps volunteer who began training thoroughbreds fulltime four years ago. "I allow them to be horses, to do what comes natural. I put them in their natural environment so that they can frolic together, eat grass and definitely talk to each other.

"I tell them that I'll give them two weeks of devotion on the farm if they will give me two minutes of devotion on the horse track."

Del Castillo realizes most trainers and many owners laughed at her unorthodox training methods. "I would say the first couple years I was like the Country Bumpkin coming to the big city. I had no money at all and had to do everything myself.

"I know some veteran trainers were laughing and snickering. But I didn't care. When I was in the Peace Corps in Colombia, I taught the poor natives that they had to make do with what they had. I was in the same boat. I didn't look for excuses."

On her 14-acre farm outside Winter Haven, she built barns, a mini-paddock and make-shift starting gates. She did it all — training the horses, riding them, feeding them, swimming them, bathing them and doctoring them like her own children — with the help of her three children.

In 1976, all the hard work started to pay off. First Prediction, a $2,500 castoff who had been given to a children's home in Central Florida, proved that Del Castillo's methods worked during a Cinderella racing career that produced $270,000 in earnings. "First Prediction saved my farm, she was a heavenly gift,"

said Del Castillo. "When I was first galloping First Prediction through the orange groves, I thought I was going three miles a day, but I was actually going closer to 5½ miles."

Little wonder First Prediction went on to become known as the "Iron Maiden" with more than 70 career starts.

Make no mistake, Del Castillo trains her eight to 14 thoroughbreds each year to run forever.

"I like to have a solid foundation in my horses before I take them to a race track," said Del Castillo, who was born in Oregon but raised in San Francisco where she worked with polo ponies before joining the Peace Corps. "By working them three miles through heavy sand, up and down hills and around tight turns, I am building a racing machine. I don't believe in drugs, so when my horses reach a point where they want to tear through the three-mile course, then I know they're ready to go to the race track."

That presents another problem, getting them to the tracks in South Florida. And, often, it's not to race, but just to get work out of a real starting gate. "I don't mind the drive down," she says of the 220-mile trip. "It's something that has to be done."

It can seem a short trip home if her horse wins. "Nothing beats winning, nothing." It can be a very long trip home if her horse loses, or maybe doesn't even get into the race.

But the long and short of it is that Del Castillo believes in her method.

"I train a lot of young fillies, and

some are hyper and delicate and tend to tie up or get nervous when they run. But when they are home, they are with their friends and can talk and play together. It's not their natural life style to be cooped up at a track 24 hours a day. God meant for them to graze and to be moving all the time. I know it may sound silly, but I think it's important to let horses be horses."

Asked if she would like to become a conventional-type trainer, Del Castillo was quick with an emphatic "NO."

"But I would," she added, "like for owners to have enough confidence in me and my training methods to let me have their horses from age 18 months to 2½ for what I think is solid progressive type training. I also would love for an owner come to me and say, 'Here is $20,000 or $30,000, go out and buy me a good horse.'"

There is one point to her training methods that can not be overlooked. Even if her horses do not make the grade on race tracks, they do as family horses/pets. "They are raised in such a placid setting, they can do something else other than be race horses. So I always try to find them a nice home," she said.

And there is a personal benefit that would make her reluctant to trade places even with Hall of Fame trainer Woody Stephens.

"The best part of the day is working the horses," she said. "Tearing through orange groves is a fantastic ride through nature. It's thrilling, a natural high without doing drugs."

SEPTEMBER 1988
THE MIAMI HERALD

271

Racing *Daily* Form

Nine Clash at Gulf In F-M Turf Event

By WILLIAM C. PHILLIPS

GULFSTREAM PARK, Hallandale, Fla.—Cynthia Phipps' For Kicks, who was a good third behind a pair of stakes-winning rivals on the turf in her only race at the meeting, will be solidly supported in the wide-open betting field of nine older fillies and mares named to compete at a mile on the turf in the allowance feature here Thursday.

For Kicks was the pacesetter in a mile and a sixteenth race on the grass the opening day of the meeting, January 8, and held on gamely in the drive to be third behind Without Feathers and Vana Turns. Both of those fillies won on the grass in their next starts.

For Kicks was still a maiden and she tired after showing speed and finished unplaced when she first tried the grass in the third start of her career at Belmont Park last spring. The 4-year-old Topsider filly since then has won four of six races at distances from seven furlongs to a mile and a sixteenth on the dirt at Belmont Park, Aqueduct and Calder. She is trained by Angel Penna Jr. and is to be ridden by Jorge Chavez at 119 pounds.

She is opposed by Holly Ricon's Ana T., 122, Earlie Fires; D. E. Hager 2d's Stop and Smile, 119, no rider; and six contenders who are each to carry 115 pounds. They are M. Miller's Luckie's Girl, Jorge Duarte; Stanley M. Ersoff's Miss K. L. Taylor, Doug Valiente; Janet del Castillo's First Prediction, no rider; Firmanento Farm's Kalerre, also Valiente; T. Asbury's Bug Bug, no rider, and

Big Bucks Racing Stable's Lost Weekend, no rider.

Two of the rivals to For Kicks have shown speed on the grass at the meeting and can be expected to challenge her for the early lead.

Stop and Smile came back after tiring in her first start to lead from the start and to widen her margin to better than two lengths over a good allowance field in a mile and a sixteenth race on January 19. Incidentally, she was the first to win on the turf at Gulfstream this winter by leading from the start. The 6-year-old daughter of Libres Rib appeared to be overmatched in the first division of Saturday's Grade III Suwannee River and dropped back after showing early speed to finish last.

This will be the fifth race for First Prediction since she resumed racing in the fall. The 7-year-old On to Glory mare is a stretch runner and the class of the field going back a couple of years when she won two stakes on grass over this course.

Bug Bug was in front into the stretch run of a mile and a sixteenth race captured by the stakes filly Orange Motiff on grass here on January 29. She lost by a little more than four lengths and finished fifth. The 4-year-old Ginistrelli filly similarly held the early lead in the Atlantic City Oaks on turf last summer at Atlantic City and in the Tropical Park Oaks at Calder in the spring.

VOL. 19. No. 40   HIGHTSTOWN, N.J. THURSDAY, FEBRUARY 9, 1989

Edge?   First Prediction (middle), a stakes winner, may be the class of the filly-mare turf feature at Gulfstream. 272

First Prediction Tops F-M Feature On Grass at Gulf

By WILLIAM C. PHILLIPS

GULFSTREAM PARK, Hallandale, Fla.—First Prediction, a dappled gray 5-year-old who is owned and trained by Janet del Castillo, will attract the most attention when 10 fillies and mares go postward in the mile allowance feature on the turf here Friday. Another four are listed as also eligibles.

Del Castillo, who trains her horses under the orange trees at Winter Haven in the central part of the state and vans them to the track to race, entered her stakes-winning earner of $204,700 to carry 122 pounds. The mare will be piloted by her regular rider, Julio Pezua.

First Prediction, who obviously thrives on the unorthodox method of training, closed with characteristic speed in the final run and won a mile and a sixteenth race by a length last out on April 16. The race was transferred from the grass to the main track.

But she is also adept on the grass. This past winter at Hialeah she got up approaching the wire for a neck victory over Christmas Dancer, who will be one of her main rivals on Friday. She was beaten by the same short margin in a three-way photo with Anka Germania and Chaldea over the Hialeah turf course in a division of the Grade III Columbiana Handicap, and in her last start at that meeting she took second behind Singular Bequest on the grass in the Key Largo.

The others who drew into the field are J.S. Carrion's Christmas Dancer, 117, Earlie Fires; Dr. Keith C. Wold's Opera Diva, 122, Robert Lester; Cam M. Gambolatti's Stuttering Sarah, 122, no rider; Gladys Ross' Frau Agustina, 115, no rider; W.P. Sise's Lycka Dancer, 119, apprentice Jorge Milian; Gray and Yingling's Betsy Mack, 115, Robert Breen; Horse Haven's Social Occasion, 108, apprentice Jorge Santos; Virginia K. Payson's Imprudent Love, 117, Lester, and Frances A. Gen-

ter's Truly, 117, Jose Velez Jr.

The also eligibles are Wimborne Farm's Grande Couture, coupled as an entry with Imprudent Love, 115, Earlie Fires; Knoll Lane Farm's Tea for Top, 119, Mile Gonzalez; Peter Barbarino's Lucky Touch, 117, no rider, and Hardesty and Walden's Bereavement, 117, Fires.

Christmas Dancer, third and fourth in a couple of other turf races at Hialeah, comes off a sharp second to True Chompion at a mile on the grass here March 22. She held a daylight lead before she was overtaken by First Prediction in their previous meeting at Hialeah and she has the speed to either take the lead or be near the pace in this event. She is a 5-year-old daughter of Sovereign Dancer and trained by J. Bert Sonnier.

This will be the first race for Truly since the 5-year-old In Reality mare was second behind Algenib in a race taken off the turf and run at seven furlongs on a sloppy track March 24. She won four of 16 races in 1986, including the Impatiens and Vizcaya handicaps and lost the Black Velvet Handicap on the main track there to First Prediction by a nose in August.

273

Del Castillo's training style unorthodox

By Lisa A. Hammond
The Ledger

EAGLE LAKE — Most racehorses learn to run during one-mile jaunts within the confines of a racetrack. Janet Del Castillo's thoroughbreds train by galloping for three miles in the deep sand of an orange grove on her Rancho Del Castillo.

Her methods, including swimming the horses in Eagle Lake, are considered unorthodox.

"People feel sorry for me when I have to train on the farm and not at the track, but I wouldn't trade them," she said.

Her horses negotiate the sharp turns of the orange grove which, she says, makes the gradual curves of the race track a breeze.

"People say the sand will bow the horses' tendons, but my horses are very sound. Galloping through the deep sand and up the hills strengthens all of their muscles, and going around the sharp turns makes them surefooted," Del Castillo said.

The grove and ranch are located off of State Road 540 on Crystal Beach Road.

"I love the orange grove," she said. "To be able to support my family doing this is just heavenly."

She often treats herself to an orange plucked off a tree after she rides.

Del Castillo, 41, is a tall, stocky woman, who radiates strength. She has shoulder-length brown hair with a few streaks of gray. She seems very motherly and kind, especially to the horses, which she strokes with her large hands and calls her "little babies."

She began by training polo ponies when she was in high school.

"I started cleaning stalls so I would be allowed to gallop the polo ponies," she said.

Later her uncle, who owned a quarter horse ranch in Virginia, got her family involved with quarter horses, which she took to the Green Swamp for match races.

Her association with thoroughbreds began when her ex-husband, Dr. Hernando Del Castillo, acquired some.

"I watched how the trainer trained these horses and I couldn't believe that the horses could run. I think they really damage them structurally," she said. "I think they need a better foundation, which is why I train the way I do.

"I want to put guts in them," she said.

Trainer Dwaine Glenn of K-ville said Del Castillo's practices are based on a sound theory.

"Anytime you run a horse in deep sand like that, you're going to leg them up real well," Glenn said. "It's an endurance program — it does help them. I see nothing wrong with it."

Glenn said more orthodox methods are often used because the trainers don't have the facilities to train the horses any other way.

Del Castillo's horses do not get drugs, liniments, or leg wraps, all common practices in horse racing.

"If a 2-year-old needs leg wraps, he shouldn't be training," she said.

Janet Del Castillo, right, and Vicki Portlock, an exercise girl, run some horses through an orange grove on Del Castillo's ranch near Eagle Lake.

She has been training thoroughbreds for about 10 years and says experience has been a great teacher.

"I used to gallop them all the time," she said. "But I learned that no matter how fit they are, they won't run any faster than God will allow them to run. They won't run faster than their natural ability."

The proof, of course, is in the race results, and Del Castillo's evidence is First Prediction, a horse she refers to as "sweetness and light."

First Prediction, owned and trained by Del Castillo, is a 7-year-old gray mare who has won two stakes races. Only 3 percent of thoroughbreds ever win a stakes race.

"She is a dream come true. People wait for years for a stakes horse, and I never knew what I had," Del Castillo said. She bought the delicate mare, which is gray with dark flecks, from a children's home for $2,500. First Prediction has won more than $270,000.

First Prediction has displayed heart, a racehorse's most elusive quality, in both her racing style and in coming back from injuries.

"One time she started at 26 lengths behind, and ended up losing by three lengths," Del Castillo said.

First Prediction has also had to recover from physical setbacks.

"She had a bone chip in her knee from being kicked in the pasture, and then she got a virus and foundered (an inflammation of the tissue that attaches foot to hoof)," Del Castillo said. "People said she would never race again."

First Prediction's rehabilitation took place in Eagle Lake. Del Castillo would attach a long lead to the horse's halter and stand on a dock while the horse paddled around in the lake. Swimming exercised the horse without straining her sore feet and legs.

"She loves to swim now. Sometimes she'll lay over on her side and just float," Del Castillo said.

First Prediction returned to dry land to win several races at Gulfstream Park, including a stakes race, the Very One Handicap, which took place on Mother's Day of 1988. Del Castillo said that race was especially meaningful to her.

"She is really my baby, and it was wonderful to win a stake on Mother's Day," she said.

First Prediction now is trained almost exclusively by swimming because galloping causes her muscles to "tie up." The small, sprightly mare, who looks more like a pet than a racehorse, has won 12 races in her long career, including a $30,000 allowance race on Feb. 21 at Gulfstream.

She races most often at Gulfstream, Calder and Hialeah, where she is viewed as an underdog.

"Whenever I haul this horse down to Miami, they think she's a pony horse," Del Castillo said.

Del Castillo uses a chart to keep track of the 12 to 15 horses she trains. Assistant Eric Low, two exercise riders, and Del Castillo's children, Nando, 20, and Victoria, 17, help out at the ranch.

Most of the other horses Del Castillo trains run in claiming races at Tampa Bay Downs.

"First Prediction is the only big-league horse I've had," she said.

Lisa Hammond was an intern for The Ledger during the winter months. She is a student at Northwestern University in Evanston, Ill.

a nice Background story!

274

Tampa Bay

Training in the Orange Groves

I magine this scenario, if you will:

You're sitting on a beautiful bass lake in central Florida, casting artificial worms and crank baits against the cattails while in search of that trophy largemouth. The lake is all but deserted.

You're 90 miles from Ocala, 50 miles from Tampa Bay Downs and more than 200 miles from Miami. The furthest thing from your mind is horses and horse racing.

But suddenly you hear a sound, a familiar sound you've heard a hundred times before. It starts as just a murmur, but in a matter of moments it grows louder and more distinct.

It's the sound of horse's hooves, and from the pattern of the sound, it's obvious these horses are in a strong gallop or are working. You look around for a training track, for some sign of a racing strip, but all you see are orange trees.

After some investigation you find out that you had indeed heard race horses at work and that those charges came from the Rancho Del Castillo, a unique training facility located high on a hill overlooking Eagle Lake and the surrounding rolling landscape of central Florida.

JANET DEL CASTILLO
An off-beat trainer

The story of Rancho Del Castillo and it's master, Janet Del Castillo is one well worth repeating.

From the Peace Corps to the Race Track

It seems that many years ago a young Peace Corps volunteer found herself in the wilds of Columbia. While working with the natives there, she met a doctor who she later married. The couple eventually settled in Winter Haven. The husband wanted some race horses so they went into business the usual way, by contacting a trainer and buying some stock.

"To make a long story short," continues Janet Del Castillo, "the horses were soon beat up and injured from racing and wound up on the farm here. My husband wanted to get rid of them but I persisted, stalling him for a time.

"After he went to work I would work with the horses, learning as I went along. I snuck them over to the track to work once they were recovered, hurrying back before my husband got home."

Although the marrriage failed to survive, Del Castillo's interest and love for thoroughbreds not only lived, it blossomed. Using training methods and philosophies considered radical and outlandish by many of her peers, Del Castillo went about training and developing horses the way she wanted to, with only a modicum of success.

Then along came First Prediction. "I got her from the Children's Home, believe it or not," the trainer recalled. "They had two fillies they couldn't keep and I took them both for $5,000 on the cuff."

That modest purchase went on to become a top stakes and handicap distaffer for Del Castillo, earning more than $260,000 during her career and recently came back from a bout with founder to race again with top grass company at Gulfstream Park.

Developing Sound, Healthy Horses

And where did the pounding hooves come from?

"I gallop my horses through an orange grove," Del Castillo explained. "It's exactly one mile around, with a half mile stretch where we cluck 'em and let them work."

Del Castillo calls her training style the "Montessori school of horse training" and her horses are permitted to develop at their own individual pace. She doesn't race horses at two and admits it takes her charges several races to acclimate themselves to racing once their careers start.

"Because I'm here on the farm I can take my time with my horses. I don't believe in pushing young horses and I believe the results speak for themselves. I rarely use medications, hardly ever have a horse on Lasix and I don't believe I've ever had a horse of mine bow a tendon.

"Here at the farm they're allowed to graze in the paddocks, we swim them in the lake after training and we do everything to give them a natural environment.

"I substitute time, patience and healing powers Mother Nature has given the horse over speed, medications and shortcuts. I know one thing: I develop sound, healthy race horses. We may train in the groves but it's training all the same."

━━━━━━ Doug McCoy

Doug McCoy is RACING ACTION's Tampa Bay correspondent.

The View From *Racing Action May 20 ot*

Florida

First Prediction Makes Grade

T his is the tale of a woman and a horse.

It is also the tale of good things coming to those who do things, "my way" and the "hard way."

Best of all, it is the story of charity, the good side of horse racing, the nice people involved and their rewards.

The woman raised in San Francisco during the 1950s always loved horses. She cared for and trained polo ponies in Northern California while growing up. She joined the Peace Corps in the mid-1960's, served in the proverty of South America doing whatever she could.

In fact, it was while there that she met her husband and aided him delivering babies by candlelight in Columbia. Her name is Janet Del Castillo.

The horse is a mare. A gray mare foaled in 1982 by On To Glory out of the Hagley mare Around The Bend. She was just another one of the yearlings in breeder Paul Marriott's large operation and when the herd was culled, her destiny was to be donated as a yearling to the Florida Children's Home in Cintra, Florida. Her name is First Prediction.

JANET DE CASTILLO
Trains in groves

Dr. Hernando Del Castillo and his family returned to the United States and bought a farm, Rancho Del Castillo, in Winter Haven, Florida and went into the thoroughbred business with the expectations of raising a champion. Janet took out a trainer's license, but there were no champions.

"When the horses (they were just cheap claimers) did not win the Kentucky Derby right away, my husband lost interest in racing," she said. "But we had over $25,000 invested and I didn't want to give up just like that."

Then she got a break.

While working at the Florida Children's Home, still helping others, she spotted a gray yearling filly that she thought might have some ability on the race track and invested in her and took her back to her farm in Winter Haven. The filly was First Prediction.

First Prediction's road to success has not been traditional; uncoventional would be more apt.

"I can train horses in an orange grove," Janet said, "and have them as fit as any that train at the race track."

First Prediction's success story on the track is just as unbelievable. She could really be called the "Iron Mare," for in nearly 60 starts, she has earned over $250,000 and done it the hard way—on the rubber-based strip at Calder, the main tracks at Gulfstream and Hialeah, and the grass courses of all three South Florida race tracks.

Her most recent string of wins began in an even more bizarre manner. It seems Gulfstream Racing Secretary Tommy Trotter was having a tough time filling the Rampart Handicap because no one wanted to challenge Wayne Lukas' Life At The Top and Woody Stephens' I'm Sweets. He approached Del Castillo, and though she had another race in mind for First Prediction, she said that she would be there.

When we questioned her on why she accepted this spot she responded, "Did you ever hear of a trainer using a handicap race as a tightener for an allowance race?"

Unfortunately, everything did not go right, as First Prediction did not reach a contending position for her patented late charge and trailed throughout.

But 11 days later, she made the six-hour van trip from Winter Haven down to Gulfstream and won an allowance race.

Then on Mother's Day, after a lengthy van trip, First Prediction—under the brilliant handling of Julio Pezua—was up to win The Very One Handicap by a nose at one mile on the turf.

As First Prediction came back to the winner's circle, hundreds of fans circled around and cheered the winning horse, jockey and owner in a display of emotion most befitting the holiday.

Oh yes, in a story with a happy ending such as this, what began as a charitable venture continues on that way. That's because Janet Del Castillo makes a donation to the Florida Children's Home after every win.

━━━━━━ Derk Ackerman

Racing Action Contributing Writer

Peace Corps Service In Trainer's Past

By Graham Ross

OLDSMAR — The first thing that Tampa Bay Downs trainer Janet Del Castillo projects is a free spirit. She is a happy soul but one with a sense of adventure — a trait perhaps first noted on Nov. 18, 1963, when she left her San Francisco upbringing on a trip to Kansas City as a Peace Corps volunteer.

Four days later President John F. Kennedy was shot, and a lot of other dreams died for a lot of other children of the '60s, but Del Castillo was one of those who kept the flame burning — serving honorably in the most rural area of Colombia, dependent on villagers for all human contact and existence itself.

"You learned to depend on others — and they on you — for everything that kept us all alive. If you didn't learn to speak the language you didn't eat, so you learned quickly, but you also learned to deal with things at their simplest level," Del Castillo now recalls. "Basically it was the 'in-order-to-make-lemonade-you-start-with-lemons' kind of lesson in life repeated throughout the two years I was there.

"But I also learned not to be so quick to judge other people's way of doing things while I was in Colombia. You'd start to build a roof on a hut and the villagers would tell you to wait until the moon was right — and if you resisted the temptation to scoff, you could learn that sap flows better when the moon is right, and would help hold the roof in place."

But while in Colombia Del Castillo met and married a doc-

tor, returned to this country, and mostly through her husband's initiative, became involved with thoroughbreds at their farm in Winter Haven. When the marriage failed, Del Castillo became a horse trainer by default, using training methods as unorthodox as her Peace Corps past and her life with the villagers.

"I take my horses on three-mile gallops through the orange groves overlooking Eagle Lake," Del Castillo offers, as one of her training exercises, and I find that the middle mile is the hardest. That middle mile is pretty much tells me a lot about each horse — whether or not they are going to want to go that third mile"

Another somewhat unusual training regimen — swimming her horse in Eagle Lake after training — led to an unusual experience for one of her three children, who range in age from 21 to 17 years old. "My kids always helped with the training of the horses from the time they were 14. They did everything. No matter what, they pitched in," Del Castillo now recalls.

"For some reason, my son always wanted to be one of those smiling, happy kids you always see on television commercials for soft drinks, and I've always tried to teach my kids the power of imagery: the ability to make things come true by thinking positively about them and working to make them happen.

"One day a television camera crew came to town, and ended up filming a Mountain Dew commercial at our farm, with my son riding one of our horses around Eagle Lake towing a water skier in the lake itself. It was a great commercial, and a dream come true for my son."

And what of her own dreams — this child of Camelot — beyond the usual fantasies of horse trainers? "I'd like to have my cartoon strip, that I call "Mulliken Stu," become syndicated," Del Castillo says. "It's centered around thoroughbreds being raised on our farm by kids, and the idea is to present the world of thoroughbreds as a fun thing, full of family involvement, not as a threat to families.

"That's how we all need to project thoroughbred racing —

showing its health and its basic communication with nature," Del Castillo concluded.

She explained all that following a guest apearance on the Tampa Bay Downs' Saturday Morning Glory Club recently, on

a day when she had no horses entered and no real reason to make the hour-long drive from her farm to the race course, other than to help promote the sport which she initially inherited by default.

Mercedes Won In Beam Stakes

OLDSMAR — Florida Derby winner Mercedes Won, owned locally by Oldsmar resident Christopher Spencer, came out of his third-place finish in the Tampa Bay Derby "better than he went into it," according to Spencer, and will be in northern Kentucky for a planned next engagement in the upcoming Jim Beam Stakes at Turfway Park on Saturday, April 1.

"He came back bouncing," Spencer said of Mercedes Won following the Tampa Bay Derby on March 19; "he just had too much to overcome. It would have been nice to win one in front of the home folks, but that's racing luck and it wasn't meant to be."

Spencer plans to remain in the northern Kentucky area until after the Jim Beam.

Trainer Janet Del Castillo shows a condition book to one of her thoroughbreds running at Tampa Bay Downs.

Photo by Bob Cicero

27
77

'Horses need to romp on grass.
They need each other's
company.'

JANET DEL CASTILLO

It's a strictly down-home operation

Del Castillo believes in her methods despite skeptics

By TOM AINSLIE

In a 14-acre orange grove on the sandy shore of Eagle Lake, near Winter Haven, Fla. a non-conformist named Janet Del Castillo raises, schools and trains thoroughbreds in unusual ways.

Even when 60 miles from Tampa Bay's Downs, 220 from the eastern Florida tracks. They van to the track on race day. That evening they come home to recuperate in grassy paddocks, swim in the lake and gallop every few days on the trails among the orange trees.

"It is important to treat horses as horses," says Del Castillo. "They need to romp on grass. They need each other's company. Individual confinement to racetrack stalls for 23 hours a day is unnatural".

She does not race 2-year-o. 's. She asks no horse for speed until he is almost 3. Her horses race on food and water, unmedicated.

These methods arouse skepticism, but her horses dispel it. They win their share. None has bowed a tendon or broken down in a race. They last for season after season. She never pays more than $2,500 for a yearling. But she has won stakes.

Her best buy was First Prediction, a 2-year-old filly that had been donated to a children's home where Janet was a volunteer worker. The filly, a by Gin to Glory, a half-brother to Ruffian. Icrapade and Buckfinder. In a six year-career, she competed in more than 100 races, winning or placing in 13 stakes and earning $312,000.

The Del Castillo approach is novel but not new. Before racing

was urbanized in enclosed stadiums, horses trained at home. Some harness races, quarter horses and thoroughbreds still do. What sets this woman apart is her sense of bounden duty to advance an idea that might benefit fellow horsefolk, the breed and racing itself.

To encourage experimentation by others, she is writing an instruction manual called, "The Backyard Racehorse." She also conducts seminars. She recently regaled a two-day gathering of enthusiastic horsefold at the New Jersey farm of a friend and follower, owner-trainer Ann Cain. She was interviewed there.

"Thousands of Americans already have horses on their own property", said Janet. "Not only thoroughbreds, but horses of all kinds-- pleasure horses, cutting horses, draft horses, you name it. When these horse-lovers learn how gratifying it is to school and care for an actual racehorse, and how practical it is, we'll recruit new stable owners to our sport. Matter of fact, we already have."

Obviously, not everyone with a horse has enough acreage for serious conditioning. But many do, says Del Castillo, and others have access to useful trails, hills and bridle paths. If shipping back and forth between home and track is not feasible, horses properly schooled at home are welcome in the trackside stable of good trainers. And can return home for furloughs.

"Before its first start, a horse needs to be at the track a few times :: become acclimated to the environment and accustomed to producing speed on a dirt oval." Del

Castillo points out. "But, before and after those workouts and all the races that follow, home is the best place."

As the reader may have surmised, these ideas come from no shrinking violet. Janet Helene Mulgannon Del Castillo is a strapping, strong-minded individual who speaks her mind. She is 40-something, with three grown children and a divorce from the Colombian physician whose family name she retains.

She grew up in San Francisco, where her father was a Federal narcotics agent. She became horse-happy at an early age, walking and rubbing polo ponies. While an art major at San Francisco State she opted for real life, joined the Peace Corps and spend two years of privation in a Colombian village. She nursed the sick, struggled to establish rudimentary sanitation and warmed to the dignity and generosity of the poor.

She returned home and married the young Colombian doctor whom she had assisted in the village. He revived her interest in horses when he decided in all seriousness: that they should buy an inexpensive yearling, and win the Kentucky Derby. When that failed, he dropped the project. But she was hooked and has had racehorses ever since.

All right now. What exactly are the advantages of "backyard" schooling and conditioning". And what does it take to develop winners who go the track only to race?

"The purpose of training," says Janet Del Castillo, "is to fulfill a horse's potential without breaking him down. At home you give your

horses the natural environment in which their bodies and spirits thrive. Frolicking and grazing with each other makes them more resilient, less hectic, less frightened

"But the main factor is the severe disadvantage of trying to strengthen equine bone, muscle and attitude at a track. Conditioning is a cycle of stress-recovery-stress-recovery. At a track, the horse stressed by a hard race or workout is confined to a stall, sometimes with pain-killing medication, and walked under the shed a few minutes a day until asked once again to strain himself at high speed. That program, combined with the frequent after-effect of medication, can hasten the onset of physical problems. But a horse conditioned at home recovers naturally from routine trauma, free to walk and jog his way through the discomfort.

"Another major advantage is economic. The expense of shipping to and from the track is far less than the cost of keeping a horse in training there. And then there is the joy of having your horse around and knowing that no other arrangement could be more constructive."

As to the Know-how, she describes it as love for horses plus command sense. The main technique is gradually increased exertion that begins before age 2. At her own place, Del Castillo has cut a trail that winds up and down grades, with many ozarp turns. She gallops young horses slowly for three miles every three or four days, monitoring the. reactions. After a year, as the 2nd birthday approaches, they are :appy, rugged animals, ready for :peed.

JANET DEL CASTILLO has been training in Florida from her home base.

The Road Less Traveled

Racehorse trainer Janet Del Castillo says at-home conditioning is the best route to the winner's circle.

By Laura Hillenbrand

Janet Del Castillo's multiple stakes winner First Prediction thrived under her owner's unconventional "backyard race training" regimen. Del Castillo (right), conditioned the mare through swimming and long gallops on her farm.

From the moment she first visited a racetrack backstretch, Janet Del Castillo was uneasy about the physical and mental demands placed on conventionally trained racehorses. Kept in their stalls 23 hours a day, pushed to destructive speeds early in their lives and oftentimes plied with medication to add a competitive edge, most equine athletes are not allowed enough time to "be horses" in Del Castillo's view.

Nonetheless, it wasn't until the former polo pony trainer faced a tricky personal dilemma that she discovered that a completely different training style was feasible—and profitable.

In 1978, a divorce left Del Castillo with three children to raise on her own and a barn full of racehorses to train. Complicating matters was the fact that her home, an orange farm located in Winter Haven, Florida, was a 4½-hour drive from the nearest racetrack. But she solved her problems by drawing on her experience as a Peace Corps volunteer and the maxim she had once taught to others.

"In the Peace Corps, my mission was to teach people to look at their problems and cope with their problems with what they have," she says. "If you have lemons, make lemonade."

In surveying her lemons—a 14-acre orange grove and small barn miles from the nearest racetrack—it occurred to Del Castillo that her horses might train just as well, or even better, on the heavy sand trails between her orange trees. Then, to the scorn of many trainers, owners and journalists, she packed up her horses, shipped them to her farm and began making lemonade. With the help of her children, she galloped her horses into condition on the meandering trails of her orange groves and swam them in a nearby lake, ferrying them to the track only for races and occasional timed workouts.

More than a decade later, a brilliant, multiple-stakes-winning mare and a "matchless record" of training sound, durable horses have silenced the naysayers. And Del Castillo is spreading the word about her concept of a "backyard racehorse."

Del Castillo's offbeat training approach does not consist of simply keeping racehorses on the farm. Blending practical experience with common sense, her program is designed to engender the endurance, strength and physical maturity needed to withstand the breakneck speeds of racing.

"Horses have a capacity to do more than what is good for them," she explains. "On the track, [trainers] go straight to speed. The horses start pulling themselves apart. That's damage you can't undo. You have to allow them a certain amount of growth time."

Thus, Del Castillo's horses are not raced or asked for speed drills before they are three years old. Instead, the trainer uses swimming and long gallops at graduated distances and weights to give them the "substructure to allow them to hold up to their own speed." And, once horses are fit, Del Castillo gallops them only every three to four days.

"All you have to do is keep their wheels greased," she says.

The trainer also takes a commonsense approach to her horses' stabling arrangements. Unlike track-dwelling athletes, who are usually out of their stalls only for training or racing, Del Castillo's horses are turned out for much of the day, an arrangement that allows them to stretch, graze and socialize at will. "I try to inhibit the horse as little as possible," she says. "Horses are very social animals. When they are emotionally undernourished, they develop neurotic habits to cope with it.

"People think a horse has to be jumping out of his stall and acting like an idiot to be a good runner. Those things don't go hand in hand," she continues. "My horses are relaxed, but when they go to the racetrack, they know what they're there for."

While one set of unusual circumstances spurred the development of Del Castillo's unique training approach, another led to her greatest triumphs—as well as the long-awaited vindication of her methods.

In 1984, a Florida breeder donated two Thoroughbred fillies as pleasure-horse prospects to a children's home where Del Castillo was a volunteer. The home's director soon determined that he could not house the fillies, and asked Del Castillo if she was interested in them. Although in such a precarious financial position that she feared losing her home, Del Castillo saw enough potential in the fillies to buy them, on credit, for the bargain-basement price of $5,000.

One of the fillies did indeed prove to be best suited to life as a riding hack, but the other, a little gray named First Prediction, thrived on the backyard training regimen and became Del Castillo's most accomplished runner.

First Prediction, who won several stakes races and earned more than $300,000, almost single-handedly put her trainer on the map and proved the legitimacy of her once-maligned training approach. Dubbed the "Iron Maiden," the mare was phenomenally sound, racing more than 100 times between ages three and eight, while sometimes competing as often as three times in two weeks.

So far, First Prediction is the only stakes-class campaigner to emerge from Del Castillo's barn, but the trainer has also had notable success with her less celebrated charges. Although she has been able to afford only obscurely bred runners, almost every one of her horses has made it to the winner's circle during its racing career—an extraordinary statistic for any racing stable.

In addition, Del Castillo has managed to avoid the soundness troubles that frequently plague racing operations. She reports, for example, that none of her horses has a tendon problem, an affliction common among conventionally trained runners. And, although she does use medication when necessary, such instances are rare. "I try to combine common sense and medical know-how," says Del Castillo, "The horses I train last."

Currently at work on a backyard training manual, Del Castillo is also planning a series of seminars for those interested in learning more about her philosophy and techniques.

While admitting that backyard training is not for just anyone with a horse, barn and pasture, Del Castillo believes that her program can bring much-needed new blood to racing. "I'm trying to appeal to competent horsepeople. I want to encourage horsepeople," she says. "People have illusions that only the rich and the criminals are involved, but there are many, many people like me in the sport."

A strong selling point is the comparative cost of backyard training as opposed to conventional race training. On-track training can cost as much as $100 per day, Del Castillo says, while training a racehorse at home costs no more than keeping a pleasure horse. Plus, she points out, racehorses normally spend months at the track, running up bills before they are even old enough to have their talent gauged.

In contrast, her program calls for a horse to be shipped to a professional trainer at the track only when the animal is ready to begin speed training and racing. If a horse turns out to be a poor racing prospect, he has cost his owner far less than a conventionally prepared horse would have, Del Castillo says, and his relaxed upbringing will make him an excellent pleasure horse.

Basically, the trainer says, she wants to share some of the enjoyment she has derived from racing. Looking out the window of her home, Del Castillo's eyes rest on her Cinderella horse, First Prediction, now in foal to Preakness winner Gate Dancer. "The joy I've had with this you could never buy." ■

For information regarding seminars, contact Janet Del Castillo, Rancho Del Castillo, 3708 Crystal Beach Rd., Winter Haven, FL 33880; telephone 813-299-8448.

Backyard Racehorse: Hands-On Training

Janet Del Castillo
Winter Haven, Florida

The logistics of training a horse at the racetrack work against both the trainer and the horse. The track closes at 10:00 a.m., so any significant work must be done by that time. The daily cost and maintenance at the track forces trainers to come up quickly with answers for impatient owners. Trainers are trying to develop athletes and this is not done overnight – a great deal of patience and guidance are necessary. While an idea that I have to alleviate some of these problems may not be for everyone, it may prove to be a solution to limited training time and some of the other pressures trainers experience. What I'm talking about is called hands-on training, which allows the competitive horse owner (who owns horses from other disciplines, i.e., jumpers, rodeo competitors, endurance riders), to consider training their own racehorse up to a certain point. By my own experience and observations, I know that a racehorse can be trained in other than racetrack circumstances until it is about 28 to 32 months of age. Trainers should be happy to receive horses with a sound backyard training foundation as they will be fairly fit and ready to go into speedwork at the racetrack.

What's Involved?

Being turned out daily is an important part of the training of the young horse. "Benevolent neglect" is essential; I advise saddling and riding a young horse no more frequently than every 3 days. This allows the hands-on trainer to be aware of any stress or overwork done in the early training of a young horse. One can differentiate "stocking up," typical of horses adapting to the progressive stress being put upon them, from over-stress to joints and tendons. There are many signs the hands-on trainer should be aware of that will warn him or her well in advance of problems to joints and tendons. Given proper rest between "stresses" is what allows the horse to build a system that can withstand its own high speed.

No speed work whatsoever should be done until the horse is 30 to 32 months of age. Up to that point, the backyard trainer's (owner's) goal should be a horse with a good foundation achieved by slow, steady progressive training. Ideally, a 2- to 5-mile route over hill and dale is the best way to establish this. The horses that I train in this manner must achieve certain goals within this route

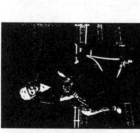

Janet Del Castillo off the track. In the hands-on training process she recommends saddling and riding the young horse no more than once every 3 days.

before I allow them to go on to more work and/or speed. Riding a horse every 3rd day allows the body rebuild time for any slight pulls or strains the trainer might not be aware of. Having the horse out a good portion of the day allows it to walk out naturally from any stiffness and lets the trainer observe the animal's movement. If swelling is a result of a strain, it will persist.

Continued

At the track it is easy to be fooled about the status of legs and joints. Common practices of poulticing and wrapping legs may hide many potential problems on young horses. This is not a criticism of track trainers; horses will stock up, even sound ones, if stalled a great deal. The trainers are just trying to keep their horses comfortable, but the wrapping and poulticing may hide heat and/or strains and stresses. If the horse is not obviously lame, then it goes out to the track again and perhaps becomes more severely injured. I don't think a 2-year-old should be wrapped during its normal training regime. If this type of horse has swellings or strains, it should be turned out until the swelling and/or strains are gone, at which time training may resume (it may only be a couple of days until the limb is normal again). Obviously, this is difficult for trainers to do at the track as most backsides do not have paddocks to turn out horses in.

Letting the Owner Take Over

If owners have been competitive in showing, rodeo, and/or hunter jumping – and have been successful in those fields – they might consider buying a yearling (Thoroughbred, Arabian, Appaloosa, or other racehorse) that they could do a great deal of preliminary training with themselves. By doing most of the work at home, these owners will initially save thousands of dollars in training fees and when their horse goes to a track trainer, it will be a little older than most and will have been well handled and used to a great many more circumstances than the typical track-trained animal. Most trainers will be happy to get a 32-month-old animal that hopefully has already been through the flus and colds suffered during its first 2 years of life and, after a few days

of getting adapted to the racetrack routine, is ready to breeze. Within about 2 months at the track, the trainer should have an idea of whether or not there is talent to pursue in the animal. If no gift of speed is apparent, the horse may go back home to be a hunter jumper or whatever else the owner had in mind. If, however, the horse had been racing, many Thoroughbreds start racing, only a small percentage win and/or pay their way), then it will start bringing in checks to help defray its costs. The track trainers should be glad to have sound horses to hone into speed. No one really likes to "hold a horse together" for one more race.

Running to Win

A good trainer is one who manages to allow the horse to develop into its natural ability without breaking the horse down in the process. Many horses are capable of pulling themselves apart long before they are mature enough and sound enough to run. That is why a good trainer is tuned into how much stress the horse is enduring. The trainer should allow the horse to evolve comfortably and naturally into its speed. When its mind grows into having the concentration necessary to run full out 6 furlongs to a mile-and-a-half and likes what it's doing, then you have a runner. Defining a horse's personal best at that point is important so that it is not put in competition that is over its head. Keep the horse happy and run it at a level where it is capable of winning.

Racing is a challenging, difficult business. The hands-on training methods I suggest will allow some owners a more active role with their horses, cost them less money, and give the horses a better chance of making it to the races. Racing can utilize the energies and economic clout of pleasure horse owners to give a boost to the industry, and we all win.

Janet Del Castillo is currently holding training seminars at her farm in Winter Haven, Florida, while working on a "Backyard Race Horse" training manual. For information about seminars and/or manual please write: Janet Del Castillo, 3708 Crystal Beach Rd., Winter Haven, FL 33880; (813) 299-8448.

The Equine ATHLETE encourages trainers and others to send us their opinions and ideas for this feature in our newsjournal. All readers are invited to respond to the comments printed here. Please address your materials to: The Equine ATHLETE, P.O. Box 4457, Santa Barbara, CA 93140-4457.

IL LIBRO

Dalla parte del cavallo: purosangue fai da te sul manuale di Janet Del Castillo

BACKYARD RACE HORSE di Janet Del Castillo ovvero un manuale "fai da te" di allenamento del purosangue dalla parte del cavallo

Jo Kristel

Il mondo del purosangue è e decisamente carente dal punto di vista della trattatistica sull'allenamento del cavallo da corsa, argomento che è sempre stato considerato esclusivo e segreto appannaggio degli allenatori, detentori di un'arte spesso tramandata oralmente di padre in figlio. È pertanto con grande stupore che abbiamo scoperto che negli Stati Uniti è stato pubblicato un manuale per l'allenamento "in casa" del purosangue.

Il testo è stato scritto da Janet Del Castillo, una ex volontaria nel corpo di pace americano, che da diversi anni allena purosangue nella sua tenuta costellata da aranceti sulle rive sabbiose del Lago Eagle vicino a Winter Haven in Florida. Nella sua fattoria di 14 acri Janet ha fatto tutto da sola: ha costruito scuderie, paddock, gabbie di prova ed ha dovuto combattere per anni contro lo scetticismo di allenatori e proprietari che sono talmente abituati al metodi tradizionali di allenamento da non riuscire nemmeno ad immaginare un'alternativa. E Janet un'alternativa non solo l'ha immaginata, ma l'ha anche messa in pratica lottando duramente per anni finché i successi dei cavalli da lei allenati non hanno dimostrato che il suo metodo funziona. I suoi cavalli non soffrono di tendiniti, non si rompono durante gli allenamenti. Durano anno dopo anno, non sono costati più di 2500 dollari da yearling, ma hanno vinto delle stakes. «È importante trattare i cavalli come cavalli - dice Janet - essi devono poter correre nei pascoli, hanno bisogno della compagnia reciproca, e la segregazione per 23 ore in una scuderia di un ippodromo è contro natura. Anche quando i suoi cavalli corrono, vivono a casa e raggiungono in van le piste il giorno della corsa, la sera stessa ritornano a casa per recuperare le energie in ricchi prati, possono nuotare nel lago e galoppano nelle piste circondate dagli aranceti. Janet non fa correre i cavalli a due anni e non chiede loro velocità finché non hanno compiuto i tre anni. I suoi soggetti non assumono farmaci.»

Janet ha voluto fare conoscere i suoi originali sistemi di allenamento ed ha scritto un manuale "Backyard Race Horse" dove viene trattato tutto quello che un proprietario dovrebbe sapere per potersi occupare personalmente della preparazione dei propri cavalli per le corse.

A Complete **HANDS-ON MANUAL** for the **COMPETENT HORSEMAN** Train Your Own **RACE HORSE**! by **Janet Del Castillo**

I primi capitoli del libro trattano delle Aste e dell'acquisto di purosangue suggerendo un metodo pratico, ma molto razionale per leggere i cataloghi e per valutare la conformazione fisica di un puledro. Successivamente viene affrontata l'organizzazione delle scuderie e delle strutture di allenamento. Quindi l'educazione del puledro viene trattata dal momento dello svezzamento ai due anni di età. L'allenamento viene programmato in modo estremamente razionale e progressivo allo scopo di potenziare al massimo la resistenza del cavallo, riducendo al minimo il rischio di traumatismi all'apparato osteo-tendineo. I cardini della filosofia di Janet sono: ritardare il più possibile l'allenamento veloce, da effettuarsi solo quando le strutture ossee, tendinee e muscolari del cavallo non abbiano raggiunto la condizione sufficiente a non subire danni dalla velocità ed intervallare l'allenamento in modo tale che qualora il lavoro abbia forzato un po' troppo alcune strutture, queste abbiano il tempo di recuperare prima dell'allenamento successivo.

Janet non è un veterinario, ma le parti più tecniche del suo manuale sono state sottoposte ad una versione di diversi veterinari della Cornell University e dell'Università della California a Davis e dobbiamo riconoscere che le sue teorie abbinano un grande amore e rispetto per il cavallo ad un programma di allenamento estremamente razionale e teso a sviluppare la massima potenza e resistenza conservando quella serenità mentale, che purtroppo la vita che il purosangue conduce in un ippodromo non può sicuramente conservare.

Consigliamo a tutti gli interessati, proprietari, allenatori, veterinari e chiunque ami profondamente i cavalli, questo manuale di... sopravvivenza del cavallo che la razza equina, se potesse leggerlo, sicuramente approverebbe. Grazie Janet, i purosangue ti ringraziano.

Chi desideri ricevere il libro potrà rivolgersi a "Cavalli & Corse" o richiederlo direttamente all'autrice scrivendo a:

Janet Del Castillo
3708 Crystal Beach Road
Winter Haven FL 33880
Fax. (813)293-2749

L'autrice Janet Del Castillo con First Prediction

This is the Italian Racing Form! They (the editors) are very interested in "Backyard" Race training!

280

Country People
SECTION

Horses Benefit from Fruits of Her Labor

JANET DEL CASTILLO of Winter Haven, Florida has bucked the odds when it comes to training Thoroughbreds.

Most trainers run their horses at the closest racetrack. Not Janet. She works her horses in the orange groves on the family farm.

"It's the perfect environment for them to build up muscle and stamina," Janet says. "Galloping through the deep sand and up the rolling hills of the groves gives strength to all their muscles."

Makes sense—especially when you consider Janet got the idea from raising her own children. "I thought about raising strong, healthy kids and applied the same thinking to horses. The best place for them to develop and grow is right in their own backyard!"

Horsing Around

At the farm, the horses are turned out early in the morning and given the freedom to frolic in the pasture.

Janet only works them every 3 or 4 days, and often includes a swim in a nearby lake as part of the routine. "I found that it's good therapy, especially if a horse has an injury."

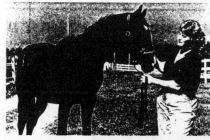

GALLOPING GROVES. Janet Del Castillo chooses to train her Thoroughbreds at home instead of at the racetrack. She runs them through the orange groves on the family's Winter Haven, Florida farm.

To support her claim, she points out one of her Thoroughbreds that had a bone chip in its knee and suffered from inflammation. "People said she'd never race again," Janet recalls.

> "*Sometimes she'll lay on her side and float in the water!*"

She took the horse to the lake, attached a long lead rope to the halter and let the horse paddle around, getting exercise without straining the injury.

"She really loves to go to the lake and swim now," Janet affirms. "Sometimes she'll actually roll over on her side and just float!"

Proof's in Pace

When her horses aren't floating or frisking in the orange groves, they're often winning races. "First Prediction", a gray mare Janet bought on credit in 1984, is a prime example.

A Florida breeder had donated First Prediction and another filly to a children's home where Janet was a volunteer. The director of the home decided that he couldn't house the horses and asked Janet if she was interested in them.

The other filly turned out to be best suited for pleasure riding. But First Prediction went on to win dozens of races, earning over $300,000. Not bad for a "backyard" horse!

"My horses get to run free and act like horses every day, and I think that gives them an edge," Janet informs. "There are many ways to train Thoroughbreds, but I think my 'backyard regimen' will soon become more popular with other trainers."

No doubt. Why buck a winning trend?

281

ORDER FORM

Prediction Publications
3708 Crystal Beach Road
Winter Haven, Florida 33880
(813) 299-8448

SEND TO:

_____

_____

_____

Telephone:_____

Backyard Racehorse $40.00

Number of Copies: _____ = _____

Florida Residents add 6%   _____
Shipping:
Priority Mail $2.90   _____

Total Enclosed   _____

For information regarding The Newsletter or Seminars
at Rancho Del Castillo or in your area please contact
Prediction Publications
I am interested in The Newsletter ☐

I am interested in Seminars   ☐

Drop me a line!

282